D0173540

The
Giant Book
of Useless
Information

The Giant Book of Useless Information

Magpie Books, London

Constable & Robinson Ltd
3 The Lanchesters
162 Fulham Palace Road
London W6 9ER

www.constablerobinson.com

This paperback edition published by Magpie Books,
an imprint of Constable & Robinson Ltd 2010

Copyright © Constable & Robinson Ltd, 2010

All rights reserved. This book is sold subject to the condition that it shall not,
by way of trade or otherwise, be lent, re-sold, hired out or otherwise circulated
in any form of binding or cover other thant that in which it is published and
without a similar condition including this condition being imposed
on the subsequent purchaser.

A copy of the British Library Cataloguing in
Publication Data is available from the British Library

ISBN 978-1-84901-897-5

Cover designed by Ken Leeder
Printed and bound in the EU

3 5 7 9 10 8 6 4 2

PEFC
PEFC/16-33-111
CATG-PEFC-052
www.pefc.org

Contents

Crazy Animals

Love Aquarium. At the Sea Life London Aquarium, staff have been playing music by soul legends like Barry White and Marvyn Gaye underwater in an attempt to put a shark in an amorous mood. Zorro, a six-year-old zebra shark, arrived from Sea Life Belgium, arriving on Valentine's Day. The curator at the aquarium, Paul Hale, had a potential mate lined up, a single shark called Mazawabee, but they showed no interest in one another. The staff thought that seductive music, such as Marvin Gaye's *Let's Get It On*, would encourage the two to be more than just friends. Hale was quoted as saying that 'research suggests that fish can not only hear music but can appreciate different tunes and melodies so we have decided to see if some good old-fashioned love songs will get them in the mood!'

Frog Frenzy

Children discovered hundreds of dead frogs in the Dutch village of Montfort. The corpses were in a fishing pond. According to frog expert H. van Buggenum the frogs had died from an excess of sexual activity. The hormones of the frogs and toads make them return to 'pairing ponds' to mate. Males crawl in groups onto each female. The result is that she is either crushed or suffocated. But the males suffered too. In the frenzy of frogs travelling to the pond many had been crushed. It is normal for a few deaths to result, but in this case the death toll was in the hundreds.

Gay Penguin Rights

A zoo in Germany had to reverse a decision to break up apparently homosexual penguin pairs following protests from gay rights groups. The Bremerhaven Zoo had observed three penguin couples in which both animals were male. They flew in four female penguins to try and encourage breeding. They intended to introduce the female birds in the hope that the males would switch their preferences, but the experiment was cancelled after complaints. An open letter to Bremerhaven's Mayor described this as 'organized and forced harassment through female seductresses.' The zoo director Heike Kueck said: 'Everyone can live here as they please.' He said they never planned to forcibly separate the couples and that the final choice would be down to the animals themselves.

Doggy Love

In Sao Paulo, Brazil, there is a love motel for amorous dogs. It offers specially decorated rooms for dogs of pet owners who want to provide a special experience for their canine friends. Robson Marinho, owner of a local pet shop, constructed the motel on the floors above the shop. A sign outside announces the presence of the 'Pet Love Motel'. The rooms are decorated in a similar

Thought For the Day

A man with one watch knows what time it is; a man with two watches is never quite sure.

Lee Segall

fashion to human love motels with satin sheets, romantic music on tap, heart-shaped ceiling mirrors, dimmer switches, and throw cushions. The windows have thick curtains to ensure absolute discretion. Marinho was quoted as saying: 'I am absolutely certain this is the first love motel for dogs in the world. The owner has to know what kind of DVD will excite his or her dog. We also have a wedding agency that matches up dogs and if the female dog doesn't get pregnant, we offer artificial insemination services.' A room for your dogs costs $41 for two hours.

Dolphin Heroes
A group of dolphins saved a group of New Zealand swimmers when they were threatened by a great white shark. The dolphins circled protectively around Rob Howes and three other lifeguards who were training 100 meters offshore at Ocean Beach near Whangarei. The dolphins raced in and herded the four swimmers together. One said 'They started to herd us up, they pushed all four of us together by doing tight circles around us.' They didn't initially realize that the dolphins were protecting them from a shark. Rob tried to move away from the group, but two of the bigger dolphins herded him back. At this point he spotted a great white shark swimming towards them. It was nine feet long and perfectly capable of killing him. 'I just recoiled. It was only about two meters away from me, the water was crystal clear and it was as clear as the nose on my face.' For 40 minutes the dolphins continued to protect the swimmers before the shark moved away. Research shows that dolphins will attack sharks to protect their young. The swimmers owed their lives to the dolphins' decision to extend this protection to them.

Fish Morgue

In Tripura, India there was a scandal when it was discovered that some of the fish eaten locally had been stored with a human corpse. Fish traders were storing hilsa, a river fish, in the local hospital morgue. The fish was kept in cooling boxes alongside human corpses. The hospital and its employees were charging about $.20 per kilogram per night for this service, and thus undercutting private storage charges. Unfortunately, when the scheme was reported in the local press there was an outcry. A reporter who had gone undercover as a fish trader tricked hospital employees into demonstrating how they stored the fish together with corpses in morgue boxes. One worker was suspended and an inquiry was ordered by central government.

Frisky Horse

A twenty-four-year-old man in Poland died after he tried to calm down a sexually aroused horse. The horse reacted badly and the man was bitten to death. It had been towing a cart through the village, but it became wild and started to buck. An autopsy showed that the man died either from a severed jugular vein or a spinal injury.

Smoking Dog

A Chinese man faced prosecution after training his pet puppy to smoke cigarettes. Zeng Ziguang, a 23-year-old chef from Wuchang, Hubei Province, taught Blackie to smoke in order to keep him company. The dog became addicted to tobacco and would smoke a packet of cigarettes a day. Zeng said 'he hated the smell of smoke to begin with. But I trained him to get used to it by blowing smoke at him. Gradually Blackie got used to the smell and I started putting the lit cigarette into his mouth. Each time he did that, I would reward him with food.' Neighbors called for him to be arrested for being cruel to animals. One told the local *Changjiang Daily* 'he is a terrible pet owner.'

Jarhead the Bear
According to the Florida Fish and Wildlife Conservation Commission a bear cub in Weirsdale, central Florida. had to be rescued after getting its head stuck in a plastic bottle for ten days. Nicknamed Jarhead, the cub was close to death after consuming no food or water for over a week. The black cub had been digging through rubbish for food when its head became wedged. For days he was seen in and around the town on the edge of the Ocala National Forest with his head clearly trapped in the container. Baited traps were used to locate the family of bears, a mother, Jarhead and his sibling, following concerned reports from residents. The protective mother stayed away from the traps for more than a

Natural Thoughts

If a man walks in the woods for love of them half of each day, he is in danger of being regarded as a loafer. But if he spends his days as a speculator, shearing off those woods and making the earth bald before her time, he is deemed an industrious and enterprising citizen.

Henry David Thoreau

week before finally venturing out. Biologists managed to shoot her with a tranquilizer gun. They grabbed the cub and successfuly removed the container from his head. Once the mother had woken up, the proverbial bear with a sore head, they released the family into a more remote part of the forest for safety. Mike Orlando, an FWC biologist who helped in the operation, said: 'It was a lot easier said than done. The residents were really great about calling us when they saw the bears, but it seemed like we were always about 20 minutes behind.' The FWC pointed out that 'although the story appears to have a happy ending, it truly illustrates one of the worst things that can happen when wildlife gets into garbage.'

Swan Love

Swans tend to mate for life, though they occasionally make strange decisions about who to choose. Petra, a swan who lives on

---

Obscure English Language Facts

Alphabetical Order

Aegilops, (8 letters long) is the longest word to have all of its letters arranged in alphabetical order. Shorter words of this kind include **beefily** and **billowy** (7 letters), **abhors, accent, access, almost, biopsy, bijoux, billow, chintz, effort,** and **ghosty** (all 6 letters).

Spoonfeed (at 9 letters long) is the longest word to have all of its letters in reverse alphabetical order.

Weird And Crazy Laws

In Kingsville, Texas, there is a law against two pigs engaging in sexual congress on the property of the city airport.

In the reign of Peter the Great, there was a special tax on beards. Any man who chose not to shave regularly was required to pay the 'beard tax'.

If you take your giraffe to Atlanta, Georgia, remember not to tie it to a telephone pole or street lamp. To do so would be illegal.

Dueling is not currently against the law in Paraguay. However, both parties in the duel must be registered blood donors.

In 1838, an ordinance was passed in Los Angeles requiring a man who wanted to serenade a woman to first obtain a license.

In the 17th Century, Japan existed in almost total isolation from the rest of the world. Citizens were not allowed to leave their homeland, under penalty of death. In the 1630s, a decree was issued preventing the construction of large ocean-worthy ships which might encourage emigration or trade with the outside world.

In Canada, it is against the law to pay any debt higher than 25 cents in pennies.

In Illinois, it is against the law to offer a cigar that has been lit to cats, dogs, or any other domesticated animal that is being kept as a pet.

For long-forgotten reasons, Idaho has a law that forbids any citizen from giving another citizen a box of candy weighing in excess of 50 pounds.

Don't try to organize a whale hunt in Oklahoma. This is not a legal activity in the state.

Aasee lake in Germany, fell in love with a swan-shaped pedalo. The lovestruck single female spent a summer swimming alongside the pedalo whenever it was launched out onto the lake. Concerned about how she would react to separation, when pedalos were put in storage for the winter, staff decided to set up a mini-shelter especially for Petra and the pedalo. Petra was happy to move into the love nest for the winter and continued to accompany the pedalo everywhere the next year.

The Moth Whisperer

The barbastelle bat, found in various parts of Europe, has evolved in a most unusual way. It has lowered its voice so that some moth species are unable to hear it. This allows the flying mammal to swoop and catch the moths undetected. To navigate in the dark, bats use echolocation. This means they send out sound waves and listen for echoes bouncing back to them. Over millennia, some moths have evolved rudimentary ears which allow them to hear the bat calls and avoid the predators. Tiger moths even use special ultrasonic clicks which can effectively jam bats' sonar. However, the barbastelle has now evolved a counterstrategy. Its whispering allows it to get around the moths' defenses. Study leader Holger Goerlitz, a biologist at the University of Bristol, said: 'evolution is putting larger pressure on prey to evolve adaptations to win against the predator, so therefore it's rare when you find cases in nature when a predator is winning in the arms race.'

Pea-Size Frog

One of the smallest frogs in the world is the species Microhyla nepenthicola. Smaller than a pea, and tiny enough to perch on the tip of a pencil, the species was discover on pitcher plants in the Malaysian rain forests of Borneo. The species has actually been captured before but it was only recently understood that it is a separate species. Co-discoverer Indraneil Das, a herpetologist at Universiti Malaysia Sarawak in Malaysia, said 'I saw some specimens in museum collections that are over a hundred years old. Scientists presumably thought they were juveniles of other species, but it turns out they are adults of this newly discovered microspecies.'

 # Memorable Movie Quotes

Lytton Strachey: I tend to be impulsive in these matters . . . like the time I asked Virginia Wolf to marry me.
Dora Carrington: She turned you down?
Lytton Strachey: No, she accepted. It was ghastly.
Carrington

Major Strasser: What is your nationality?
Rick Blaine: I'm a drunkard.
Captain Louis Renault: That makes Rick a citizen of the world.
Casablanca

Hey, maybe you haven't been keeping up on current events, but we just got our asses kicked, pal!
Aliens

Hilarious Misprints

The season for grass fires seems to have arrived, so stamp out that cigarette-end before you throw it down.
Herne Bay Press

Arthur Kitchener was seriously burned Saturday afternoon when he came in contact with a high voltage wife.
Surrey News

For sale. Lovely rosewood piano. Owner going abroad with beautiful twisted legs.
North Wales Advertiser

PARKYNS – to the memory of Mr Parkyns, passed away September 10. Peace at last. From all the neighbors of Princes Avenue.
Leicester Mercury

If the motion were passed, no strike action would be taken by NALGO without a ballet of all its members.
Bristol Evening Post

Community Bands Together To Help Burn Victim's Family
Bay City Times

SLEEP WELL – For the Rest of Your Life!
Prevention Magazine

We apologise for the error in last week's paper in which we stated that Mr Arnold was a defective in the police force. This was a typographical error. We meant of course that Mr Arnold is a detective in the police farce, and we are sorry for any embarrassment caused.
Ely Standard

A heavy pall of lust covered the upper two-thirds of Texas last night and was expected to drift south-east over the state by morning.
Yankton Press

Terror Leader In Iraq Declares War On Tape
AP

UFO Sightings and Stories

The Clayton Incident. On 6th June 1966, hundreds of people in Westall, Clayton, South Victoria, Australia spotted an alleged UFO in the sky. Students and teachers at two schools in Victoria fled their classrooms and reported seeing the object in the sky for up to twenty minutes, before it descended into a nearby field. Soon afterwards the object climbed rapidly upwards and flew away towards the northwest. Some observers later suggested that the departing craft was pursued by five mysterious aircraft. Local police attended the site, and later in the week uniformed men visited the site. These were probably representatives of the Australian army and air force. After samples had been taken, the vegetation in the field was burnt, either to destroy evidence or cleanse the area. People who witnessed 'The Clayton Incident' still gather for regular reunions.

The Flatwoods Monster
On 12th September 1952 six local boys and a local woman reported witnessing a UFO land. They subsequently saw a strange-looking creature near the site in West Virginia. It was variously described as being man-sized, with a flared body that looked like it was wearing a skirt, having a green color, and with stubby arms like a lizard. The creature has been given various

names, including the Flatwoods Monster, the Braxton County Monster or the Phantom of Flatwoods.

The First British Crop Circle Report in Britain
The farm of John Scull lies within sight of the White Horse, on the Wiltshire downs in England. In mid-August 1980, Mr Scull was walking around the edge of his oat field when he was outraged by the sight of what looked like wanton vandalism. Someone had been trampling his oats on a vast scale. But, when he surveyed the damage at close quarters, he realized that it was more organized than it looked. There were three immense circles, each sixty feet in diameter, spread out over the field. The ripening oats had been neatly flattened in a clockwise direction, yet without breaking the stalks – the horizontal oats were continuing to ripen.

It looked as if some practical joker had worked out an elaborate hoax – elaborate because the circles must have been produced manually rather than mechanically; there was no sign of the disturbance that would have been made by some kind of machine. In fact the circles were surrounded by undamaged oats, which made it hard to see how anyone had approached. But then, all cornfields have 'tramlines' – double lines made by the

---

The Fame Name Game

What did Richard Jenkins change his name to?

Answer: Richard Burton

farmer's tractor as he adds fertilizer or weedkiller – and a careful hoaxer could have trodden carefully along the tramlines without leaving any signs of disturbance.

But to what purpose? What kind of a madman would want to spend a whole night making three sixty-foot circles – presumably with long planks, or a piece of rope stretched from the center? The *Wiltshire Times* ran a story on this on 15th August 1980, together with a photograph. This was the first time that crop circles came to wide public attention in the UK.

The Grinning Man

Residents of Elizabeth, New Jersey were startled on 11th October 1966 to catch a glimpse of a strange tall man who had no nose or ears in their neighborhood. This strange apparition followed closely after a number of reports of a UFO in the same area. The incident has become known as 'The Grinning Man' because of the expression on the face of the suspected alien.

Taking Out The Trash?

On 12th January 1975, there was an incident in North Bergen, New Jersey that some consider an authentic alien encounter. George O'Barski was driving towards his home just across the Hudson River from Manhattan, when his radio was overcome by static. He tried to retune his radio, but broke off when he saw to his left a dark round object with tall windows. The object was making a humming sound and travelling at the same speed as his car, and bright light poured from the windows. As O'Barski watched, the UFO hovered over a playing field, in a stationary position close to the ground. A panel opened in the side of the craft and a ladder emerged. O'Barski claims that he saw ten identical small figures climb down, wearing helmets that obscured their faces. He watched as each of them dug a hole in the ground and placed a bag inside. They then hurried back into their ship which rapidly ascended into the sky.

Some time later O'Barski told the story to an old acquaintance, Budd Hopkins. Hopkins was interested in UFO sightings and began to investigate. He discovered that the event had been seen by other witnesses who could corroborate O'Barski's story. A doorman at an apartment complex bordering the park said that he had seen the object, and heard a high-pitched vibration, which appeared to shatter a window in the lobby as the UFO departed. Budd Hopkins later became a well-known figure in UFO and alien abduction research, and this case is considered one of the best-documented tales of a UFO sighting. Did George O'Barski witness aliens involved in some kind of interplanetary experiment? Or were they perhaps just having a spring clean and taking out the trash?

Strange Events in Poland
On 10th May 1978, Jan Wolski of Emilcin, Poland, was driving a cart drawn by horses when he encountered two short, green-faced beings. They got into his cart and began talking in a strange language. Wolksi described them as having slanting eyes and prominent cheekbones, and being slightly shorter than a grown man. They made him drive to a clearing where he claimed he saw a large UFO hovering just above the ground. The craft was white, about fifteen feet in height and 'as long as a bus'. He claimed that he was taken aboard the ship where there were already two other

humans. He was forced to undress and wait on one of eight to ten benches located around the craft. He was then examined with a tool resembling two dishes.

After the abduction, Wolski returned home to his family and told them of what had just happened. He told them to come see the site. His sons went to fetch other neighbors, and together they went to investigate. Where the craft had been the grass was flattened and there were unusual paths coming in towards it from all directions. Wolski spoke about this experience in an interview recorded by two Polish UFO investigators later that year. The audio tape of the interview was kept in a private archive for many years before being released. The Emilcin UFO Memorial, which commemorates Wolski's experience, was constructed in 2005, a monument to the strange events of that year.

The World's Oddest Animals

Aye-Aye The Aye-aye is the world's largest nocturnal primate, and can be identified by its rodent-like teeth and long fingers. It looks a bit like a woodpecker, and is characterized by a unique method of finding food; it taps on trees to find grubs, and it then chews holes in the wood and inserts a long middle finger in order to retrieve them. It has large ears and a small patch of gray hair, making it one of the less attractive primates, as it looks like a kind of troll or gremlin.

Venezuelan Radiation

On 24th October 1886 a letter appeared in *Scientific American* magazine claiming that the US Consul to Venezuela had witnessed a bright object accompanied by a humming noise above a hut in the Venezuelan village of Maracaibo. The people in the hut later came down with a mysterious illness similar to what in modern times would be called radiation sickness. It was also claimed that all the trees surrounding the hut withered and died within nine days.

Alien Grave

On 4th September 1897 people living in the area of Aurora, Texas reported that a UFO had crashed in nearby fields. Locals also insisted that the pilot, believed to be an alien, was secretly buried in the local cemetery.

Tunguska Explosion

A massive explosion near the Podkamennaya Tunguska River in Russia on 30th June 1908 was widely believed by many to be the explosion of a crashed UFO. Others, however, think that it was more likely to be an asteroid or meteorite collision. The damage left behind by the Tunguska explosion extended over hundreds of miles. The actual explosion seems to have happened a few miles

The Fame Name Game

What did Allen Stewart Konigsberg change his name to?

Answer: Woody Allen

above the ground – rather than a crater, the scientists investigating the incident found that millions of trees had been flattened and the ground scorched. The impact on the ground of a meteorite ten meters across exploding is thought to be roughly equivalent to that of the atomic bombs that were dropped on Japan at the end of the Second World War.

Roswell Uncovered

The famous 'Roswell' UFO incident happened on 7th August 1947. Many have claimed to have seen a UFO landing near Roswell, New Mexico and legend has it that United States Army Air Forces captured a flying saucer and hid the truth from the citizens of the country. Roswell and the famous Area 51 in Nevada have been the inspiration for many films, songs and books. In spite of the literature surrounding this incident, the truth has never been established. Some believe that it was a military experiment that went wrong and that the UFO stories were deliberately put out by the government to create a harmless diversion from the real truth.

The Disappearance of Flight Number N3808H

On 28th June 1980, Jose Maldonado Torres and his friend, Jose Pagan Santos, took off from Los Americas International Airport in the Dominican Republic in a small aircraft. They were going home to Puerto Rico. Some time later, a Mayday signal was picked up emanating from flight N3808H. Iberia Airlines Flight IB-976 from Santo Domingo to Spain responded to the Mayday. Torres said that a strange object was clearly visible in front of them. This peculiar object had forced them to change course several times as it was interfering with their instruments. The Iberia captain then relayed a message from San Juan flight control asking N3808H to turn on their transponder. N3808H replied they didn't have one. So the Spanish captain asked for their call sign and estimated position. N3808H's reply was that they were approximately 35 miles off the coast of Puerto Rico.

This was the last that was ever heard from the flight, which subsequently disappeared without trace. Aviation experts confirm that the last radar position of N3808H was indeed 35 miles to the west of Puerto Rico. A search was mounted by various parties, including relatives of Santos, based on this final radar position. Neither man was ever found, nor was any wreckage from the plane. There were no records of any unidentified objects that could have explained the mysterious object they had reported seeing, and that they had believed to be interfering with their navigation.

Fort Knox Disappearance
On 1st July 1948, the US Air Force sent a fighter pilot to investigate a UFO sighting over Fort Knox, Kentucky. The pilot was killed mysteriously while pursuing the UFO.

Historic UFOs
One of the first recorded claims of UFO sightings was on 8th December 1886. José Bonilla was observing sun spots at the Zacatecas Observatory in Mexico where he was director, when he saw around 283 objects crossing the sun. He claimed that so many of them appeared simultaneously it was impossible to count them. He did, however, photograph them and the photographs

Amazing Animals

Never take a cow upstairs. It is possible for them to walk upstairs but not downstairs, because the knees of a cow can't bend sufficiently for going down.

Pigs are physically unable to look up into the sky.

The first bird that was ever domesticated by man was the goose.

A group of geese on the ground is a gaggle, while a group of geese in the air is a skein.

There are more chickens in the world than there are people.

Chickens absorb vitamin-D from sunshine through their combs.

A female pig gestates in three months, three weeks, and three days.

A donkey can see all four of its own feet at all times because of the positioning of its eyes.

The underside of a horse's hoof is called a frog. The frog peels off a few times a year and is replaced with new growth.

A 1200 lb horse eats about seven times its own weight each year.

A donkey will sink in quicksand but a mule won't, which makes a mule a useful animal in areas that are prone to quicksand.

A quarter of the horses in the US died in an equine virus epidemic in 1872.

The average hen will lay 225 eggs a year.

Roosters can only crow if they are able to fully extend their necks.

are still in existence today, and are regarded by many as the oldest images of UFOs in the world.

Light On The Horizon

On 15th September 1991, a camera located at the back of Space Shuttle Discovery's cargo bay was pointing towards the Earth's horizon. A glowing object, unobserved by any of the astronauts, who were busy on the craft, suddenly appeared just beneath the horizon. It slowly moved from right to left at a slight slant upwards in the picture. Moments before this a number of other glowing objects had been visible, although indistinct. There was a flash at the lower left of the screen, and the main object, along with the others, changed direction abruptly and moved rapidly away, as though responding to the flash. Another streak of light then moved through the area where the main object had been, and one more streak became visible for a few seconds on the right hand side of the screen. A minute after the main flash, the TV camera rotated down automatically. This produced a fuzzy picture of the side of the cargo bay rather than any more views of the moving lights. Finally the camera refocused and suddenly ceased to film. The lights have not been explained as natural phenomena.

Flying Saucers

The UFO sighting for which the name 'UFOs' was first used happened on 24th June 1947. A man named Kenneth Arnold saw what he called an 'unidentified flying object'. The term UFO came into general usage soon after.

Moose Lodge

At the Loyal Order of Moose Lodge, in Massillon, Ohio Rosemary Lyons and a co-worker were taking a smoking break on the evening of 11th May 2007. They saw what they believed to be a UFO in the sky above the lodge. It appeared to be 60 feet in diameter and they observed it for over 20 seconds. The object was round and glowed underneath and made no noise. There were no reports of aircraft or other manmade objects that could have explained this sighting.

Himalayan Mystery

In 1926, Nicholas Roerich's travel diary mentions that he and his companions encountered a silver metallic disc hovering above the Himalayas (possibly in Nepal). They observed the disc through binoculars for some time until it disappeared beyond mountain peaks.

The Tinley Park Lights

There have been five mass UFO sightings in Tinley Park and Oak Park, Illinois, which are both suburbs of Chicago. There were hundreds of witnesses who reported seeing three silent, shining objects which were between red and orange in color and sphere-shaped. The objects hung in the night sky and moved slowly

---

Thought For the Day

Do not seek to follow in the footsteps of the wise. Seek what they sought.

Matsuo Basho

about in 'formation' for approximately half an hour at a time. For each sighting, the objects were at low altitude, and could be seen from the ground within a circle 25 miles in diameter.

Wartime Mysteries
During the 1940s many fighter plane pilots reported small metallic spheres and colorful balls of light were spotted repeatedly. These were on occasion photographed, by various military air crews around the world during World War II.

Color Craft
In 1950, Great Falls, Montana, United States, the manager of Great Falls' baseball team took color film of two UFOs

The World's Oddest Animals

Pink Fairy Armadillo *The smallest species of armadillo in existence, the Pink Fairy Armadillo or Pichiciego, is typically a mere 90-115mm long, excluding the tail, and is pale rose or pink in color. It is found in central Argentina where it inhabits dry grasslands and sandy plains populated with thorn bushes and cacti. If frightened it can bury itself completely in a matter of seconds. The Pink Fairy Armadillo burrows small holes near ant colonies in dry dirt to feed mainly on ants and ant larvae nearby. Occasionally it feeds on worms, snails, insects and larvae, or various plants and roots.*

apparently flying above Great Falls. The film has been analyzed by the US Air Force and independent investigators and no explanation has ever been given.

Lights on Film
On 25th August 1951 in Lubbock, Texas lights were repeatedly observed flying over the city. They were witnessed by science professors from Texas Tech University as well as being caught on camera by a Texas Tech student. Their origins have never been discovered.

The Disappeared
In June 1953, at Otis Air Force Base in Falmouth, Massachusetts, a US Air Force radar operator and pilot bailed out of their aircraft over Otis Air Force Base because of engine failure. There have been claims that the men were chasing a UFO. The airplane and both operators were never seen again.

UFOs on Film
Over the period from May to September 2008 a night guard at the Yeni Kent Compound near Istanbul, Turkey, repeatedly filmed UFOs over Turkey in the hours of darkness. Many witnesses corroborated the two and a half hours' worth of video, and the Sirius UFO Space Science Research Center has described the film as 'most important images of a UFO ever filmed'.

The CIA Investigates
In 1952, there was a wave of reported sightings of UFOs in the United States in the Washington DC area. The cases made

headline news across the country. So many people contacted various government agencies regarding UFOs, that daily government business was affected. On 1st August 1952 the *New York Times* reported that 'regular intelligence work has been affected.' Various newspapers, including the *Baltimore Sun*, *Washington Star*, *Denver Post*, and the *Los Angeles Times*, reported the opinion of Air Force Chief of Staff Hoyt S. Vandenberg that the recent spate of UFO sightings and reports was an example of 'mass hysteria'. The military was concerned that the confusion generated by these UFO reports could be exploited by communist foes.

Documents show the CIA becoming involved after a request by the National Security Council. This development came about because President Truman personally expressed concern over the sightings at a NSC meeting. The CIA's study was primarily conducted by their Office of Scientific Intelligence (OSI). They gave this matter such importance that they authorized an ad hoc committee in late 1952 which eventually led to the formation of the Robertson Panel by the CIA in 1953, a body which monitored UFO sightings.

The Goblins
On 21st August 1955, a family in Kentucky, USA, encountered a group of strange, goblin-like creatures. The creatures are reported to have attacked the family as the family shot at them.

The Mind Bending Quiz

1   Who has more daughters, George W. Bush or Tony Blair?
2   What is the total of the numbers in a row in a Sudoku puzzle?
3   What is the emblem of Canada?
4   Where was the Genie in the 1999 hit of Christine Aguilera?
5   In which US state was the first National Park established?
6   Which Brothers made the first controlled powered flight?
7   Born in Yugoslavia, Monica Seles eventually played for which country?
8   Which part of the body is associated with Achilles?
9   Which was the first full length feature film designed completely on computer?
10 To the nearest million, what is the population of Portugal?
11 Jenny and Oliver were the tragic young lovers in which movie?
12 In which part of the human skeleton are the metatarsals?
13 Which Fonda won an Oscar for *On Golden Pond*?
14 Which was the first country in the world to introduce national conscription?
15 Which Julia won an Oscar for *Erin Brokovich*?

(Answers on Overleaf)

Answers

1 George W. Bush. 2 45. 3 Maple Leaf. 4 Bottle.
5 Wyoming. 6 Wright Brothers. 7 USA. 8 Heel.
9 *Toy Story*. 10 Ten. 11 *Love Story*. 12 Foot.
13 Henry. 14 France. 15 Roberts.

How did you do?

12-15
King of the World

8-11
Super Trooper

4-7
Medium Cool

1-3
Head in the Clouds

Brief Histories

The Black Death. In 1346 eastern Asia and China were afflicted by a terrible plague. It was a deadly combination of bubonic plague (carried by fleas, particularly those on black rats) and pneumonic plague, in which the bacilli are spread through the air as infected victims breathe and sneeze. The plague traveled westwards across Asia during 1347. By autumn, Turkish tribes in the Crimea were affected. At a siege of Genoese merchants at a fortified trading post in Caffa, they catapulted plague victims over the walls instead of the usual massive stones. The Genoese were terrified and broke out from the siege, returning to Europe. Unfortunately they brought the plague back with them.

The first European outbreak was in Sicily in October 1347. The most common route of infection was through trading routes, so the ports of Genoa and Venice were hit next, in January 1348. Gradually the disease spread across Europe, with rumours of its deadly effects preceding it. A huge proportion of affected towns and villages tended to be killed by the plague. One rumour blamed water poisoned by the Jews for the illness, and this led to several massacres, starting with one in France in 1348. As Jews suffered similar attacks and pogroms across Flanders, France and Germany, many fled to Poland, where they were given asylum by the King Casimir III.

In late summer 1348 the plague reached England, after infected victims or flea-carrying rats had been carried on a ship from Calais. From eastern England the disease would also follow trading routes into Norway and Sweden in 1350. It was a period of great fear and superstition and economic collapse, although some of the survivors would eventually benefit from the shortage of workers as serfs and villeins were now able to demand higher wages for their labour. There were further outbreaks through the rest of the century, but none were as terrible as that first one in which up to a third of Europe's population died.

The Roosevelt Dime
Franklin D. Roosevelt was left partially paralyzed after a bout of polio in 1921. Roosevelt could afford excellent private treatment but he knew that there were many who couldn't. This was a time when there was no cure or vaccine available for polio. In 1938, he helped to create the National Foundation for Infantile Paralysis (later known as the March of Dimes). It helped to care for polio patients and funded research looking for a cure. It was money raised by the March of Dimes that helped Jonas Salk to discover a vaccine for polio. After President Franklin D. Roosevelt died in 1945 there was a write-in campaign involving

Natural Thoughts

Among creatures born into chaos, a majority will imagine an order, a minority will question the order, and the rest will be pronounced insane.

Robert Brault

letters from the public to the United States Treasury Department suggesting that Roosevelt's portrait should be featured on a coin. Due to his involvment in the March of Dimes, the dime was chosen. The new dime was first released on 30th January 1946, Roosevelt's birthday.

The Vikings

The Vikings came from Scandinavia. Their name came from the Old Norse word for piracy, as when they sailed away to rape and pillage other lands they were 'going Viking'. From AD 700 to 1100 the Vikings were a powerful force in Europe. Many left Scandinavia and settled in other countries, including Britain, Ireland, Greenland and Iceland. They weren't always pirates. Many settled peacefully in new lands as farmers, craftsmen or traders.

In 865, a great army of Vikings invaded England and stayed for 14 years of battles against the local kings and warlords. In 892, a fleet of 300 Viking ships returned to fight against King Alfred the Great of Wessex. It was only his resistance that prevented the Vikings from becoming the dominant caste in England. Eric Bloodaxe, the last Viking king on British soil was driven out in the late 10th Century. After his death in battle, the Vikings in England finally recognised the English monarchy. However, one could argue that the Vikings were the final victors in this long battle. In 1066 William the Conqueror, Duke of Normandy, invaded Britain, defeating King Harold in the Battle of Hastings. These particular Normans were descended from Vikings who had settled in France. So while the Viking Age was now finished, the British monarchy for centuries to come would be of Viking blood.

The 'Tin Lizzie'

Henry Ford's Model T was aimed at the average American so it needed to be sold at an affordable price. Marketed from 1908 to 1927, it was the first mass-produced car and acquired the nickname of the 'Tin Lizzie' after a famous 1922 car race. Car dealers often held races at which new models were unveiled. In Pikes Peak, Colorado in 1922, a championship race was held in which a Noel Bullock raced his old Model T. The car was named 'Old Liz' because of its rather shabby condition, and in the crowd the name 'Tin Lizzie' caught on. Bullock won the race in his old car even though he was competing against newer models. This gave such a good impression of the Model T's durability that the national press picked up the story, and the nickname 'Tin Lizzie' stuck.

Pablo Picasso

Pablo Picasso (1881–1973) was a Spanish artist who had a revolutionary impact on painting, drawing, sculpture, and ceramics. Born in Malaga, in southern Spain, his father was an art teacher who was also an artist. The young Pablo was something of a child prodigy, and produced impressive art from a young age. Following his Spanish childhood, he moved to Paris at the age of 19. He would also spend periods in Barcelona and Madrid. His most famous early paintings came in the melancholy style known as the 'blue period'. They featured a predominance of the color blue, as Picasso started to move further from realistic styles. After this his work and the palette of colors he was using became slightly more cheerful in the 'rose period'. Then came a radical break when, along with his friend Georges Braque, he embarked on the completely different style of Cubism in which objects were represented by cubes, cones, and cylinders as well as by scraps of objects from real life. While this was his most shocking departure he would continually experiment with styles such as Surrealism and abstraction, and different techniques such as collage, mural painting, sculpture, and ceramics. One of his most monumental works was *Guernica*, the giant painting he created in 1937 as a protest against the Spanish Civil War. *Guernica* traveled the world, being displayed in different galleries and drawing attention to the tragedies that his native Spain was undergoing. Picasso's work was suppressed under the Nazis, but most of it survived, along with his reputation, and he remained an admired figure until his death in 1973. His final words, which were turned into a song by Paul McCartney, were 'Drink to me, drink to my health, you know I can't drink any more.'

Hoover Flags
After the 1929 Wall Street Crash, President Herbert Hoover was attempting to prevent the country from falling into an economic depression. The fact that the Great Depression lasted much of the following decade suggests that not enough was done, and

Thought For the Day

The charm of history and its enigmatic lesson consist in the fact that, from age to age, nothing changes and yet everything is completely different.

Aldous Huxley

Hoover's name was used as an ironic nickname for many of the results of that crisis. The economic crisis led to the homeless living in shanty towns, also known as 'Hoovervilles'. If the homeless used newspapers to keep warm they called them 'Hoover blankets'. Shortages of gas and money for gas led to the increased use of horses and carts, which became known as 'Hoover wagons'. Meanwhile poor and destitute wanderers would turn their pockets inside out to indicate poverty, which was useful both to deter thieves from wasting their time and in provoking pity and perhaps charity. The turned-out empty pockets acquired the name 'Hoover flags'.

A Brief History of Tug-of-War
The game tug-of-war has been played for at least two millennia and probably dates back to the Ancient Greeks. More recently it has even been an Olympic event. In 1900 it was an official sport at the Paris Olympic Games. It was not the greatest of successes as it only remained an official Olympic sport until the Antwerp Olympic Games in 1920. Many other Olympic events have been removed over the years, including lacrosse, golf, rugby and polo while newer events such as 'beach volleyball' and 'synchronized swimming' have been added as replacements. Tug-of-war continues to be a popular sport on a local level, being contested at many fairs and festivals.

Gerald Ford's Real Name
The 38th President of the United States, Gerald Ford changed his name in his twenties. He was originally called Leslie King Jr., after his father. His mother and his biological father were

The Fascinating Body

The jaw muscle is the most powerful muscle in the human body. And the jawbone is also the hardest bone in the body.

When honey is swallowed, it reaches the blood stream within 20 minutes.

The sensation of pain travels through the body at approximately 350 feet per second.

Blonde beards tend to grow faster than beards of darker hair.

From the ages of 30 to 70, your nose often lengthens and widens. The difference can be as much as half an inch.

When you touch something, electrical impulses that convey the sensation of feeling travel from the surface of the skin toward the spinal cord at a rate of up to 425 feet per second.

Each red blood cell lives an average of four months. In this time it travels between the lungs and other tissues 50,000–100,000 times before it returns to the bone marrow to die.

We blink once every two to ten seconds. While reading a sentence, the eyes swing back and forth up to 100 times a second, and during each second the retina can perform the equivalent of 10 billion calculations, as compared to a computer.

The average square inch of skin contains over 600 sweat glands and 20 blood vessels.

The hardest substance in the body is tooth enamel.

Your kidneys filter about 500 gallons of blood every day.

Your hearing becomes less sharp when you have overeaten.

divorced because of the abusive behavior of the father. This was shortly after Ford was born in 1913. Two years later his mother met Gerald Ford Sr. and she married him soon afterwatds. The family called him Gerald Ford Jr. rather than Leslie King Jr., wanting to move on from the past. However, his name was not officially changed until another twenty years later, on 3rd December 1935, when Ford was 22 years old.

The Rise of Nazi Germany
Germany was a turbulent place after the economic problems of the late 1920s. The Nazi party were on the rise, but had not cemented their grip on power. The German parliament building (the Reichstag) burned down on 27th February 1932. A Dutchman called Marinius van der Lubbe was arrested and confessed to the crime. Hitler claimed that it had been backed by a Communist plot. As a direct result President Hindenburg was persuaded to sign the 'Presidential Decree for the Protection of the People and the State', which allowed the power of arbitrary arrest. As a result leading Communists were arrested. The last election of the Weimar period in Germany was held on 5th March 1933. The Nazis didn't get a true majority of the vote but following the ban on the Communist party, none of its members

 # The Fame Name Game

What did Julia Elizabeth Wells change her name to?

Answer: Julie Andrews

could take their seats in the Reichstag, and this allowed the Nazis to take control. In March 1933 the Reichstag passed the enabling law, giving Hitler the power to pass new laws without the consent of the Reichstag. Astonishingly 80% of the Reichstag voted in favor, with only the Social Democrats voting against it.

Hitler now imposed a tyrannical regime. Since 1871 Germany had been a federal state, but Hitler imposed loyal Nazi members as 'Reich governors'. In May and June 1933, he banned trade unions and the Social Democratic Party. Not satisfied with this, a month later Hitler banned all parties except the Nazi party. Finally he consolidated his grip on power with the Night of the Long Knives on 30th June 1934, in which his opponents were killed or arrested. In 1934, the SA or brownshirts wanted to take over the army. Heinrich Himmler, head of the SS (the Schutzstaffel, Hitler's personal guard unit) wanted more power and argued for the SS to be removed from SA control. Himmler told Hitler that the SA was planning to overthrow him. Hitler arrested Rohm, the leader of the SA, while the SS arrested and killed other key SA figures and critics of Hitler within the Nazi party. Finally on 2nd August 1934 President Hindenburg died. At this point Hitler assumed presidential powers and called himself Fuhrer (leader).

The Third Reich

One of the first acts of Hitler after he became Fuhrer was to insist that the army should swear an oath of loyalty to him personally. From this time onwards opponents of the regime, in which group he included communists and socialists, were liable to arrest and being sent to a concentration camp without trial. Homosexuals, vagrants, beggars and the 'work-shy' received the same treatment.

Hitler was an anti-semite and passed the Nuremberg laws in 1935. These made it illegal for Jews to marry or have relationships with 'Aryans' (by which he meant people of Germanic descent). The Reich Citizenship Law stated that Jews could not be German citizens and thousands were arrested and sent to concentration camps.

The Nazis regarded modern art, jazz music and music by Jewish composers as degenerate and all were banned. In 1933 the Nazis organized a book burning, taking works they disapproved of from libraries for the bonfires. Many writers, artists, film directors and musicians fled from Nazi Germany in response to their attack on freedom of expression.

The Nazis were obsessed with education. School children were indoctrinated with Nazi ideology, including the Nazi version of history and their racial theories. They also created the Hitler-Jugend (Hitler Youth), a scout-like organization which soon became compulsory for boys of 14 and above. As well as camping, hiking and learning to tie knots, they studied Nazi ideas. For girls they created the Bund Deutscher Madel (League of German Girls).

Thought For the Day

Alice came to a fork in the road. 'Which road do I take?' she asked.
'Where do you want to go?' responded the Cheshire cat.
'I don't know,' Alice answered.
'Then,' said the cat, 'it doesn't matter.'

Lewis Carroll, *Alice in Wonderland*

The Fall of Nazi Germany

Following a period of increasing tension over the situations in
Austria and Czechoslovakia, and the false peace that Chamberlain
negotiated with Hitler, war became inevitable. On 1st September
1939, the German army invaded Poland. Two days later, Britain
and France declared war, as Poland was overrun. On 17th
September, the Russians invaded Poland from the east and by early
October the country was fully occupied. In April 1940 the Germans
occupied Denmark and moved on to Norway, which fell in early
June. In May 1940 Germany invaded the Netherlands, Belgium and
France. This was a period of astonishing success for the Germans.
Britain fought on, but there was a widespread expectation that it too
would soon fall to the Third Reich's armies.

Following the Battle of Britain and the failure or abandonment
of German invasion plans, the war moved on to sea and other
parts of the world. Late in 1942 the British won the key battle of
El Alamein in Egypt, a turning point in North Africa. In
November of the same year the Russian army surrounded the
Germans at Stalingrad. A significant part of the German army
surrendered there in January and February. After these setbacks
Germany was fighting a defensive war. Meanwhile British and
American bombing started to destroy German cities and industry.
Through the final years of the war the allies gradually pushed the
Germans back, but these were some of the bloodiest years of the
war with some terrible bombing raids and battles.

In 1945, Germany lay in ruins, its cities reduced to rubble, its
industry destroyed, and millions of innocent people dead. In the
concentration camps 6 million Jews and many others had been
murdered. Hitler committed suicide in his Berlin bunker on 30th

Leaders Have Their Say

Time and again we see leaders and members of religions incite aggression, fanaticism, hate, and xenophobia – even inspire and legitimate violent and bloody conflicts.
Hans Kung

Wise leaders generally have wise counselors because it takes a wise person themselves to distinguish them.
Diogenes of Sinope

Leaders come in many forms, with many styles and diverse qualities. There are quiet leaders and leaders one can hear in the next county. Some find strength in eloquence, some in judgment, some in courage.
John W. Gardner

The trust of the people in the leaders reflects the confidence of the leaders in the people.
Paulo Freire

I know that we shall meet problems along the way, but I'd far rather see for myself what's going on in the world outside, than rely on newspapers, television, politicians and religious leaders to tell me what I should be thinking.
Michael Palin

Without initiative, leaders are simply workers in leadership positions.
Bo Bennett

It is our experience that political leaders do not always mean the opposite of what they say.
Abba Eban

The masses are in reality their own leaders, dialectically creating their own development process.
Rosa Luxemburg

April 1945 at a point when defeat was a matter of days away, and was thus not brought to trial for his many crimes.

The Discovery of Insulin

Diabetes, or 'sugar disease', used to be a fatal illness, but now diabetic people can live a full life. This is down to research in the early 1920s, when Frederick Banting and his assistant Charles Best were researching diabetes at the University of Toronto. They managed to isolate insulin and tested it on diabetic dogs by first artificially lowering the dogs' blood sugar levels. Meanwhile the researcher John Macleod and James Collip, a chemist, worked to prepare insulin for human use. On 11th January 1922, the first human experimental dose of insulin was administered to Leonard Thompson, a 14-year-old boy who was dying of diabetes. The insulin worked and saved his life. In 1923, Banting and Macleod were awarded the Nobel Prize for their work on discovering insulin.

The Internet

As recently as the mid-1990s relatively few people had personal computers and they were still seen as something relatively futuristic. Whereas today almost every home has a computer and our world is dominated by the internet revolution. Most

The Fame Name Game

What did Frederick Austerlitz change his name to?

Answer: Fred Astaire

businesses and organizations have a .com domain name and there are different types of domain for different countries and types of organization. The very first .com company was actually set up in the mid-1980s. Symbolics.com registered their domain name on 15th March 1985. At that stage, the internet was known as ARPANET.

The World's Oddest Animals

Frill-Necked Lizard *The Frill-necked Lizard (also known as the Frilled Dragon or Frilled Lizard) is so named for the large ruff of skin which normally lies folded back against its head and neck. The neck frill is formed by long spines of cartilage which support the skin, and if the lizard is frightened, it opens its mouth showing a bright pink or yellow lining, and the frill spreads out, displaying its bright orange and red scales. It is thought the frill may also aid in heat regulation. The lizards may grow up to one meter in total length and mainly walk on four legs. However, if they become frightened they begin to run on all fours and then accelerate onto the hind-legs. In Australia this has led to it being known as the 'bicycle lizard' because of this strange-looking behavior. Males are significantly larger than females when both young and mature. These animals can be aggressive and are known to hiss and lunge! If this fails to scare off the threat, the lizard may flee on two legs to a nearby tree where it climbs to the top and relies on camouflage to keep it hidden.*

In its most basic form it had gone online in December 1969 as part
of the Advanced Research Projects Agency (ARPA) and connected
just four major computers at universities in the southwestern US
(UCLA, Stanford Research Institute, UCSB, and the University of
Utah). By June 1970, MIT, Harvard, BBN, and Systems
Development Corp (SDC) in Santa Monica, Cal. were added, with
more gradually following. Part of the intention behind its dispersed
design was to provide a communications network that could
function even if some of the sites were destroyed, for instance by a
nuclear attack (this was still the time of the Cold War). With a
network, if a direct route was destroyed, then routers could direct
traffic via alternative routes. In its early days the internet was used by
computer experts, engineers, scientists, and librarians. Using it
involved learning a complex system, and there were no websites or
flashing lights. Email was first adapted for ARPANET in 1972. The
huge breakthrough came 18 years later. Tim Berners-Lee, a British
engineer and computer scientist, succeeded in marrying the idea of
hypertext with the existing domain name system and protocols of the
internet. On 25 December 1990, in collaboration with a student at
CERN, where he had been working, he was responsible for the first
successful communication via the internet between an HTTP client
and a server. It was this and the subsequent development of HTML
(the basic language of website design) that allowed the internet to go
on from its modest beginnings to conquer the world.

A Brief History of Shakespeare
William Shakespeare (1564–1616) was born at Stratford-upon-
Avon in a house that tourists can visit today. His mother Mary
was the daughter of a local yeoman farmer while his father John

was a wool dealer and Bailiff of the Borough. From the age of seven to fourteen, Shakespeare was well educated at Stratford Grammar School. At the age of eighteen he married Anne Hathaway, who was seven years older than him but already three months pregnant. Hathaway's family owned a farm just outside Stratford. It was not a happy union, and Shakespeare eventually ran away to London where he became an actor. He did well in London, becoming actor-manager and part-owner in the Blackfriars Theater and eventually the Globe Theater. In his day he was best known as an actor, but it is as a playwright that he has achieved immortal fame around the world. He wrote whatever style the audience wanted, including historical romances, fantastic comedies, and tragedies but his talent and gift for language always shone through. He made a great deal of money from the business of acting and writing plays in his life, and retired a wealthy man in approximately 1613. It is rumoured he contracted a fever after a heavy drinking binge with Ben Jonson and Michael Drayton and that this led to his death at the age of 52. He is buried in the Holy Trinity Church in Stratford.

The Might of the Roman Army

Roman soldiers had to be men, at least 20 years old and they couldn't get married while in the army. Every Roman soldier was declared a Roman citizen, and this was one reason why most soldiers came from countries other than Italy. Many came from Africa, Gaul, the Balkans, Spain, the Middle East and Germany. Minimum service was 25 years, after which soldiers could retire with a pension or a gift of a farm. There were about 30 legions in the Roman Army, with between 4000 and 6000 legionaries in each. The officer in charge of the whole legion was called a legate. Each legion had ten cohorts made up of six troops of about 80 legionaries. These troops were called centuries and were led by a centurion. His status was shown by a stick he carried, with which he might choose to beat any disobedient soldiers. Most of the fighting took place on foot, with horse-mounted soldiers only usually deployed to chase enemies who tried to flee. The Roman soldier's usual weapons were the gladius, which was a short sword, and a javelin, a long spear for throwing. At the peak of the Roman Empire, the Roman Army was the most formidable fighting force in the world, well equipped with machines for breaking sieges by throwing stones or fireballs at their enemies. The Empire stretched across most of Europe, North Africa and the Middle East up into Asia Minor, and it was the military might of the army that made this possible.

 # Memorable Movie Quotes

When the phone ain't ringing, that's me not calling.
Lost and Found

Don't cry at the beginning of the date. Cry at the end of the date like I do.
Jerry Maguire

I was married. My husband cheated on me left and right. He made me feel like I was crazy all the time. One day, he tells me it's MY fault he saw other women. So I picked up a knife and told him it was HIS fault I was stabbing him.
Living Out Loud

Weird And Crazy Laws

In the Greek capital Athens, any driver deemed either 'poorly dressed' or 'unbathed' may be punished by having his (or her) driving license confiscated.

Technically it is illegal to sell dolls of ET or Chewbacca in France, since there is still a law on the statute book forbidding the sale of dolls that have non-human faces.

On the Channel Island of Jersey men are not allowed to indulge in knitting during the fishing season.

Britain passed a law in 1845 making it a capital offense to attempt to commit suicide. Offenders who survived the original attempt could end up being hanged for their efforts.

If you ever find youself in possession of an alligator in Michigan, bear in mind that it is not permitted to chain it to a fire hydrant.

In Turkey, in the 1500s and 1600s, it was illegal to drink coffee. The punishment for transgressing this law was death.

In Alabama it is not legal to carry a comb in your pocket. Like many peculiar laws there is a sensible explanation – the law was passed after a tragic case in which a teenager died after being stabbed with a comb.

If you want to organize a camel hunt, steer clear of the state of Arizona, where this activity is forbidden.

Some archaic laws are still in existence that we can be grateful that few citizens know of or adhere to. In Indiana, for instance, bathing during the winter is prohibited.

Urban Myths

Urban myths are the stories that get passed around, and gradually mutate through Chinese Whispers until no one is sure whether the original story was true, or just made up in a barroom or children's playground somewhere. Some of these stories are funny, some are terrifying and others are just gross. We can't verify the truth or falsity of the stories in this chapter, but for the sake of amusement, here is a selection of the most common urban myths.

Envelope Glue Roach Eggs

An office worker got a paper cut on her tongue as she licked an envelope. The next day her tongue was painfully swollen and she remembered the paper cut. She took pain killers and used medicated mouthwash, but her tongue kept getting worse. Eventually she decided she really had to go to see her doctor. The doctor thought it was a slight infection and tried to make an incision to release what he assumed would be pus from the swelling. But he made a disgusting discovery when he cut into the tongue. About thirty tiny roaches crawled out of the incision. This was because roaches had laid their eggs in the stationery cupboard and some had stuck to the envelope glue. (This story is usually told to try to scare people off licking envelopes...)

Razorblades at Halloween

There are many urban legends about children getting injured by Halloween candy. An early story concerns a Connecticut girl in the 1960s. The claim is that she was given an apple with a razorblade hidden inside it and was badly cut when she tried to eat the apple. After that people were warned to check fruit carefully to see if any offensive items such a razorblade or needle could have been inserted into it. A later story concerned a Florida boy who was given candy that had been injected with poison. This boy supposedly nearly died after becoming very ill from eating the candy. In the early 1980s the story went round that candy was being laced with Tylenol and a number of children were poisoned. The common thread of all these stories is an attempt to harm the children who trick or treat on Halloween.

The Stolen Kidney

A traveler in Mexico befriended a young local man in a bar. The traveler's new friend seemed generous and fun loving and so the traveler went with his new friend to a smaller bar for a late night drink. During the evening, the traveler lost consciousness, and couldn't remember where he was or exactly what happened. He finally regained consciousness in a small room in a downbeat house. As he woke up, the traveler noticed a sharp pain in his right side. Looking down he saw a large fresh scar but had no idea of how it got there. He immediately went to seek medical help. The paramedics took him to the local hospital where he was examined by a doctor. The doctor told him that he had had a kidney removed the previous night. When the traveler pointed out that there was nothing wrong with his kidneys, the doctor concurred. However, he explained that organs were often stolen for large cash sums. The traveler was unable to track down his new friend (who turned out not to be such a great guy) or even the house in which he had awoken.

Alligators in New York's Sewers
A family from Manhattan went to Florida for a vacation and bought a couple of tiny baby alligators for their children. They believed both to be female. They returned with the new pets to New York and kept them in the same tank. When they started to grow, it became apparent that one was getting much bigger and that they had a male and female alligator. They started to fight with each other and they also began to outgrow the tank. The family didn't know what to do, so flushed them down the toilet. These alligators ended up in the sewer system, mated and survived on rats. There have been numerous unconfirmed reports of alligators living in the New York sewer system, descendants of these two.

Airline Promotion
In the early days of air travel, one airline set up an offer whereby the wives of traveling businessmen would be able to travel with

Natural Thoughts

The moment a little boy is concerned with which is a jay and which is a sparrow, he can no longer see the birds or hear them sing.

Eric Berne

their husbands for free. The names of couples who took up the offer were kept in a database and a while later the airline decided to offer a repeat promotion of the same offer, sending letters to the home addresses of the couples. Of the wives who were approached, 95% responded by asking; 'What airplane trip?'

The Pancake Car

Late one night during a very hot summer, a family were woken by a huge crash. At the end of their road two large heavy-goods trucks had smashed into each other. The police were called and arrived with an ambulance. Once they had checked out the scene, the police told them that both truck drivers had been killed. The ambulance took the bodies away and the police told the family that the crash scene had to be investigated and that the trucks would not be removed for a few days. After a few more hot days, the trucks were still there, there was a terrible smell and the area became full of flies. When the family called the police back, they winched the trucks up and discovered there had been a third vehicle involved. A small car had been crushed beneath one of the trucks, the three occupants of the car had been lying there dead in the flattened car and their bodies had started to rot.

The Fame Name Game

What did Betty Joan Perske change her name to?

Answer: Lauren Bacall

The Vanishing Hitchhiker

On a remote desert road in Arizona a driver stopped for a hitchhiker who was standing by the road, in the middle of nowhere. There were no buildings in the area and the hitchhiker was completely alone. The driver invited the hitchhiker to get in the car. The man got in but didn't say where he was heading for and sat in the back seat. After a while they started to chat, and the hitchhiker took a peculiar stone out of his pocket to show it to the driver. It was covered with strange symbols and the hitchhiker said it was a fortune-telling rune that had been used by Native Americans a long time ago. After the driver had taken it in his hand, the hitchhiker asked for it back. 'You're returning from a business meeting in California,' he told him. This made the driver uneasy as it was true. Then the hitchhiker told him his wife's name, where she was and how many children he had. The driver couldn't work out how he could have told any of this from the impersonal hired car he was driving so was a bit freaked out.

At the next gas station he stopped for refreshments. Back at the car the hitchhiker told him his family were in danger and should leave the house. He then got out to go to the bathroom. After a half an hour, the driver went to search for him, but he had completely disappeared. The driver then phoned home in a panic and asked his wife to get the children out of the house. Later that afternoon an airplane hit the house, in a freak accident.

Halloween Body

One icy Halloween night, on a highway near to Chicago, drivers reported seeing a tasteless Halloween decoration hanging from a bridge. The life-sized body of what looked like an old witch was hanging by a piece of rope, swinging as the traffic passed below. After calls to local radio stations complained about the bad taste of this, police were sent to take the decoration down. However, they made the unpleasant discovery that it was a real body. A local woman had committed suicide by jumping off the bridge with a rope tied around her neck. The misfortune was that, because it was Halloween, no one had thought it might be a real person.

The World's Worst Burger

A man bought a chicken burger from a well-known chain and ate it on his way to work. He arrived before finishing his meal and kept the remainder of the meal in his bag for later. During the afternoon he developed a serious fever and started to feel dizzy and sick. The symptoms were so worrying, one of his colleagues took him straight to the hospital for a doctor to look at him. The doctor diagnosed symptoms of serious food poisoning and asked him what he had eaten that day. The man showed him the remains of the chicken burger that were still in his briefcase. Upon examination, the meat of the burger had a giant abscess in

Obscure English Language Facts

The Other Half of The Alphabet
Nonsupports (11 letters long), is the longest word in the English language that only uses letters from the second half of the alphabet. The 10-letter runners-up include **prosupport**, **soupspoons**, and **zoosporous**.

it, some of which the man had bitten through. It was the pus that oozed out of the abcess that had caused the food poisoning.

Exam Swap

During an exam, a college student realised that he didn't know any of the answers because he had simply been revising the wrong subject areas – he needed to write three essays but was going to struggle to complete any. In desperation he committed three of the questions to memory, and then wrote a letter to his parents telling them that he was in the exam room and had finished early so wanted to write and tell them how well he thought he had done. He handed in the letter, took some spare answer paper with him and then ran to the library where he researched and wrote the necessary essays. He sent the essays to his mother. In turn, she posted the exam answers back to him. At this point he took them to his professor, with the stamped dated envelopes, explaining that he had made an awful mistake. He claimed he had finished the exam early and had written the letter in the time remaining. The gullible professor chose to believe the story, accepted the belated exam paper, and the student ended up with straight 'A's. (Warning: Many college professors and teachers have heard this story and are unlikely to fall for an attempt to duplicate the trick.)

Play Snake

A family were enjoying a day out at a restaurant that had one of those play areas with polystyrene balls. Their three-year-old boy played there for a while. When it was time to go home, the boy complained of a pain in his hand. The mother looked quickly at his hand and saw two little scars which she thought must be scrapes or scratches. They luckily didn't live far away because the boy rapidly became weak and started to struggle to breathe. They diverted to the hospital where the doctor identified the marks on his hands as snakebites. The restaurant was informed of the situation, searched the play area, and uncovered a poisonous snake that had been concealed under the play balls.

Leave Room To Rise
A thirteen-year-old boy had a secret plan to bake his mother a birthday cake. He bought the ingredients in secret and started following the recipe when he got home from school. When his mother got home two hours later her son was standing outside the kitchen door doing nothing. She asked what was going on and he confessed his secret plan, and told her he was following the recipe. They looked at the recipe book together and he pointed to the bit where the book said 'leave room to rise'. He had spent two hours leaving the room repeatedly and waiting for the mixture to turn into a cake, but had been constantly disappointed.

The Chandelier Bug
Two businessmen were in Moscow working on a new building contract they were bidding for. They were concerned about being bugged as this was during the cold war period and the Russian secret service was notorious for its surveillance techniques. They searched the room and found a suspicious bulge under the carpet. They were convinced that this was a bugging device, so they carefully unscrewed it from the floor. However, when they picked it up it turned out to be empty, with no wiring. They then went downstairs for dinner, but in the dining room of the hotel

Hilarious Misprints

The accident occurred at Hillcrest Drive and Santa Barbara Avenue as the dead man was crossing the intersection.
Los Angeles Times

Save regularly in our bank. You'll never reget it.
Advertisement

The bride was gowned in white silk and lace. The color scheme of the bridesmaids' gowns and flowers was punk.
Toronto Post

Wrap poison bottles in sandpaper and fasten with scotch tape or a rubber band. If there are children in the house, lock them in a small metal box.
Philadelphia Record

Two men were admitted to hospital suffering from mild buns.
Essex Chronicle

Unless the teachers receive a higher salary increase they may decide to leave their pests.
The Times

Peanut butter grilled corn – spread ears lightly with peanut butter. Wrap each ear with bacon slice; fasten with toothpick. Place on grill, turning until done – about 10 minutes. Or let everyone grill his own ears, using long skewers to do so.
The American Weekly

Man, honest. Will take anything.
Advertisement

Today's weather: A depression will mope across Southern England.
The Guardian

Astronomers Say Comet Should Be Visible To The Naked Idaho
Los Angeles Examiner

they found a strange scene. The huge chandelier in the center of the room had come crashing down onto the tables below. Luckily no one was hurt, but the damage was considerable and the chandelier looked to be beyond repair. At this point the businessmen suddenly put two and two together and swiftly went elsewhere for their dinner.

The Accidental Mugger

Early one morning in a city park, a man was jogging when another jogger passed him, bumping into him slightly on the way past. The man immediately checked for his wallet. It was missing, so he ran after the other jogger and tackled him to the ground. He started shouting that he wanted his wallet. Terrified, the other jogger handed over a wallet before running away at great speed. The man ran home to boast to his wife about how he had nearly lost his wallet but had fought for it. She calmly pointed him to the kitchen table, where his wallet had been lying all along. In his hand he had the other jogger's wallet, that he had taken from him by force.

Necklace Embarassment

Nurses are not allowed to wear jewelry whilst working for a very good reason. In one East Coast hospital, a nurse was giving a male patient a bed bath when her gold necklace got entangled in his pubic hair. With her head stuck, she couldn't get the necklace undone. As she attempted to pull herself free, the man moaned in pain. At this unfortunate moment, the man's wife walked into the room and started to scream at them, which was unsurprising given what she thought what they were doing. After a brief, violent altercation another nurse arrived and cut the chain free. From that day on a jewelry ban was imposed.

Zombie Funeral
In Mexico, a funeral was held for a young man who had died in a fight. As the priest was finishing the ceremony, a young man came into the chapel. All the women began screaming and the mother of the dead boy fainted clean away. One of the men told the priest that the person they were laying to rest that day was the young man who had just walked in, he was a living corpse. Once everyone calmed down, the young man identified himself as the person whose funeral it was supposed to be. He had been staying with friends and had wondered why all his family and friends were gathered in the chapel as he passed. His mother had very poor eyesight, and had wrongly identified a dead body at the police station as her son.

Wheelbarrows
For many years a security guard at a large factory noticed that one of the workers left each night with a wheelbarrow filled with

 **Thought For the Day**
He who has seen present things has seen all, both everything which has taken place from all eternity and everything which will be for time without end; for all things are of one kin and of one form.

Marcus Aurelius

straw. Each night he felt obliged to search carefully through the straw to make sure that the man didn't have any tools or other equipment hidden there – part of his job was to prevent workers stealing from the plant. Ten years later, this particular worker had his leaving party as he was retiring. When he said goodbye, the security guard finally asked him what he had been doing all those years taking straw out in a wheelbarrow. The man replied, 'Stealing wheelbarrows.'

Ice Coins

In the 1970s in England, electricity companies often made people have an electricity slot meter in their flat. This forced people to pay for their electricity as they used it, thus preventing the need for bill collection. One London family who lived in an upstairs apartment found a way to fool the meters. The mother created a mould of a fifty pence coin then used this to make replica coins out of ice. They were delighted to find that the meter accepted the ice coins and that they were able to keep the heating on all winter as a result. However, in the spring, when they were moving a wardrobe across the room, the floor started to sag and then collapsed under the weight, taking most of the contents of the room down through into the apartment below. It turned out the

 The Fame Name Game

What did Robert Zimmerman change his name to?

Answer: Bob Dylan

downstairs neighbor had been complaining all winter to her landlord about the large water stain that had been spreading on her ceiling. As the coins had melted they had soaked the floorboards through and the final result was the collapse of the entire floor.

Moving the Bed

An elderly lady living in one of the poorer suburbs of Paris was happy to find a cheap quilt at her local flea market. She took the quilt home and covered her bed with it, glad of the heat it gave her in the cold winter. However, during the night she woke up to find that the quilt had fallen onto the floor. She pulled it back up and went back to sleep, but the same thing happened again several times during the night. She started to suspect that the quilt was somehow moving itself, so took a pair of scissors and cut the quilt open. It looked at first to contain a lot of dirty feathers. But when she looked closer she realised that it was infested with maggots. As they wriggled en masse, the quilt was moving itself along. She took the quilt out and burned it and spent the rest of her winter in her old coat and blanket.

Out of Body Experience

A young man went missing and his mother called the police. A search party was organized and after extensive local investigations he was declared officially missing. He was known for not being the cleverest young man, so his mother was worried about him. However, he turned up two days later looking ragged and confused. He told anyone who asked that he had been dragged away by aliens. They had apparently taken him to a room where he was given food that burnt his mouth and kept forcing him to drink a strange golden liquid. Then he lost consciousness, woke up in a field feeling terrible and gradually made his way home. He couldn't remember anything from the moment when he started to drink the golden liquid. He seemed puzzled as to why everyone was so interested in this tale. When the police asked him to retrace his movements, they discovered a small Mexican bar near the field where he had woken up. All that had happened was that he had fallen in with a group of Mexicans, gone to their bar, and then had confused the police by using the immigration term 'aliens' to describe them.

Blind Confusion
Early one morning a woman was just getting into a shower when the door bell sounded. She went naked to the door, and used the the entry phone to ask who was there. A male voice answered 'Blind man!' She was in a hurry to get ready for work and figured it was only a blind man begging for money so she opened the door without a dressing gown or towel. It turned out that the rather surprised looking visitor was a man from the company she had called to fit some new blinds.

Getting Plastered
A group of junior doctors went on a stag night, with their friend, the groom-to-be. The aspiring husband became extremely drunk and passed out late in the evening. His friends then decided to play a joke, and took him to the hospital. There they wrapped his leg in plaster, and when he awoke they told him he had fractured his tibia when he fell down some stairs. The groom was forced to go through the marriage ceremony on crutches with half of his left

trouser leg cut off. The friends decided that this was as far as the joke should go, so after he had set off on honeymoon on crutches, they called his hotel to tell him that the plaster was fake and could be removed. However, he had guessed they might play some kind of trick and had given them the wrong hotel address, so he ended up spending the entire honeymoon on crutches.

The Curse of Tecumseh
There is a folktale that a death curse from a Native American Indian threatens US presidents elected in years that are divisible by twenty. There have been exceptions, but many US presidents elected in years ending in zero have been killed or have died while in office. Tecumseh is believed to have placed a curse on the Great White Fathers after suffering defeat at the Battle of Tippecanoe in 1811:

• **William Henry Harrison**
  Harrison, elected in 1840, died aged 68 after his inaugural speech. He talked for an hour and 40 minutes in freezing

Natural Thoughts

We are all but recent leaves on the same old tree of life and if this life has adapted itself to new functions and conditions, it uses the same old basic principles over and over again. There is no real difference between the grass and the man who mows it.

Albert Szent-Györgyi

damp conditions, then became ill, and died of pneumonia
exactly one month later in April 1841.

- **Abraham Lincoln**
Lincoln was elected in 1860 and was assassinated by John
Wilkes Booth in 1865, not long after his re-election.

- **James A. Garfield**
Garfield was gunned down in a railroad station waiting room
in Washington DC in July 1881, following his 1880 election.
He died of his injuries in September of the same year.

- **William McKinley**
After being re-elected in 1900, William McKinley was shot as
he shook hands with supporters following a speech in
Buffalo, in September 1901. He died of his injuries around
ten days later.

- **Warren G. Harding**
Harding came to office in 1920 but died of an apparent
stroke or heart attack in 1923. At the time, there were some
rumours that he had been poisoned by his wife.

- **Franklin D. Roosevelt**
During his third term in office in 1940, Franklin D.
Roosevelt suffered a major cerebral hemorrhage and
eventually died not long after beginning his record fourth
term in 1945.

- **John F. Kennedy**
Kennedy, elected in 1960, was assassinated by Lee Harvey
Oswald in 1963.

Perhaps the curse has now lifted. Ronald Reagan was elected in
1980 and didn't die while he was in office, though he did survive

an assassination attempt by John Hinckley in 1981. The bullet missed his heart by a matter of inches. And George W. Bush (elected in 2000) is still in good health after two full terms of office.

Trunk Call

Police in New York raced to get to a store where the owner had pressed the panic button, to alert them to a robbery. The thief ran out of the back door of the store as they entered from the front. The back of the store looked onto a narrow alley from which only Spiderman could have climbed out. The alley led back to the street, but it was competely empty with no sign of the thief. The man appeared to have simply vanished into thin air. However, two days later the police heard banging in the trunk of their patrol car. When they opened it up they found their robber, looking pale and weak. He had hidden in the trunk as soon as he ran out of the alley, calculating that it was the last place they would think to look. However, he had then been unable to open it from the inside and, after two days of waiting for a chance to escape, had concluded that surrender was the best option.

The Fame Name Game

What did Malcolm Little change his name to?

Answer: Malcolm X

Amazing Animals

The spots on a Holstein cow are like fingerprints, in that no two cows have the same pattern of spots.

Twelve or more cows are known as a 'flink.'

The longest recorded flight made by a chicken is thirteen seconds.

A duck's quack doesn't seem to echo. There is no scientific explanation for this to date. If any budding scientists need suggestions for their next research project, a Nobel Prize surely awaits.

Chickens with red ear lobes lay brown eggs. White eggs come from hens with white feathers and ear lobes. The shell color makes no difference to the quality, nutrients or flavor of the egg.

When a female horse and male donkey mate, the offspring is called a mule, but when a male horse and female donkey mate, the offspring is called a hinny.

Goats' eyes have rectangular pupils.

Hamsters are fond of crickets as a snack.

Pigs, walruses and light-colored horses can get sunburned.

Horses are unable to vomit.

A pig's penis is shaped like a corkscrew.

A pig's skin reaches its thickest at the back end of the animal, where it is a sixth of an inch.

A capon is a castrated rooster.

Quirky Tales From History

S kate Man. The first roller skates were attempted two centuries ago by Joseph Merlin. His first public demonstration ended in disaster. As a renowned maker of violins and harpsichords, the Belgian-born Merlin moved to London in 1760, where he dreamed up the idea of replacing the blades on ice skates with metal wheels. To dramatize his invention, Merlin dressed as a minstrel and made a spectacular entrance on skates at an elegant masquerade ball. He dazzled the other guests as he wheeled gracefully about the ballroom floor while playing a violin. Then, as his admirers watched in horror, Merlin lost control and sailed headlong into a crystal mirror, demolishing it and his handcrafted violin while also reportedly breaking his nose.

Joseph Merlin (1735-1803)

Skinny Dipping Away
One summer day, the young Josef Scheffel set out on a hiking trip along the right bank of the Rhine. The day grew unbearably hot so Scheffel removed his clothes in a secluded spot and dove in for a swim. Having grievously underestimated the river's current, however, he barely managed to regain the shore – on the opposite (left) bank. Entirely naked, the young poet was obliged to seek assistance at the nearest inn, where he soon found himself

being questioned by the district military policeman, who also happened to be visiting: 'Where did you come from?' the officer demanded. 'From the opposite bank, Sir,' Scheffel replied. 'And what's your name?' 'I'm the writer, Josef Victor von Scheffel.' 'Indeed?' the officer cried 'Show me your papers!'

Josef Victor von Scheffel, (1826-1886) German writer

De-cloaked Clergy

Even nuns and clerics were not immune from the Las Vegas-like madness of 18th-Century Venice. Nuns wearing pearls and low-cut gowns could be seen fighting among themselves for the honor of serving as mistress to a visiting papal nuncio. One evening, in a casino in 1762, the Abbe Grioni bet all his clothes on the turn of the wheel, lost, and promptly returned to his monastery completely naked.

Abbe Grioni, (18th Century) Venetian monk

Hegel's Soliloquy

Even on his deathbed Hegel remained abstractly philosophical. 'Only one man ever understood me,' he remarked, with a pause, 'and even he didn't understand me.'

Georg Wilhelm Hegel, (1770-1831) German idealist philosopher

Thought For the Day

You can't wake a person who is pretending to be asleep.

Navajo Proverb

Shortsighted

In 1845 the amateur astronomer, the Earl of Rosse, built a
telescope with a lens six feet in diameter. Dubbed the Leviathan,
it was easily the largest telescope of its day. Rosse was applauded
for his efforts; however, the results he achieved were less than
stellar. The problem? He built it in Ireland – where the weather
was so bad he could hardly ever use it.

Earl of Rosse, (1800-1867) Irish astronomer

Calling Aliens

The famous 19th Century mathematician Karl Friedrich Gauss
once proposed that ten-mile strips of trees delineating the
Pythagorean Theorem should be planted in the Siberian steppes
– so that they might be visible to alien beings on other planets.
In 1840, the Austrian Joseph Johann von Littrow recommended
setting immense geometrical fires in the Sahara for the same
purpose.

Karl Friedrich Gauss (1777-1855)

Godless

At the height of the Industrial Revolution in the 19th Century,
child labor was prevalent in England's factories and coal mines.
One day Robert Owen the famed industrialist (and utopian
socialist) encountered a twelve-year-old breaker boy, exhuasted
from separating shale from coal, completely covered in toxic black
coal dust. 'Do you know God?' Owen asked him. 'No,' the boy
replied. 'He must work in some other mine.'

Robert Owen, (1771-1858) Welsh-born British
manufacturer and social reformer

Demanding Rule

Ferdinand I of Austria suffered from such severe bouts of insanity that, during his reign, a council managed affairs of state. Unsurprisingly, this untenable state of affairs ended in revolution and Ferdinand was forced to abdicate in favor of his nephew, Francis Joseph. According to historian A.J.P. Taylor, among the most lucid utterances of his entire reign was 'I am the emperor...and I want dumplings!'

Ferdinand I, (1793-1875) Austrian emperor (1835-1848)

Toothless and Helpless

The Duke of Marlborough, who lived in considerable style at Blenheim Palace, once visited one of his daughters in her relatively modest home. Early one morning, she was astonished to hear her father hollering down the stairs, complaining that his toothbrush was 'not working': it was not foaming as it should, the duke explained, angrily demanding a replacement. Marlborough's daughter was obliged to explain that foam was produced only when 'toothpaste' was applied to the brush – a task usually performed by the duke's valet.

John Spencer-Churchill Marlborough, British aristocrat (1897-1972)

On the Throne

Despite its lack of modern amenities, the Belgian writer Maurice Maeterlinck once graciously accepted an invitation to visit a French chateau whose remote location would enable him to relax and write in peace. Having arrived while his hostess was away, Maeterlinck asked the maid to direct him to the washroom. She led him down a corridor, at the end of which stood an immense, apparently solid oak throne – from behind which she retrieved a large cloak and face mask. 'Here you are, monsieur,' she said. 'You wear these so no one knows who is sitting here.' Maeterlinck politely thanked the woman and was miles from the chateau by the time his hostess had returned.

Count Maurice Maeterlinck, (1862-1949) Belgian poet and dramatist,
Nobel Prize recipient (Literature, 1911)

The World's Oddest Animals

Proboscis Monkey *The Proboscis Monkey is so called for the distinctive quality of the male's large prominent nose. The purpose of the large nose is unclear, but some believe it to be a result of sexual selection as the female Proboscis Monkey seems to prefer big-nosed males, thus propagating the trait. Both genders have large bellies but males are much larger than females, reaching 72 cm (28 inches) in length, with a tail as long again, and weighing up to 24 kg (53 lbs). Females are up to 60 cm long, weighing up to 12 kg (26 lbs). Diet causes their large bellies, as their digestive system is divided into several sections, with distinctive gut flora, to digest leaves. This digestive process releases a lot of gas, resulting in the monkey's 'bloated' bellies. This also means that the Proboscis Monkey is unable to digest ripe fruit, like most other simians. Instead they consume seeds, fruit and leaves.*

The Breakfast Club
Doctor John Harvey Kellogg prescribed daily yogurt enemas to patients at his Battle Creek, Michigan sanitarium. He also invented breakfast cereal. Both corn flakes and graham crackers were designed to inhibit masturbation, based on the notion that bland food and self-abuse were somehow incompatible.

John Harvey Kellogg, (1852-1943) American physician
and social reformer

Life on Mars?
The American publisher, William Randolph Hearst, always in search of sensational stories, once sent a telegram to a leading astronomer asking 'Is there life on Mars? Please cable 1000 words.' The astronomer replied 'Nobody knows' and repeated it 500 times.

William Randolph Hearst, (1863-1951) American newspaper and
magazine publisher, art collector

Honored Writings
A young poet once sent Hermann Bahr a historical tragedy, along with a request for his opinion: 'If you find any faults, please be honest with me. Words of criticism from such a source would make me feel ennobled.' Bahr returned the manuscript with this comment: 'I'd like to make you at least an archduke.'

Hermann Bahr, (1863-1934) Austrian playwright, author, and theater
director

Churchill's Wrath
Winston Churchill once pilloried one of Prime Minister Stanley Baldwin's policies in the House of Commons. 'History will say

that the right honorable gentleman was wrong in this matter,'
Churchill bluntly declared. 'I know it will, because I shall write
the history.'

Stanley Baldwin, (1876-1947) British Prime Minister

Scientists Squabble

In 1921, a curious editorial appeared in the *New York Times*
critiquing the revolutionary work of rocket scientist Robert
Goddard: 'Professor Goddard does not know the relation
between action and reaction and the need to have something
better than a vacuum against which to react,' it declared. 'He
seems to lack the basic knowledge ladled out daily in high
schools.' Goddard knew the *Times* was wrong. He had used
airtight chambers to show that a rocket could indeed fly in a
vacuum, thanks to Newton's third law. Sure enough, after the
Apollo 11 mission (in 1969), the *Times* published a retraction:
'Further investigation and experimentation have confirmed the
findings of Isaac Newton in the 17th Century, and it is now
definitely established that a rocket can function in a vacuum as
well as in an atmosphere. The *Times* regrets the error.'

Robert Hutchings Goddard, (1882-1945) American
physicist and inventor

Biro's Are Better

While working as a journalist in the early part of the 20th
Century, Hungarian born Laszlo Biro was often annoyed by
fountain pens. He began to wonder whether the troublesome
object could be replaced with something more convenient. The
result was the 'biro' (ballpoint pen). The commercial version of

Laszlo's invention was launched in Argentina. Ironically, however, Biro neglected to use his invention to file for North American patents and, as a result, lost what would have amounted to a sizable fortune.

Laszlo Biro, (1899-1985) Hungarian inventor,
noted for his invention of the ballpoint pen

Larry's Mates
Although Laurence Olivier, often named the finest actor of the 20th Century, was often asked for advice from aspiring performers, he categorically refused to oblige... with one exception. The extent of Olivier's advice to his fellow thespians was to 'Relax your feet.' Though he was knighted in 1947 and made a life peer in 1970, Olivier remained a humble man – refusing to carry on a conversation with anyone who would not address him simply as 'Larry'.

Laurence Olivier, (1907-1989) British actor

Not Right in the Head
The turn of the 20th Century marked the height of oddball treatments for neurasthenia, hysteria, and other newly named neurological disorders. Ford Madox Ford, never one to stint himself, saw nineteen specialists between 1903 and 1906 and underwent treatments which ranged from being fed one grape every quarter of an hour for sixteen hours out of the day to having indecent photographs of a singular banality flashed before his eyes.

Ford Madox Ford, born Ford Hermann Hueffer, (1873-1939)
American writer and editor

The Fascinating Body

The human brain doesn't grow after the age of 18.

Blood is only red in the arteries after it has left the heart and is full of oxygen. In the veins on the way back to the heart, it is purplish, because it has picked up carbon dioxide and other waste from body cells.

The average human bladder can hold up to 13 ounces of liquid.

It takes 72 different muscles all acting together to produce human speech.

During a lifetime, the average human will grow 600 miles of hair.

There have been many experiments into why and how people blush, but scientists still disagree as to the causes and mechanism involved.

One 1970s group of scientists reported that you could cure the common cold by freezing your big toe.

Babies are born without kneecaps. They don't start to develop until the age of two.

Every human living today spent about half an hour as a single cell.

The main cause of blindness in the United States is diabetes.

It is impossible to verify that any disease ever identified has been eradicated forever.

The way that human skin is attached to facial muscles is what gives people dimples.

The dead skin cells an average person sheds in a lifetime would fill eight five-pound flour bags.

Virginia Woolf's Permanent Breakdown

In the 20th Century, literary people seemed particularly susceptible both to nervous breakdowns and the quacks who treated them. Viginia Woolf famously saw five different doctors and underwent the so-called Weir Mitchell cure, from which she later extracted a measure of revenge by mocking the doctor in *Mrs Dalloway*.

Virginia Woolf (1882-1941) British novelist

Nixon Caught Out

Dick Tuck (whose business card once featured a mock dictionary entry for 'political prank') was the 20th Century's premiere political practical joker. Tuck pulled off his best-known prank in Los Angeles in 1962, during Nixon's California gubernatorial campaign. The press reported that five years earlier Howard Hughes had lent the candidate's brother $205,000.

The loan, which had not been repaid, was widely seen as an attempt by Hughes to curry favor with Nixon. At a rally in Chinatown, Tuck distributed signs and fortune cookies that read 'Welcome Nixon!' over a row of Chinese characters. Nixon smiled broadly for the cameras, until he was informed that the

The Fame Name Game

What did Israel Baline change his name to?

Answer: Irving Berlin

Chinese script said, 'How about the Hughes loan?' Nixon grabbed a sign and, on camera, ripped it up. Later, Tuck learned, to his chagrin that the Chinese characters actually spelled out 'What about the huge loan?'

Dick Tuck, (1924-) American practical joker

Churchill's History

Shortly after Harold Macmillan was chosen as the new Conservative leader (over Rab Butler), a private secretary entered Churchill's office and found him muttering: 'Intelligent, yes. Good-looking, yes. Well-meaning, yes, but not the stuff of which Prime Ministers are made.' 'But would Rab have been any better?' the secretary interjected. 'I was thinking,' Churchill replied, 'of Melbourne.' (Churchill often spoke of such historical figures as Walter Raleigh and Henry VIII as though they were his contemporaries; Lord Melbourne had died in 1848.)

Winston Leonard Spenser Churchill, (1874-1965) British politician and writer, Prime Minister (from 1940)

Coast to Coast

In the middle of the 20th Century, Los Angeles was considered by many New Yorkers to be little short of a cultural wasteland. H.L. Mencken had called it 'Moronia', Aldous Huxley had commented that 'thought is barred in this city of Dreadful Joy and conversation is unknown'. Woody Allen was to remark that the city's only contribution to culture was the practice of turning right at a red light, made legal in the 1947 vehicle code.'

Woody Allen, born Allan Stewart Konigsberg, (1935-)

Freudian Slip

Sigmund Freud was not without his critics. Among them was Dr. Sophie Freud, Sigmund's own granddaughter. 'In my eyes,' she once remarked, 'both Adolf Hitler and Sigmund Freud were false prophets of the 20th Century.'

Sigmund Freud, (1856-1939) Austrian physician,
father of psychoanalysis

 # Memorable Movie Quotes

The key here, I think, is to not think of death as an end. But . . . but . . . think of it more as a very effective way of cutting down on your expenses.
Love and Death

Stop trying to hit me and hit me!
The Matrix

All men are mortal. Socrates was mortal. Therefore, all men are Socrates . . . which means that all men are homosexuals . . .
Love and Death

Weird News Stories

Loving Snakes. An Arizona man decided to demonstrate his courage to his friends by kissing a rattlesnake that they had come across in the wild. The man picked up the snake and planted a kiss on its 'lips'; unsurprisingly, he was bitten, on the tongue, by the shocked beast. In an effort to remove the venom, the man tried a drastic and unorthodox method. He attached his tongue to the battery of his car.

Arizona Republic

Doggie Bag
A department store in Japan will, for the equivalent of about £50, prepare a gourmet carry-out meal for your pet dog. A popular menu consists of premium rare beef, unsalted ham sausages, cheese and white chocolate for dessert.

Wall Street Journal

Arms Trade
British troops participating in the recent UN actions in the Gulf were forced to wear thick, green camouflage uniforms, obviously unsuited to the desert environment. This was because four years before the British government had sold all the army's desert uniforms to Iraq.

Los Angeles Times

Fussy Eaters

The US Army has regulations concerning almost all aspects of a soldier's life. Here are some extracts from those regarding the baking of cookies: 'They shall be wholly intact, free from checks or cracks . . . The cookies shall be tender and crisp, with an appetizing flavor, free from burnt or scorched flavor . . . They shall have been uniformly well baked with a color ranging from not lighter than chip 27885, or darker than chip 13711 . . . The color comparison shall be made under sky daylight with objects held in such a way as to avoid specular reaction.'

Ann Arbor News

Beam Me Up

In late 1977 the play-offs to determine who would play Anatoly Karpov in the Chess Championship of the World were taking place between Victor Korchnoi and Boris Spassky. After having lost three games in ten days, Korchnoi made an extraordinary claim. In front of the world's media, he alleged that the KGB were beaming microwaves at him while he was thinking about his moves, to confuse his thought and affect his play. He supported his claim by pointing out that Spassky got up and left the stage after each of his moves, evidently to get out of range.

Daily Mail

Thought For the Day

A stumble may prevent a fall.

English Proverb

False Teeth

Police investigating strange cries in the night coming from the cemetery of St. Mary's Church, Felling, Durham, found a full set of clothes and a pair of false teeth, but no sign of the owner. A senior officer commented: 'There are no reports of anyone looking suspiciously undressed.'

Daily Mirror

Get That Man

Until 1990 prison inmates in Texas were used as bait for training attack dogs The practice was only halted after six injured prisoners sued the state. During an investigation, it emerged that the Vice-Chairman of the Texas Board of Criminal Justice was one of the dog-handlers. So enthusiastic was the VC about his 'hobby' that he even had jackets printed for himself and his fellow trainers featuring the slogan: 'The Ultimate Hunt'.

Los Angeles Times

Keep a Lid on it

In 1922, a meteorite was seen to fall near Omsk in Russia. But when scientists tried to determine where the object had landed, they drew a blank. The rock was eventually located by Professor Dravert of the Omsk Mineralogical Institute. A local farmer was using it to weigh down the lid of the barrel in which he fermented his sauerkraut.

Sunday Express

Pigging Out

Detective Constable Bernard Startup, of Linden Avenue, Oldham, was disturbed at 9.30pm on 5th August 1972 by a knock at his door.

The man on his step alerted DC Startup to the fact that a huge hairy pig was eating the young fir trees in his garden. As the pair watched, the alarming animal stretched too far in search of food and fell into the fishpond. While it was thus distracted, Startup blocked off the entrance to his garden with his car, and phoned his colleagues. The ammal was eventually tranquillized by a vet.

This oddity became a mystery when it was discovered that the 200 lb beast was a wild boar, a species supposedly extinct in Britain for 400 years. The animal was taken to Marwell Zoological Park when no collector or zoo claimed it as their own.

Aldershot News

The Fame Name Game

What did David Robert Hayward-Jones change his name to?

Answer: David Bowie

The Mind Bending Quiz

1   What was the third *Lord of the Rings* movie called?

2   What is a young penguin called?

3   Which hurricane devastated New Orleans in September 2005?

4   Hybrid tea and floribunda are types of what?

5   What is a nun's garment called?

6   How do letters alter when reading down an eye-test chart?

7   Mars is called what color planet?

8   If you have laryngitis what do you lose?

9   Which director Alfred's first Hollywood movie was *Rebecca*?

10 Which Kate is the daughter of Goldie Hawn?

11 What is Frank Sinatra's widow's first name?

12 What color does the skin become if someone suffers from jaundice?

13 Which town is closest to the Everest base camp?

14 Sir Humphry Davy discovered that laughing has which effect?

15 In 2000 U2 received the keys to which city?

(Answers on Overleaf)

Answers

1 *The Return of the King.* 2 Chick. 3 Katrina.
4 Roses. 5 Wimple. 6 They get smaller. 7 Red.
8 Your voice. 9 Hitchcock. 10 Hudson. 11 Barbara.
12 Yellow. 13 Namche. 14 Anaesthetic. 15 Dublin.

How did you do?

12-15
Leader of the Pack

8-11
Everyday Hero

4-7
Supporting Cast

1-3
Where Is My Mind?

Curious Information

A **Fertile Mule.** According to Encyclopedia Britannica, mules – the offspring of a horse and a donkey – are sterile. In 1930, Old Beck, a mule owned by the Texas Agricultural and Mechanical College, proved this wrong by giving birth to two offspring, one sired by a donkey, one by a horse.

Fort Eiffel
All the gold in the world could be placed under the curved base of the Eiffel Tower.

Hotspot
Ladak in Kashmir – high in the Himalayas – has the greatest temperature changes in the world. The temperature can drop from 160 degrees in the daytime to 45 degrees at night, and it is possible to experience a drop of 90 degrees by walking from the sunlight into the shade.

Boxing Clever
During the whole time he was world champion, boxer Jack Dempsey fought for only 138 minutes. This was because few opponents survived his savage style of fighting for more than a few minutes. On 8 February 1926, he knocked out four men in one round each, and repeated this stunt again four days later.

Harmless?

Apparently, cobra venom is quite harmless to drink. But please don't try this at home...

To Kill a Vampire

Do vampires still walk in Romania? In 1974 a gypsy woman told of her father's death when she was a girl. According to custom, she said, the body lay in the house awaiting the ceremonial final dressing by the family. After this ceremony it would be carried to the grave uncovered, so that everyone could see that the man was truly dead.

When the family lifted her father's legs to put them in his burial clothes, the limbs were not stiff. Neither were his arms or the rest of his body. Rigor mortis had not set in. The family stared horrified at him and at each other, and the fearful whispering began.

The story spread among the villagers – people who remembered, or thought they remembered, the vampires that used to roam in the darkness of night. One unmistakable sign of a vampire is an undecomposed body, kept lifelike by the regular feasting on the blood of the living. Fear licked through the

Thought For the Day

The obscure we see eventually. The completely obvious, it seems, takes longer.

Edward R. Murrow

Scientific Snippets

A single ounce of gold is capable of being stretched into a wire 50 miles long.

Sea water weighs about a pound and a half more per cubic foot than fresh water at the same temperature, because of the additional mineral salts it contains.

Shippingport Atomic Power Station in Pennsylvania went on line in 1957. It was the first nuclear facility to generate electricity in the United States, and was only closed down in 1982.

The air we breathe is 78% nitrogen, 21.5% oxygen, 0.5% argon and other gases.

The Chinese were using aluminium to make things as early as AD 300, while in the West its use wasn't rediscovered until 1827.

Diamond is the hardest naturally occurring substance, and also one of the most valuable natural substances. Diamonds are crystals formed almost entirely of carbon. A diamond is the most enduring of all gemstones because it is so hard. Their rarity is emphasized by the fact that only four important diamond fields have ever been found – in Africa, South America, India, and the Soviet Union.

Mercury is the only metal that is liquid at room temperature.

The largest gold nugget ever found weighed 172 lbs 13 oz.

Natural gas has no odor. The smell is added artificially in order that leaks can be detected.

The three most common elements in the universe are hydrogen, helium and oxygen.

village, and the inhabitants soon came to the house armed with a wooden stake.

The family – bewildered, uncertain, and grief-stricken – fell back. The men tore off the corpse's covering sheet and, in the traditional manner, thrust the stake through the dead man's heart. The vampire – if such it was – was vanquished.

Wise Words
Franklin D. Roosevelt: 'A radical is a man with both feet firmly planted up the air.'

Quaker Oats
Did you know that Quaker Oats once removed Popeye the Sailorman from its packages of Instant Oats because the Society of Friends (the Quakers) objected to his use of violence to settle disputes?

Here's The Bell, Here's The Steeple...
In November 2003, a Romanian priest is said to have appealed to his young parishioners to abstain from having sex in his church's steeple. 'There are used condoms everywhere,' he supposedly complained. 'I even found some hanging on the bell's chain.'

The Fame Name Game

What did Melvin Kaminsky change his name to?

Answer: Mel Brooks

Local police chief Lucian Sfetcu, however, said little could be done to resolve the problem: 'We give out hundreds of fines for this activity.'

Holy Hose
In 1998, Church elders and several firefighters baptized 2000 people in Charlotte, North Carolina – by fire hose. 'It's not the water,' C.B. Gibson of the United House of Prayer for All People supposedly explained, 'it's the belief you have in it.'

Christ's Mass at Christmas
Did you know that our word Christmas is derived from the Middle English usage 'Christ's Mass'. In medieval England there were, in fact, three Masses celebrated on Christmas Day. The first and most characteristic was at midnight (the Angel's Mass), catching up the notion that the light of salvation appeared at the darkest moment of the darkest date in the very depth of winter. The second Christmas Mass came at dawn (the Shepherd's Mass), and the third during the day (the Mass of the Divine Word). The season of Advent, the forty days of leading up to Christmas, has been observed in the Western Church since the year AD 500. St. Nicholas was a very popular medieval saint, and his feast day came in Advent (6th December), but he did not play his part in Christmas as Santa Claus until after the Reformation.

Weird And Crazy Laws

Another example of strange local laws comes from Fairbanks, Alaska, where it is illegal to let your moose use the side walk. This law was passed in the early days of the town when the bar owner used to give his pet moose alcoholic drinks. The moose would become drunk and stumble around the town, creating havoc. In the same town it is illegal for a moose to have sex on the city streets – one can only guess at the reasons why this law was passed, though it can be conjectured that the same moose may have been the guilty party. Finally it is illegal in Fairfield to play the game of crackaloo. This is the case whether a moose is involved or not.

In Cleveland, Ohio, a hunting license is needed even if you only want to catch mice.

If you have been eating garlic in Toronto, Canada, make sure you check what day it is. On Sundays it would be illegal to subsequently ride a streetcar.

Residents of Massachusetts who are prone to snoring should remember to close and securely lock all bedroom windows if they want to stay within the letter of the law. Snoring with open windows isn't allowed there.

In Atwoodville, Connecticut a local law prohibits citizens from playing Scrabble while waiting for a politician's speech – perhaps past politicians were offended when their audience preferred to continue with their game rather than listen to them talk.

North Carolina forbids extramarital sex, but both the married partner and their accomplice must be prosecuted.

Celebrity Scandals

Winona Ryder Loots Saks. In December 2001, Winona Ryder made the mistake of embarking on a shoplifting spree in posh Beverly Hills über-store Saks. She was captured on surveillance cameras piling up armfuls of clothes, then popping into the dressing rooms where she cut out the security tags. Still carrying the pile of designer gear, she attempted to leave but was stopped by security staff. It emerged that she was trying to take over $6000 of merchandise with her. A tabloid furor resulted including a flurry of unproven statements about the star's private life. Ryder herself made light of the incident and turned up for her court hearing wearing angelic white.

Sinead O'Conner Rips the Pope
On 3rd October 1992, Sinead O'Connor shocked the conservative American audience of *Saturday Night Live*, when she tore up a photograph of Pope John Paul II. This was deemed so shocking that the incident has never since been aired on American television. Comedy Central sometimes re-run the incident by substituting the dress-rehearsal footage, which features O'Connor holding up a picture of a little girl, but not tearing it up.

During the show, O'Connor sang an a cappella version of Bob Marley's *War*. While singing a line about evil, she held up a picture of the Pope, shouted, 'Fight the real enemy', and ripped it into pieces. The audience was stunned into silence. In the furore that followed, O'Connor was publicly threatened with violence. Her intention had been to draw attention to child abuse within the Catholic Church. In 2002, the Church would be shaken by a scandal that involved child-molesting priests, and there have been many subsequent revelations about alleged cover-ups of this abuse. Sinead O'Connor continues to vocally oppose the Vatican.

Minnelli-Gest Marriage

Oscar-winner Liza Minnelli was already notorious for spending most of the 1980s in one rehab facility or another. Then there was her apparent addiction to weddings. In March 2002, she married concert promoter David Gest, who had his own 'addictive' relationship with plastic surgery, for which Michael Jackson's cosmetic surgeon was his preferred option. Michael Jackson and Elizabeth Taylor formed the wedding party and Minnelli and Gest duly tied the knot in a rather chaotic ceremony. The happy couple began married bliss with their own VH1 reality show but only one episode was ever produced, reportedly because of Gest's 'controlling issues'. Two years later the inevitable divorce arrived. David sued his ex-wife for $10

Natural Thoughts

Man is the only animal who enjoys the consolation of believing in a next life; all other animals enjoy the consolation of not worrying about it.

Robert Brault

million, claiming she'd beat him so badly while drunk that he needed hospital treatment for nerve damage. Liza counter-sued, with allegations including a poison plot, a $2 million theft and a cleaning obsession.

Matt Damon Dumps Minnie Driver on Oprah

The 1997 hit movie *Good Will Hunting* was the catalyst for Damon and Driver's real-life love affair. However, the real-life version of the romance didn't end with Damon following his lover to the ends of the Earth. Instead, he told Oprah Winfrey and her millions of viewers that their 'relationship' was over and had been for a while, and proclaimed that he was single and available. Unfortunately, this was the first Minnie Driver had heard of it. She reacted with admirable sang froid. Speaking to the *Los Angeles Times*, she said 'It's unfortunate that Matt went on *Oprah*. It seemed like a good forum for him to announce to the world that we were no longer together, which I found fantastically inappropriate.' Well said, that lady.

Angeline Jolie Snogs Big Brother

While Angelina Jolie was accepting her Oscar for 'Best Supporting Actor' for the 1999 film, *Girl Interrupted*, she told the shocked audience that she was 'in love' with James, her older brother. After this she gave him an open-mouthed kiss. This inevitably fuelled rumors that she was having an incestuous affair with her brother. Jolie's rather tempestuous past included a lesbian affair with co-star Jenny Shimizu, and S&M games with her first husband Johnny Lee Miller, so this was simply more grist to an already overworked rumor mill. However, the two siblings

insisted that the whole thing was blown far out of proportion
saying that they were just 'very close'.

The Hoff Gets Cheesy

There was public humiliation for David Hasselhoff when his
sixteen-year-old daughter filmed him drunk, half-naked while
eating a cheeseburger in a Las Vegas hotel room. The Hoff was
going through a difficult phase in his career and had been
appearing in a Las Vegas production of *The Producers*. He had a
drinking problem and was getting divorced after a 15-year
marriage. Distressed by the acrimonious divorce proceedings, his
daughter put the film of the drunken ramble on the internet. In
it she pleads with him to stop drinking. He keeps chewing on a
cheeseburger while slurring his words. 'I have trouble in my life,'
he mutters, continuing 'this is a mess.' All the while sauce is
dripping down his chest in a rather distracting way.

Eddie Murphy and the Lady-boy

On 2nd May 1997, police in West Hollywood pulled over a car.
Inside was actor Eddie Murphy together with a pre-op transsexual
prostitute who was known to them. Murphy claimed he had
driven to a newsstand because he was suffering from insomnia,
and had offered a lift home to a Hawaiian-looking woman.
However, Atisone Seuli gave a different account to them. She
said that Murphy had offered her $200 for her time after
confirming with her that she was a transsexual. The star's wife
and child were out of town at the time. Seuli was arrested on the
basis of outstanding warrants while Murphy was released, having
done nothing illegal. Unfortunately several other transvestites

came forward to claim they had had similar experiences with Eddie Murphy. One made a notorious appearance on *The Howard Stern Show*. However, Murphy's career seemed almost entirely immune to this scandal and his success continues.

Bald Britney

Britney Spears was once the golden-haired starlet with the world at her feet but by 2003, things were starting to get out of control. The road downhill began when Britney kissed Madonna at the MTV Video Music Awards. Spears had split up with Justin Timberlake, her film *Crossroads* was a turkey and her new album was selling slower than anticipated. By 2008, Britney went into a public disintegration as the paparazzi kept happily snapping away.

Spears lost custody of her sons, was photographed getting out of cars with no underwear on, and got tickets for driving while intoxicated. One of the low points was when she shaved her head bald. An attack on the photographers and a hospitalization came soon afterwards. An intervention by her father seems to have been the first tentative step in a better direction, to the undoubted disappointment of celebrity scandalmongers worldwide. Her father wisely took control of her diet and expenditure and thankfully a period of quiet on the Britney front followed.

Wino Winehouse

Amy Winehouse's breakthrough came with debut album *Back to Black* in 2007. Before long the singer's personal life started to eclipse her impressive voice and song-writing. Photographs appeared of her staggering around drunk and drugged outside her

house, in various states of undress. Her weight loss left her
skeletal and she appeared close to complete breakdown. Paparazzi
photographs appeared daily and she seemed to be steadily losing
the plot. A temporary improvement followed when Winehouse
decamped to St. Lucia to record a new album. The world's
paparazzi continue to follow her presumably hoping for a relapse
to the worst days.

Courtney Love Trips Up

Courtney Love was interviewed for *Vanity Fair* to promote her
band Hole. She told the interviewer, Lynn Hirschberg, that she
had once gone on a drug binge with Kurt Cobain which involved
heroin and other substances. Unfortunately it became apparent
that the 'drug binge' must have happened whilst she was
pregnant with their daughter Francis Bean. Los Angeles
Children's Services removed Francis from her parents' household
in September 1992. Months of legal negotiation ensued. Cobain
left one particularly acid message on Hirschberg's phone, blaming
her for the problems they were facing. Francis was eventually
reunited with her parents, although Cobain's sad, self-inflicted
death would mean she was destined to grow up without her
father.

Marriage and Eminem

Eminem married Kim his childhood sweetheart in 1999. They
had met as teenagers in 1989, daughter Hailie Jade was born in
1994. Life with Eminem was far from peaceful though. In the 2000
song 'Kim' he described his wife's murder in unpleasant detail,
whilst on stage he frequently subjected a blow-up doll version of

Kim to violent indignities. He shouldn't have been that surprised when she started to find these antics distressing. Not long after the release of 'Kim' Eminem was arrested for an assault on a Detroit nightclub bouncer and a few weeks later Kim attempted suicide after watching her husband's onstage schtick with the doll. She started divorce proceedings along with a defamation suit for $10 million. Surprisingly they reconciled in 2004 and the lawsuit was settled out of court. But a 2006 remarriage lasted less than three months. The couple separated and got divorced over again. Kim subsequently had a daughter with a new partner.

 # The World's Oddest Animals

The Sun Bear *The Sun Bear is most often found in the tropical rainforests of Southeast Asia. It is sometimes called the dog bear because of its stature as it is a very small animal, approximately 4ft (1.2m) in height, making it the most petite member of the bear family. It also has a 2in (5cm) tail and on average weighs less than 145 lbs (65kg). Unlike other bears, the Sun Bear's fur is short and sleek, probably because of the lowland climates it lives in. Its fur is dark black or brown-black fur, except on the chest where there is a pale orange-yellow horseshoe shaped marking. Similar colored fur can be found around the muzzle and the eyes, which is the feature that gives the Sun Bear its name.*

Studio 54 Files

When the FBI raided New York City's notorious Studio 54 nightclub it has been claimed that they found cocaine concealed in the walls, garbage bags stuffed with up to half a million dollars, and secret financial accounts for celebrity drug deals. Owners Steve Rubell and Ian Schrager regularly hosted club nights for luminaries such as Andy Warhol, Liza Minneli, Bianca Jagger and fashion designers Halston and Calvin Klein. But the decadent lifestyle and ubiquitous drugs became their downfall. Following the FBI raid, they were each sentenced to thirteen months in prison for tax evasion. They eventually bounced back from a period of virtual destitution when they obtained financial backing for the boutique hotel Morgan's. This hotel became a chain worth $200 million with hotels all over the world. Steve Rubell died in 1989 but Schrager continues to be successful and affluent to this day.

TomKat On the Sofa

Tom Cruise's advocacy of the religion of Scientology had already affected his public perception, but a further blow to his credibility came when he appeared on the Oprah Winfrey Show just after beginning a relationship with *Dawson's Creek* actor Katie Holmes. Oprah referred to his new relationship, and Cruise responded by

 The Fame Name Game

What did Nicolas Kim Coppola change his name to?

Answer: Nicolas Cage

leaping over the sofa like a deranged mountain goat, shouting 'It's real LOVE!' and telling the world how happy he was. For many stars this might have seemed like a drunken moment of confusion, to be soon forgotten, but it certainly marked the moment when the media started to feel that Cruise was more to be regarded as a tiny figure of fun than a compact hero.

Tyson Sentenced

While Mike Tyson was the 'undisputed heavyweight champion of the world' he allegedly invited 18-year-old Miss Black Rhode Island, Desiree Washington to his hotel room in July 1991. Desiree contradicted Tyson's claim that the sex that ensued was consensual. On 27th March 1992, a jury accepted her account, and Tyson was convicted of rape. His sentence was to ten years in prison with the final four years suspended. While he was inside, he converted to Islam. He has never made a full comeback and has been through subsequent problems including bankruptcy.

Paris Hilton's Easy Ride

Paris Hilton is rarely out of the news for long. In February 2007, whilst on probation for a 2006 charge of driving under the influence, Hilton got behind her wheel again. She was pulled over for speeding but police soon realized she was driving on a suspended license. In court Hilton was sentenced to forty five days in jail. She claimed she couldn't bear being behind bars so the LA County Sheriff agreed to forty days home confinement instead. Not so bad given that her home is a billionaire's one with all luxuries on tap. The media was furious about the little princess's 'special treatment' and a different judge sent her back to jail. She had to be hospitalized for distress on hearing the news but did eventually go back to prison. Even then she served only twenty three days before her release for good behavior. Maybe the jail governor was as sick of her as the rest of us?

Business Woman of the Year 1995
Heidi Fleiss set up a high-class international prostitution ring which provided services for politicians and A-list actors. At her trial in 1995, Fleiss was loyal to her clients and maintained the secrecy of her client list in spite of the fact she might have got a shorter sentence by giving up names. However, TV actor Charlie Sheen, son of film star Martin Sheen, was asked to testify for the prosecution. He was alleged to have spent $50,000 on prostitutes in the course of a year. It became apparent that Fleiss had routinely sent her 'girls' round the world for clients, earning millions of dollars along the way. She was sentenced to just over three years in jail for charges relating to the prostitution business, and was also required to pay millions of dollars in fines. As part of her gradual rehabilitation she made a successful appearance on the UK reality show *Celebrity Big Brother*.

Janet Jackson's 'Wardrobe Malfunction'
During the halftime break in the 2004 Superbowl, Justin Timberlake ripped open Janet Jackson's corset top and part of her breast popped out. She was wearing a sunburst nipple shield, but the stunt (later defended as being just a 'wardrobe malfunction') was greeted by over half a million FCC complaints. Sometimes a moment of scandal such as this can revive a flagging career, but Jackson's next album received disappointing sales.

Hilarious Misprints

For cockroaches do not use sodium fluoride, as children or cherished pets may eat the sodium fluoride instead of the cockroaches.
Ludlow Tribune

The murder of the man and the finding of the body was followed by a series of tradgedies, including the suicide of the murdered man.
Boston Post

Committee Names Committee
Reuters

Brain Removal Study Finds Few Volunteers
Kenosha News

The landlord insisted that no female shold be allowed in the bra without a man.
Glasgow Herald

Airline Travel Safer Despite More Accidents
Reuters

Births To High School Girls Fall To Record Low
CNN

Air Traffic Controllers Can Apply For Job In Braille
The Herald

This is the model home for your future. It was panned by *Better Homes & Gardens*.
Advertisement

All Utah Condemned To Face Firing Squad
Washington Post

Athlete Who Cheated Death Dies
AOL News

Birds Make Mess, City Steps In
Colorado Springs Gazette

Giant Replica Of Anal Lock Makes Striking Feature At Chelsea Flower Show
Daily Telegraph

Alec Baldwin vs Daughter

'YOU HAVE MADE AN *** OUT ME OF FOR THE LAST TIME ... PICK UP THE GODDAMN PHONE ... I DON'T CARE THAT YOU'RE TWELVE OR ELEVEN OR WHATEVER, ARE YOU PIG ENOUGH TO PICK IT UP? I'M A GOOD FATHER, AND YOU'RE A PIG. I DON'T GIVE A ****. GOOD FATHER.

YOU THINK THIS IS ABUSE? YOU THINK THIS IS ABUSE, YOU THOUGHTLESS PAIN IN THE ***? GET MAD, YOU DAUGHTER-OF-A-***** . . . PIG. OH, ALSO, TELL YOUR MOTHER I SAID GO **** YOURSELF. This is Dad, ring me back when you get a chance.'

This answerphone message, intended for Baldwin's 12-year-old daughter, was leaked to the world in April 2007. He accused ex-wife Kim Basinger of being the source of the leak, though she denied involvement. Following a protracted 2002 divorce, both stars were subject to gag orders intended to avoid further acrimony. Baldwin's career survived the rant, and he now has a new lease of TV life following his success in NBC's *30 Rock*.

Thought For the Day

I believe that men are generally still a little afraid of the dark, though the witches are all hung, and Christianity and candles have been introduced.

Henry David Thoreau, *Solitude*, 1854

Coffin Stealers

Gram Parsons was the heir to a citrus company but instead he left home to become a drifter musician, before his death at the age of 26. He played with the Byrds, changing their musical direction, and spent a notorious period hanging out with Keith Richards while the Rolling Stones were recording. He was obsessed by California's Joshua Tree monument, where he would go to search for UFOs while tripping on acid. On 19th September 1973, his addiction to booze and morphine led him to an overdose at the Joshua Tree Inn.

Parsons' stepfather, who was a millionaire, wanted the body returned to Louisiana. However, manager Phil Kaufman and a friend (who has never been named) bizarrely hijacked the body from a loading bay at LAX airport. They drove a borrowed hearse, to Joshua Tree, as they felt that a desert cremation would have been Parsons' preference. They attempted to burn the coffin but the result was a huge fireball that attracted the attention of the park rangers. After a police chase followed, Kaufman ended up in jail for the escapade. Parsons' charred remains did finally reach New Orleans, where they were interred.

Lilo Tries To Lie Low

Lindsay Lohan has had a chequered career having been in the public eye since she was young. She was in commercials from the age of eight and a Hollywood star at the age of twelve, having appeared in the 1998 *The Parent Trap* remake. A three-film Disney deal followed, including *Freaky Friday* and the wonderful *Mean Girls*. As a teenage star, Lohan was constantly mobbed by paparazzi. She was an easy target as she was fond of partying all night, and drank heavily at times. She ended up in hospital in November 2004 for 'exhaustion'. Three years later she was back, going into rehab for alcohol and drug abuse. Four months after this she crashed her car into a tree and fled the scene. Back in rehab she was asked to wear an 'alcohol-monitoring' anklet. She was charged again two months later, for coke possession and DUI. For a while she tried to stay out of the public eye, though her relationship with Samantha Ronson inevitably excited the tabloid reporters. At time of writing her luck has finally run temporarily dry, as she is serving a 90 day sentence for violating the terms of her probation, although it is widely suggested that her career may be revitalized if the prison sentence finally acts as a forced period of rehabilitation.

Sid Vicious
Sid Vicious was twenty when he met Nancy Spungen in 1977. They turned themselves into the ultimate 'rock and roll couple', and unfortunately their understanding of this included excesses of drugs. Following the final Sex Pistols US tour they settled into Manhattan's Chelsea Hotel for a heroin and alcohol binge. On 12th October 1978, Nancy Spungen was found dead from a knife wound in her abdomen in their hotel bathroom. Sid was accused of the murder and slit his wrists. He survived and was charged but overdosed on 2nd February 1979. There was no trial so the real facts of that fateful night will never be known.

Patty Hearst
Hearst was an heiress, but lived as a student in the drop-out capital city of San Francisco. When the radical Symbionese Liberation Army kicked in her door, attacked her boyfriend,

and kidnapped her in February 1974 she became one of the world's most famous hostages. The radicals' first demand was for her wealthy father to feed the Bay Area poor, and he agreed to do this. But Patty wasn't released. The SLA released audiotapes of her pleas for release and gradually her tone changed as she started to take on some of her captors' ideas. She started to accuse her parents of neglect and eventually condemned her family, and the whole concept of family. She had now become an SLA member named 'Tania,' and before long she was photographed robbing a bank while wearing a beret and carrying an assault rifle. When the police finally 'rescued' Patty Hearst, she was sentenced to 25 years in jail, although her sentence was commuted after less than two years (and she was eventually given a full pardon by Bill Clinton). There is much dispute about whether she was a victim of brainwashing or an earnest but misguided convert. She now lives in New York with French bulldogs, one of which recently won a prize at the Westminster Kennel Club.

Woody Allen And His Stepdaughter
Mia Farrow had no reason to doubt her director boyfriend Woody Allen until when she found a series of nude photographs of Soon-Yi Previn, their 22-year-old stepdaughter, in 1992. Allen denied that there was anything incestuous about the relationship, but the media had a field day with the story. Farrow was furious and a bitter custody court case ensued. Allen married Soon-Yi in 1997 and has been quoted crediting the success of the marriage to his 'paternal feeling' towards her. All very weird indeed.

Michael Jackson's Weird Life And Death

Once the biggest pop star in the world, things seemed to start going wrong for Michael Jackson when his appearance began changing. His nose got smaller, his skin became ever whiter, and the media began to focus on his odd lifestyle at the Neverland Ranch, where he kept a menagerie of animals and entertained visitors to private fairground rides. In 1993 he was accused of abuse by Evan Chandler, with regard to his 13-year-old son, Jordan Chandler. They had become friends the previous year, and Jordan's father was concerned about Jackson's relationship with his son. This case was settled out of court, but ten years later he confessed in a documentary that he often shared his bed with young boys. This created a media firestorm. Jackson was found

Obscure English Language Facts

A Monotonous View

*Overnumerousnesses (18 letters) is the longest English word that consists of only letters that lack ascenders, descenders, and dots in lower case. Overnervousnesses has 17 letters. 16-letter words of this kind include **curvaceousnesses** and **overnumerousness** while **erroneousnesses, nonconcurrences, overnervousness**, and **verrucosenesses** come in at 15 letters each.*

innocent of charges relating to this by a jury but his career was now in trouble.

His death was almost as weird as his life. He died on 25th June 2009 at his home near Los Angeles. Cardiac arrest was the initial explanation, but a different story then emerged. On 28th August 2009, the Los Angeles County Coroner concluded that Jackson's death was a homicide caused by the combination of drugs in his body. Jackson had allegedly been given propofol, usually used as a general anaesthetic, along with two anti-anxiety benzodiazepines: lorazepam and midazolam. Law enforcement officials investigated his personal physician, Dr. Conrad Murray, who told investigators that he had been trying to wean Jackson off propofol. On 8th February 2010, Murray pleaded not guilty to charges of involuntary manslaughter, and was released from prison with bail of $75,000.

O.J. Simpson's Book

After one of the most publicly divisive trials of the century, O.J. Simpson was found not guilty of the murder of his estranged wife Nicole Brown Simpson and her friend Ron Goldman. Simpson was however found financially culpable for the murders in a civil suit, and ended up owing the victims' survivors more than $30 million. Payment for this debt was not forthcoming. One of the low points of the whole story came when publishing giant Judith Regan announced the forthcoming release of a book called *If I Did It* in which he would explain how he would have committed the murders if he had done them. The Goldman family were appalled, but they lodged a law suit which eventually gave them ownership of Simpson's 'fictional' account, and of the payments for it. Simpson has faced further troubles since then, including allegations of armed robbery.

The Death of Princess Diana

We've seen plenty of people in this chapter who suffered at the hands of paparazzi, but their involvement in Princess Diana's life was a more direct and fatal one. She was killed when the paparazzi allegedly chased her car into a concrete pillar in a Paris underpass on 31st August 1997. Her car crashed, killing her and her boyfriend Dodi Al Fayed, the son of the owner of Harrods, London's most famous department store.

A welter of conspiracy theories have followed her death, many focusing on her well-known disagreements with the royal family and her alleged suicide attempts and bulimia. It has for instance been claimed that Princess Diana was murdered by the British secret service to prevent her marrying a Muslim. However, a hugely expensive investigation eventually concluded that the blame fell mostly on Diana's driver (who had a very high level of alcohol in his blood). It's hard to ever really crush a conspiracy theory though, and many of the theorists now allege that the alcohol in the blood was introduced later or that the test results

Thought For the Day

We used to think that if we knew one, we knew two, because one and one are two. We are finding that we must learn a great deal more about 'and.'

Arthur Stanley Eddington

are unreliable. In spite of the investigation's findings, British tabloid newspapers still regularly run headlines claiming to have found new revelations concerning Diana's death.

 # Memorable Movie Quotes

We're talking paranoid delusional psychosis. I saw the guy's room. Cozy . . . if you're Hannibal Lecter.
Ace Ventura: Pet Detective

Matt: Don't be cynical. Why do you always assume the worst about people?
Gwyn: Statistics.
Miami Rhapsody

You know, I'd buy you a parachute if I knew it wouldn't open.
Animal Crackers

Facts From Around the World

The US has the world's most violent weather. NASA states that in an average year, the US experiences 10,000 violent thunderstorms, 1000 tornadoes, 5000 floods and several hurricanes.

The official name of Rhode Island is Rhode Island and Plantation Provinces. This means that the smallest state in the US has the longest name.

The volume of the oceans means that 99% of the living space on the planet is found in them. The average depth of the oceans is 2.5 miles (4km). The deepest known point is in the Mariana Trench, 6.8 miles (10.9km) down. This makes the Mariana's depth greater than the height of Mount Everest, which is only 5.5 miles (8.8km) high.

The largest country in Africa is the Sudan.

The Vicksburg National Cemetery in Mississippi is the second oldest in the US.

In the last 75 years the town of Corona, California has buried 17 time capsules. None has ever been found.

The city of Istanbul straddles the continents of Europe and Asia.

The only nation whose name begins with an 'A', but doesn't end in an 'A' is Afghanistan.

The McCoy Federal Building in Jackson Mississippi, was the first federal building in the US to be named for an African American.

The exact geographic center of the United States is close to Lebanon, Kansas, while its center of gravity lies approximately at Friend, Nebraska.

Blunders and Oddballs

Salty Dreams. The painter Buonamico Buffalmacco is said to have once lived next door to a rich wool worker whose wife worked late at her spinning wheel, often keeping him awake all night. In desperation, he devised a plan to solve the problem. Having noticed a small hole in their kitchen wall directly above the cooking pot, Buffalmacco hollowed out a cane, pushed it through the hole, and was thereby able to add a large amount of salt to the wool worker's dinner. When, after two or three such tainted meals, the exasperated man began to beat his wife for her carelessness, her screams brought a number of neighbors, including Buffalmacco, to their door. 'This calls for a little reason,' the intrepid painter declared. 'You complain that the pot is too much salted, but I marvel that this good woman can do anything well, considering that the whole night she sits up over that wheel of hers and has not an hour's sleep. Let her give up this all-night work and sleep her fill, so she will have her wits about her by day and will not fall into such blunders.' The woolworker apparently graciously accepted Buffalmacco's advice, and he thereafter enjoyed peaceful rest.

Buonamico Buffalmacco, (c.1262-c.1340) Italian painter

Spaced Out

Alfonso the Wise was famed for his patronage of the arts and sciences. He revised the Castilian legal code, sponsored the translation of many Arabic works, and compiled the 'Alfonsine Tables' that remained the most authoritative planetary tables in existence for some three hundred years. Because they were based upon a (then-prevalent but erroneous) Ptolemaic (geocentric) scheme, however, many complicated calculations were required to render the tables usable. Indeed, Alfonso is said to have remarked that, had God consulted him during the six days of creation, he might have recommended a less complicated design.

Alfonso X ('Alfonso the Wise'), (c.1221-1284) Italian King of Castile and Leon (1252-1284)

Breath of Life

The 13th-Century English scientist and philosopher Roger Bacon once contended that elderly men could be rejuvenated in a curious fashion, by inhaling the breath of young virgins. It is worth noting that, at a time when men were lucky to see their 50th birthdays, Bacon lived to be nearly 80 years old.

Roger Bacon, ('Doctor Mirabilis') (c.1214-1292) English friar, scientist, and philosopher

New Delhi

In the 14th Century, Ghiyas-uddin Tughlaq began to build the third city of Delhi: Tughlaqabad. When Tughlaq expropriated several workers who had been employed to build a shrine for the Sufi saint Nizam-ud-din, the saint placed a curse on the project, prophesying that the city would be inhabited only by shepherds.

The king promptly vowed revenge and began to march toward Nizam-ud-din's own distant city; the saint calmly told his followers not to worry. 'Delhi,' he declared, 'is a long way off' (Dilli Doorasth).

His words turned out to be prophetic; the king was murdered on route from Delhi in 1325. Moreover, the city today is indeed largely inhabited by shepherds.

Nizam-ud-din Auliya, 14th-Century Indian saint

Not Till Death Do Us Part
When Pedro I became King of Portugal in the 14th Century, he had his dead mistress exhumed for the coronation. Having been crowned queen alongside her widowed husband, she had her hand kissed by many of the noblemen in attendance before being replaced in her casket and returned to her tomb.

Pedro I, King of Portugal (1320-1367)

Right of Passage
At the height of the battle of Crecy, Edward III was told by a messenger that Edward the Black Prince, his sixteen-year-old

The Fame Name Game

What did Maurice J. Micklewhite change his name to?

Answer: Michael Caine

eldest son, was at the forefront of the fighting and in considerable danger. Edward refused to send reinforcements or to call his son back from the field of battle. His orders were to 'Let the boy win his spurs.'

Edward III, (1312-1377) English king (1327-77)

Italian Style
The 14th-Century Italian condottiere Facino Cane and his marauding soldiers were widely loathed and much feared. One day a rich gentleman, dressed in a fine doublet, complained to Cane that one of his men had robbed him and stolen his coat. Cane asked him, 'Were you wearing that doublet on the day of the robbery?' The man replied 'Yes'. Cane immediately ordered him to 'get out', adding 'it wasn't one of my soldiers who robbed you. None of them would have left you that doublet!'

Facino Cane, (1360-1412) Italian condottiere

Club Feet
Toward the end of the 15th Century, Charles VIII of France popularized men's shoes with square toes. Why? Charles hoped to hide the fact that he had six toes on one of his feet.

Charles VIII, 15th-Century French king

Happy Days
'I have passed in ease and prosperity,' the 15th-Century Sultan Ghiyas-ud-Din Khilji declared on his deathbed, 'and in a state of pleasure such has been the lot of no monarch.' He wasn't kidding: the sultan had some 15,000 wives and concubines!

Ghiyas-ud-Din Khilji, 15th-Century Ottoman Sultan

Egg Timer

Christopher Columbus once attended an elaborate banquet, held in his honor by the grand cardinal of Spain. Though treated with deference by most of the company, he was pointedly asked by an envious courtier whether he believed that someone else would have discovered the New World had he not done so first. Columbus did not reply directly, but, taking an boiled egg in his hand, invited the guests to make it stand on its end. When everyone had tried and failed, Columbus tapped the tip of the egg against the table. Partially crushed, it was soon set standing on its flattened base. The point was clear: once Columbus had shown the way, anyone could follow.

Christopher Columbus, (1451-1506) Italian explorer

Drake Burns Beards

Drake's famous exploit, namely the singeing of the King of Spain's beard in 1588, where he destroyed thirty ships in Cadiz harbor as the Spanish were fitting out for the invasion of England, was carried out in the face of Queen Elizabeth's reluctance to provoke the Spaniards. Apparently she hoped, despite the evidence of Spain's warlike preparations, to reach a negotiated settlement. She unwillingly gave the order to allow

Thought For the Day

Even a clock that does not work is right twice a day

Polish Proverb

Drake, who had been hanging around in Plymouth harbor for some time, to set off on his hostile errand.

However, no sooner had she given the order than she had second thoughts, and sent another dispatch rider to Plymouth to countermand it. Drake however had guessed that such a second

The World's Oddest Animals

Sloths Sloths are medium-sized mammals that live in Central and South America. The lazy life-style of the sloth has led to their name being used to describe under-achieving humans. They behave this way because leaves, their main food source, provide very little energy or nutrition. Sloths are omnivores; they may eat insects, small lizards and carrion, but they mostly eat buds, tender shoots, and leaves which do not digest easily. To adapt to this, sloths have huge, specialized, slow-acting stomachs with several compartments in which symbiotic bacteria break down the tough leaves. The contents of a sloth's stomach can therefore be as much as two thirds of its body weight, and can take up to a month to digest completely. Even then, leaves provide very little energy, and because of this sloths have very low metabolic rates and have unusually low body temperatures when active (30-34ºC or 86-93ºF), and even lower temperatures when resting. Sloths mainly live in Cecropia trees.

order might be forthcoming so as soon as he received the first he put to sea immediately. Initially the queen was very angry, but there was nothing she could do to stop him. Queen Elizabeth's displeasure proved to be short-lived, the Spanish Armada was utterly destroyed and the glory of Elizabethan England assured.

Sir Francis Drake, (c.1540-1596) English naval hero and explorer

Dark Side of the Moon

While anchored off Jamaica in 1504, Christopher Columbus found himself in dire straits. Though his supplies were running low, the Jamaican Indians refused to sell him any more food. Consulting his almanac, Columbus noticed that a lunar eclipse was due a few days later. On the appointed day, he summoned the Jamaican leaders and warned them that he would blot out the moon that very evening if his demands for food were not promptly met. The Jamaicans only laughed at him – until later that night when the eclipse began. As the moon disappeared before their eyes, they visited Columbus in a state of terror, whereupon he agreed to stop his magic in exchange for food. The offer was accepted and the moon 'restored'.

Christopher Columbus, (1451-1506) Italian explorer

Smoke it Away

In 1577, shortly after the introduction of tobacco from the New World, a Spanish doctor named Nicolas Monardes published a book entitled *Joyful News out of the New Found World* detailing its supposed medicinal properties for the first time.

Tobacco was a recommended treatment for headaches, arthritis, various wounds, and stomach cramps. Moreover, it is perhaps a testament to the sorry state of 16th-Century oral hygiene that tobacco was also recommended as a cure for toothaches – and bad breath! Monardes's prescriptions were followed for more than 200 years.

Nicolas Monardes, (c.1493-1588) Spanish doctor

Guzzling Aztecs

Montezuma II, the last Aztec ruler in Mexico, was famed for his gluttony. On a typical night he ate chicken, turkey, songbirds, doves, ducks, rabbits, pheasants, partridges, quail, and – according to a secondhand report – once ate an adolescent boy or two, followed by tortillas and hot chocolate.

Montezuma II, (c.1466-1520) Mexican emperor,
last Aztec ruler in Mexico (1502–1520)

Save My Nose

Arise Evans had a fungus nose. He said it had been revealed to him that the king's hand would cure him, and at the first coming of King Charles II into St. James's Park, he kissed the king's hand, and rubbed his nose on it. The king was greatly dismayed but Evans was cured.

Charles II, (1630-1685) English monarch (1660-1685)

Incendiary Alchemist

While experimenting with urine one day in 1669, Hennig Brand discovered a novel compound. Despite its remarkable incendiary properties, however, Brand was very disappointed with his experimental result and virtually ignored it. Indeed, the compound was later 'discovered' again by Robert Boyle (1627-

1691). Why was Brand so disappointed? As a merchant and alchemist, he was seeking to restore his wealth by converting base metals into gold – and all he got was phosphorus.

Hennig Brand, (1630–c.1710) German merchant and alchemist
(noted for his discovery of phosphorus)

Sparkling Beverages

One day in 1688, blind cellarmaster Dom Perignon inadvertently discovered champagne. 'Oh, come quickly!' he is alleged to have cried out. 'I am drinking stars!'

Dom Perignon, (c.1638–1715) French cellarmaster

Slowcoach

Towards the end of his life, Lord Chesterfield became so infirm that his carriage rides were conducted at a very, very slow pace. An acquaintance once encountered the Earl on such an expedition and congratulated him on being up and about and apparently able to take the air. 'I do not come out so much for the air,' Chesterfield replied, 'as for the benefit of rehearsing my funeral.'

Philip Dormer Stanhope Chesterfield, Fourth Earl of, (1694-1773)
English politician, diplomat and writer

Fallen Women

When the Elector of Hanover became England's George I in 1714, his wife could not become the Queen of England because she had committed adultery. George had her placed under house arrest in Ahlden Castle, where she remained for thirty-two years. (Those who knew the woman's fate called her the 'Prisoner of

Ahlden' and she remains known as such today.) Ironically, George himself had arrived in England with his two mistresses; adultery was a crime only for women.

George I, (1660-1727) English monarch, elector of Hanover (from 1698), King of Great Britain and Ireland (1714–1727)

Royal Teeth
Dentistry in 18th-Century Paris was so horribly barbaric that, one day after having several teeth pulled by an overzealous dentist, King Louis XIV drank some soup – and had it cascade out of his nose!

Louis XIV ('Le Roi Soleil'), (1638-1715) French monarch

Invisible Prisoner
When John Byng was court-martialed and brought before the firing squad (for failing to relieve the island of Minorca while under French attack), it was suggested that his face should be covered with a handkerchief, lest the sight of his sorrow breed reluctance in his executioners. Byng announced 'If it will frighten them, let it be done, they will not frighten me.'

John Byng (1704-1757) British Admiral

He Lost His head
As a young man, Maximilien Robespierre was so opposed to the death penalty that he gave up a promising legal career rather than work in a court which sentenced prisoners to the scaffold. Contrarily, after assuming control of the French Revolution in 1793, Robespierre, as leader of the Jacobins, launched the Reign of Terror that sent hundreds to the guillotine. His laws permitting the

confiscation of property and arrest of suspected traitors soon led to a backlash. Robespierre was arrested in 1794, and promptly met his end (ironically without a trial) on the guillotine.

Maximilien François Marie Isidore de Robespierre,
(1758-1794) French revolutionary

 # Memorable Movie Quotes

You'll meet someone. Someone very special. Someone who won't press charges.
Addams Family Values

Cindy, you know by tattling on your friends, you're really just tattling on yourself. By tattling on your friends, you're just telling them that you're a tattletale. Now, is that the tale you want to tell?
Brady Bunch Movie

First rule of leadership: everything is your fault.
A Bug's Life

Amazing Animals

Despite its reputation for being fussy, the average cat consumes about 125,000 calories a year, nearly thirty times its own weight in food and as much again in liquids. Cats cannot be vegetarians as they cannot get the required nutrients without animal products.

Cats can make over one hundred vocal sounds, while dogs only have about ten, which might explain why so many cat owners like to talk to their pets.

No new animals have been domesticated in the last four millennia.

A cockroach can survive without a head for up to nine days.

Over the average lifespan of 11 years, a dog will cost you $13,350.00 in food, vets' fees and other expenses.

The only domestic animal not mentioned in the Bible is the cat.

Pet parrots can be fed virtually any common food except for chocolate and avocados, both of which are highly toxic to the parrot.

When they are enraged, the ears of Tasmanian devils turn a pinkish-red.

There are only two animals who have blue tongues – the Black Bear and the Chow dog.

Murphy's Oil Soap is often used to clean elephants.

Most hamsters only blink one eye at a time.

Swans are the only birds that have penises.

Armadillos sleep for an average of 18.5 hours a day.

News From Weirdville

How Cool?
The coldest place on earth is neither the North nor the South Pole, but Verkovank in Siberia, where a temperature of 100½ degrees below zero has been registered. The North Pole is about 60½ below, while the South Pole often reaches 70½ below. North Dakota has also registered 70½ below.

The Whole World
In 230 BC, the Greek philosopher Eratosthenes worked out the size of the earth. He heard that the whole sun was reflected in the bottom of a deep well in Syene (now Aswan) at midday every midsummer, implying that the sun was directly overhead at that time. At midday on the summer solstice he measured the length of the shadow of a tower in Alexandria, whose height he knew. He also knew that the exact distance from Syene to Alexandria was 500 miles, and he used these facts in the calculations.

City of the Horse
Alexander the Great, besides Alexandria, also built a city called Bucephala, named after his horse Bucephalus, which was killed in battle in 326 BC.

What Did The Romans Ever Do For Us?

The bagpipe was first introduced into Scotland by the ancient Romans.

A Woman's Place?

The word 'lady' derives from the Old English 'hlaefdige' – which literally means: 'loaf-kneader.'

Three Times a Lady

There was one queen of England who never even saw her realm. She was the wife of Richard the Lionheart, Queen Berengaria, daughter of Sancho VI of Navarre. They were married in Cyprus in May 1191. The King's wanderings meant that she saw him only twice more; she lived in France and Italy and died in Le Mans, about 1230.

Eat Your Words

In 1644, Danish author Theodore Reinking was given the choice of eating his own book or being executed. King Christian IV of Denmark thought the book too democratic in sentiment. Reinking chose to eat the book torn up in his soup.

The Fame Name Game

What did Charles Lutwidge Dodgson change his name to?

Answer: Lewis Carroll

Hugh Williams

On 5th December 1664, a man named Hugh Williams was the only survivor of a boat that sank crossing the Menai Strait – between Anglesey and Carnarvonshire in Wales. On 5th December 1785, the sole survivor of another such accident was also called Hugh Williams; sixty other passengers were drowned. On 5th August 1820, a man named Hugh Williams was again the sole survivor out of twenty-six passengers in a shipwreck.

Mini Meals

Oswaldus Norhingerus, who lived in the time of Shakespeare, specialized in carving miniature objects out of ivory. He once carved 16,000 table utensils so small that they could be accommodated in a cup the size of a coffee bean. Each dish was almost invisible to the naked eye, yet perfect in every detail. Pope Paul V viewed them through a powerful pair of spectacles.

Bacon Binary

Francis Bacon was the father of the modern computer: in 1605 he developed a cipher using only a and b in five letter combinations, each representing a letter of the alphabet, demonstrating that only two signs are required to transmit information. Towards the end of the century, Leibniz developed the principle into the binary system that is the basis of modern computers. 0 and 1 can be combined to express any number.

A Mammoth Tale

From the 1660 report of Captain William Taylor, Master, *British Banner*:

'On the 25th of April, in lat. 12 deg. 7 min. 8 sec., and long. 93 deg. 52 min. E., with the sun over the main-yard, felt a strong sensation as if the ship was trembling. Sent the second mate aloft to see what was up. The latter called out to me to go up the fore rigging and look over the bows. I did so, and saw an enormous serpent shaking the bowsprit with his second animal, and a trampling of the tracks, as if the two creatures had been excited by the meeting. Then the two went on together.'

The hunter followed. Suddenly, one afternoon, he saw them. They were enormous hairy elephants with great white tusks curved upward. The hair was a dark chestnut color, very heavy on the hindquarters, but lighter toward the front. The beasts moved very slowly.

The last of the mammoths are believed to have died more than 12,000 years ago, and the hunter knew nothing about them. But did he see mammoths?

No Drumming

The magistrate of Tedworth in Wiltshire, England, could not have imagined the consequences when he confiscated the drum belonging to William Drury – an itinerant musician caught in some shady dealings – and told him to leave the district.

That was in March 1662. Hardly had the culprit left Tedworth when the drum began to produce drumming noises itself. It also flew around Magistrate Mompesson's house, seen by several people besides the magistrate. After several sleepless nights, he had the drum broken into pieces. Still the drumming continued. Nor was that all. Shoes flew through the air, and chamber pots were emptied onto beds. Children were levitated. A horse's rear leg was forced into its mouth.

The possibility that the exiled drummer had sneaked back and was causing the trouble was fairly well ruled out when it was discovered that he had been arrested for theft in the city of Gloucester and sent to the colonies. The Reverend Joseph Glanville, chaplain to King Charles II, came to Tedworth to investigate the phenomena. He heard the drumming himself, and collected eyewitness reports from the residents. No natural cause was found for the effects, which stopped exactly one year after they had started.

Somnium

The first piece of science fiction was Kepler's story 'Somnium', published after his death in 1630. Cyrano de Bergerac's *Voyage to the Moon* (published 1657), often cited as the first work of science fiction, is not only later, but fails to qualify because it is political satire rather than science fiction.

Plumpers

In the 18th Century, many elegant gentlemen wore 'plumpers' (cork pads) in their cheeks to disguise the hollows left by rotten teeth.

Thought For the Day

There's more to the truth than just the facts.

Author Unknown

Weird And Crazy Laws

In Quebec, Canada, there is a law requiring that margarine must be a different color from butter. Local dairy producers lobbied for this law to protect their business. Since margarine was being made to resemble butter, they reasoned that making margarine a less attractive color would make consumers want to stay with butter. Originally margarine had to be a rather unpleasant dark vermilion color, but eventually pale white shades were also allowed.

If you are a mourner at a wake in Massachusetts, you may not eat more than three sandwiches. In the same state, there is an ordinance declaring goatees illegal although you may have the privilege of wearing one in public if you pay a special license fee for it. There don't seem to be any laws about men in goatees eating too many sandwiches, which seems a strange omission.

In 1978 a law was passed forcing dog owners in New York City to clean up after their animals. Prior to this it is estimated that 40 million pounds of dog excrement were left on the streets each year.

In Virginia, a law requires all bathtubs to be kept in the yards, rather than inside the houses. This law presumably predates baths that are plumbed into the internal system.

In Harrisburg, Pennsylvania it is against the law to have sexual relations with a truck driver inside a tollbooth.

In Florida, it is OK to leave your elephant tied to a parking meter. However, you have to make sure you pay the parking fee just as you would if you left your car in the same spot.

Fathers and Sons
On 13th February 1746, a Frenchman named Jean Marie Dunbarry
was hanged for murdering his father. Precisely a century later, on
13th February 1846, another Jean Marie Dunbarry, great-
grandson of the other, was also hanged for murdering his father.

Gold Fever
The US Mint once printed a run of gold coins bearing the
erroneous inscription: 'In Gold We Trust'...

Bestseller
The first 'best-selling' novel was Samuel Richardson's *Pamela, or
Virtue Rewarded* (1740), which went into edition after edition, and
was translated into most European languages. Rousseau's *La
Nouvelle Heloise* (1760) surpassed it; it was so popular that lending
libraries would lend it out by the hour. The first American bestseller was *Charlotte Temple* (1791) by an Englishwoman, Susanna
Haswell Rowson, a melodramatic and badly written book that
nevertheless went through 200 editions.

Mother Goose
Mother Goose was a real person – the author of songs and jingles
published in 1716. Her name was Elizabeth Foster, and she was
born in 1665; she married Isaac Goose in 1693 and died in Boston
– where her nursery rhymes were published – at the age of 92.

Lost at Sea
Late in the 18th Century a sailing ship off the coast of West Africa
found itself becalmed in a placid ocean. The wind had dropped,

and Jean-Magnus Dens, the Danish captain, ordered his crew to lower planks off the side from which they could scrape and clean the ship. Three men climbed onto the planks and began their work. They were scraping energetically when suddenly, out of the quiet sea around them, rose an immense octopus or squid. It seized two of the men and pulled them under the water. The third man leaped desperately into the rigging, but a gigantic arm pursued him, getting caught up in the shrouds. The sailor fainted from shock, and his horrified shipmates frantically hacked at the great tentacle, finally chopping it off.

Meanwhile, five harpoons were being driven into the body of the beast in the forlorn hope of saving the two who had disappeared. The frightful struggle went on until, one by one, four of the lines broke. The men had to give up the attempt at killing the monster, which sank out of view. The unconscious sailor, hanging limply in the shrouds, was gently taken down and placed in his bunk. He revived a little, but died in raving madness that night.

Wheels that Fly

Since 1760 seamen have recounted sightings of unidentified flying objects in the form of a wheel. The Persian Gulf sighting of 1906 was one of eleven recorded reports between 1848 and 1910. Like most of the maritime accounts of mysterious luminous wheels, this one remarked on the eery silence of the phenomenon. Also in common with most other such reports, nothing was said about humans or humanlike beings in the wheels, even though the ascent and descent of these objects were obviously controlled.

Were such glowing wheels in the sky an early and less sophisticated form of flying saucer? Were they operated by beings

from other planets who kept themselves hidden or were invisible?
Were they just visions of mariners too long at sea? No one has
found an answer.

Daylight Saving
Benjamin Franklin suggested that clocks should be moved
forward in spring to save daylight hours. He died in 1790, but his
idea was not adopted in America and Europe until World War I,
to save electricity.

On Your Chest
The practice of tapping a patient's chest was invented by an
Austrian doctor, Leopold Auenbrugger, who used to watch his
father – a wine manufacturer – tapping wine barrels to find out
how full they were. Although he published the idea in 1761, it
was ignored until his book was translated into French in 1808.

Horse Cousins
All thoroughbred race horses in the world are descended from
three Eastern horses imported into England in the early

Natural Thoughts

*Many men go fishing all of their lives without
knowing that it is not fish they are after.*

Henry David Thoreau

18th Century: the Byerly Turk, the Darley Arabian and the
Godolphin Barb. Although 174 sires are mentioned in the first
General Stud Book, these are the only three whose descent has
remained intact.

Old Boots

A man known as 'Old Boots' in Ripon, Yorskshire, who lived in
the middle of the 18th Century, had such an upward curving
chin and downward curving nose that he could hold a coin
between his nose and chin.

Foreign Language

It is 1870. She is Gretchen Gottlieb, a sixteen-year-old Catholic
girl, terrified and in hiding from anti-Catholic fanatics in a forest.
'The man made my mother dead,' she says. She complains that
her head aches, she talks about a glittering knife, and then,
desperately, evades questions. 'Gretchen can't,' she finally wails.
And there it ends. Gretchen presumably was killed, and Mrs Jay
remembers nothing until her own life began in 1923. Mrs
Dolores Jay is an ordinary American housewife, married to a
minister and the mother of four children. But when she is deeply
hypnotized, Dolores Jay moves back through time past the time of

The Fame Name Game

What did Cherilyn Sarkisian change her name to?

Answer: Cher

her childhood and her infancy – deeper and deeper back until she whimpers in German. (When she is conscious, she neither speaks nor understands any German.) Dolores Jay herself can't account for it. She doesn't believe in reincarnation. She has only heard fragments of the taped hypnosis sessions, but she can't understand the language. She has never been to Germany. She has never heard of the little town of Eberswalde where Gretchen says she lived, and which exists in what is now East Germany close to the Polish border. But Eberswalde was the scene of Germany's last stand against the Soviet Union in 1945, and the town was almost completely razed. The records that once might have proved whether or not there was such a person as Gretchen Gottlieb have been destroyed.

 Memorable Movie Quotes

One man's compost is another man's potpourri.
How the Grinch Stole Christmas

It's amazing the clarity that comes with psychotic jealousy.
My Best Friend's Wedding

The most beautiful words in the English language are not 'I love you,' but 'it's benign.'
Deconstructing Harry

Hilarious Misprints

Creech Airman Beating
Victim
Las Vegas Review Journal

Bush Favors His Own
Program
Newsweek

Ban On Runny Yolks Not
Going Over Easy
Spartanburg Herald-Journal

Crashed Jet May Have Flown
Too Low
AP

Wanted. Man to take care of
cow that does not smoke or
drink.
Advertisement

Arson Suspect Is Held In
Massachusetts Fire
New York Times

Laura Chick Accuses Some
Of Her Male Colleagues Of
Sexism
Los Angeles Times

Dead Man Ignored Police Order
Arizona Republic

Bill Would Exempt Minors
From Death
Goldsboro News Argus

Death Doesn't Deter Students
From Drinking
The Roanoke Times

Frying Squirrel Blamed For
Sunday Power Outage
Muskegan Chronicle

Cost Of Being Poor Rising
Denver Post

Blind Man Says Diana
Prettiest Woman He Ever Saw
Reuters

Florida Wants Coach With
An Offensive Mind
Florida Times-Union

Britain Inches Grudgingly
Toward Metric System
Reuters

Mad Scientists' Corner

Hallucinating Elephants. In one strange 1960s experiment, Warren Thomas chose to inject an elephant named Tusko with 297 milligrams of LSD (about 3000 times the typical human dose), to see what would happen. The plan was to find out whether the hallucinogenic drug could induce musth, a state of temporary insanity in which male elephants can become aggressive. Tragically, very little was discovered, since Tusko died as a result of this huge dose.

The scientists pointed out that they had not expected this to happen. They also confessed that two of the scientists conducting the research had taken copious amounts of acid themselves without being harmed, and since elephants were considerably bigger than they were, they had expected Tusko to be unharmed also.

The Doctor Who Drank Vomit

Stubbins Ffirth, a doctor who trained in 19th-Century Philadelphia, had a theory that yellow fever was not an infectious disease. He decided to test this theory on himself by a particularly revolting route. He poured samples of infected vomit into open wounds, then drank the vomit. As it happened, he did not become ill. However, it was subsequently shown that this was not because yellow fever is not infectious. It is because it causes infection only when injected directly into the bloodstream, usually through a mosquito bite.

Open Your Eyes

In 1960 at the University of Edinburgh, Ian Oswald wanted to test extreme conditions for falling asleep. After keeping them awake by ordinary means for an extended period, he taped volunteers' eyes open, then positioned a bank of flashing lights half a meter in front of them. Electrodes were connected to their legs giving them a stream of electric shocks. Feeling that this wasn't quite enough to guarantee wakefulness, he also blasted loud music directly into their ears.

Surprisingly, all three subjects who underwent this regime managed to fall asleep within 12 minutes. Oswald's conclusion was that the monotonous and regular nature of the stimuli had allowed them to do so.

Decapitating a Rat in Facepaint

In 1924 Carney Landis, of the University of Minnesota, was researching facial expressions of disgust. He drew lines on volunteers' faces with burnt cork, before asking them to smell ammonia, listen to jazz, look at pornography or place their hands in a bucket of frogs. This was in order to stimulate exaggerated expressions on their faces.

He then instructed each volunteer to decapitate a white rat. All hesitated, and some became angry or tearful. However, in the end most agreed to do so. This showed the ease with which most people bow to authority, something which Stanley Milgram would later demonstrate in his classic obedience experiments.

However, Landis was focused on his aim of matching up emotions and expressions, a task he never fully achieved, since different people use different expressions to display their emotions.

The Berkeley Necromancer

In the 1930s, Robert Cornish, of the University of California at Berkeley, believed he had found a way of raising the dead. His experiments involved placing corpses on a see-saw to circulate the blood, while also injecting adrenalin and anticoagulants.

Cornish carried out some apparently successful experiments on strangled dogs. Then he found a condemned prisoner, Thomas McMonigle, who volunteered to become a human guinea pig. However, the state refused permission for this rather alarming experiment, fearing that it would have to release McMonigle if the technique worked and that a public outcry would be the result.

Thought For the Day

The fly that doesn't want to be swatted is most secure when it lights on the fly-swatter.

G.C. Lichtenberg

Leaders Have Their Say

Be courteous to all, but intimate with few, and let those few be well tried before you give them confidence.
George Washington

The only man who makes no mistakes is the man who never does anything.
Theodore Roosevelt

Make the lie big, make it simple, keep saying it, and – eventually they will believe it.
Adolf Hitler

Writing a book is an adventure. To begin with, it is a toy and an amusement, then it becomes a mistress, and then it becomes a master, and then a tyrant. The last phase is that just as you are about to reconciled to your servitude, you kill the monster and fling him out to the public.
Winston Churchill

Ability is nothing without opportunity.
Napoleon Bonaparte

Ideas are far more powerful than guns. We don't allow our enemies to have guns, why should we allow them to have ideas.
Joseph Stalin

Americans . . . still believe in an America where anything's possible – they just don't think their leaders do.
Barack Obama

There are many things we do not want in this world. Let us not just mourn them; let us change them.
Ferdinand Marcos

One life is all we have and we live it as we believe in living it. But to sacrifice what you are and to live without belief, that is a fate more terrible than dying.
Joan of Arc

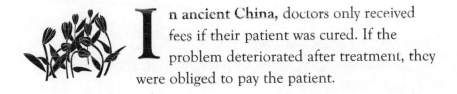

135

Fascinating Historical Facts

In ancient China, doctors only received fees if their patient was cured. If the problem deteriorated after treatment, they were obliged to pay the patient.

People have been wearing glasses to improve their vision for about 700 years.

According to Herodotus, the Greek historian, Egyptian men never went bald. The reason he gave for this was that as children Egyptian males had their heads shaved, and their scalps were thus exposed to the health-giving rays of the sun.

The Chinese used marijuana as a remedy for dysentery.

In 1956 the phrase, 'In God We Trust', was adopted as the US national motto.

The ancient Egyptians recommended putting half an onion into some beer foam then consuming the resulting mixture as a way to ward off death.

Salim (1569-1627), heir to the throne of India, had managed to acquire four wives by the age of eight.

The custom of shaking hands with strangers came from the desire to show that both the parties were unarmed.

The first wooden shoe came from the Netherlands. Appropriately enough, they were called 'klompen' and were cut from one single piece of wood.

The pharaohs of ancient Egypt wore clothes made with thin threads of beaten gold. Some fabrics had up to 500 gold threads per square inch of cloth.

The first Eskimo Bible was printed in Copenhagen in 1744.

Spider webs were used to try to cure warts in the Middle Ages.

The first parachute jump from an airplane in France was made by a certain Captain Sarret in 1918.

It is now a historical fact that Henry Ford stated that history is 'bunk.'

The Fame Name Game

What did Virginia Patterson Hensley change her name to?

Answer: Patsy Cline

Czar Paul I banished soldiers to Siberia for the crime of marching out of step.

In 1962, many schools in Tanganyika were forced to close by an outbreak of contagious laughter that lasted for six months.

The last words spoken from the moon to date were those of Eugene Cernan, Commander of the Apollo 17 Mission on 11th December 1972. 'As we leave the Moon at Taurus-Littrow, we leave as we came, and, God willing, we shall return, with peace and hope for all mankind.'

Incan soldiers invented a simple but effective version of the process for freeze-drying food. Potatoes would be left outside to freeze overnight, then thawed and stomped on to remove excess water.

The wall that gave New York's Wall Street its name was 12 feet tall and 1340 feet long. It was erected in 1653 by Dutch colonists for protection from their enemies.

Human skulls were used as drinking cups for centuries. Once the muscles and flesh had been scraped away, the bottom was chopped off. They were now suitable for drinking any beverage from, whether it be beer, water, blood or herbal tea.

The Bible does not actually say that there were three wise men or three kings; it only says there were three gifts.

The first dictionary of American English was published on 14th April 1828.

Limelight was how stages were lit before the invention of electricity. Illumination was produced by heating blocks of lime until they glowed.

Civil War General Thomas Jonathan 'Stonewall' Jackson has two separate burial sites. His left arm, which was amputated after the battle of Chancellorsville, was buried on a nearby farm. A week later, Jackson died and was then buried, along with his right arm, in Lexington, Virginia.

Time magazine's 'Man of the Year' for 1938 was Adolf Hitler.

During the California Gold Rush of 1849, miners often sent their laundry to Honolulu for washing and pressing. The extremely high costs of laundry services in California during these boom years meant that it was deemed more economical to send the shirts all the way to Hawaii for servicing.

Emir Beysari (1233-1293), an extremely wealthy Egyptian, reportedly drank wine from gold and silver cups. It is said that he never once used the same cup twice.

England's first great industry was wool. The export of wool had become the nation's largest source of income by the late Middle Ages, and many peasants were evicted from their land in 'enclosures' as landowners turned more fields into pastures for the sheep.

The first United States airplane flight from coast to coast occurred in 1911 and took 49 days.

Escape maps, compasses, and files were all smuggled into POW camps in Germany during the Second World War, by being inserted into Monopoly game boards. Real money for escapees was even concealed in the packs of Monopoly money.

Florence Nightingale was only a nurse for two years of her life. She contracted fever during her service in the Crimean War, and spent the last 50 years of her life as an invalid.

Queen Supayalat of Burma ordered about 100 of her husband's relatives to be clubbed to death, in order to ensure that her husband ascended to the throne.

Napoleon was fond of constructing his battle plans while sitting in a sandbox.

Shakespeare spelled his own name in several different ways.

Spiral staircases in medieval castles are built clockwise, because most knights were right-handed, and those who weren't were forced to use right handed equipment. A clockwise staircase gave the defenders an advantage. As the attacking army were climbing the stairs they would be unable to use the sword in their right hand effectively because of the difficulties of climbing the stairs.

Poet Henry Wadsworth Longfellow was reportedly the first American to ever have a full plumbing system installed in his house, in 1840.

The British once went to war over a sailor's ear. It happened in 1739, when Britain launched hostilities against Spain, reportedly because a Spanish officer had sliced off the ear of a ship's captain named Robert Jenkins.

3000 years ago, most twenty-something Egyptians were considered old and died by the age of 30.

The World's Oddest Animals

Angora Rabbit *This rabbit is a variety of domestic rabbit usually bred for its long, soft hair that can be turned into wool. It is one of the oldest types of rabbit, originating in Ankara, Turkey, like the Angora goat. They are now bred for wool, which can be removed by shearing or gently pulling the loose wool away. If the rabbits remain unsheared they can come to look like a huge pom-pom with no visible ears or face. These rabbits were popular pets with French royalty in the mid-1700s, and had spread to other parts of Europe by the end of the century. They were first brought into the United States in the early 1900s.*

Ancient Egyptians reportedly used slabs of stones as pillows, though whether or not they padded them is lost to history.

Spanish Flu killed over 20 million people in 1918 alone.

The Aztec Indians of Mexico believed turquoise would protect them from harm, and so warriors used green and blue turquoise stones as decorations on their battle shields.

Charles de Gaulle's final words were reportedly 'It hurts.'

In the original, more ambitious architectural design, the French Cathedral of Chartes had six spires. (It was eventually built with only two.)

Alexander the Great was an epileptic.

In ancient Egypt, people traditionally shaved off their eyebrows as a mourning symbol when their cats died.

Historians report that the Roman Emperor Gaius (Caligula) (AD 37-41) was so fond of his horse that before he died he gave him a place as a senate consul.

In 1778, the most fashionable women of Paris attached a lightning rod to their hats in blustery weather.

It took 214 crates to transport the Statue of Liberty from France to New York in 1885.

The military salute is a motion that started in medieval times, when knights in armour would raise their visors to reveal their identity.

Before 1863, the postal service in the United States was free.

Louis XIV had forty personal wigmakers and as many as 1000 wigs.

Niagara Falls stopped flowing for half an hour in 1848, when an ice jam blocked the source river.

New York was the first state to require motor vehicles to be licensed. The law was passed in 1901.

The Coliseum took its name not from its size, but from a colossal statue of Nero that stood close by. It was erected after the destruction of his palace.

The Mind Bending Quiz

1 Who played Muhammad Ali in the movie *Ali*?
2 Which vegetable is produced from the plant maize?
3 Which girl band had a hit single with *Independent Woman*?
4 Basic, Cobol, and Pascal are all types of what?
5 Which band had an *Appetite For Destruction* in 1987?
6 Which British actor died during the making of the Oscar-winning *Gladiator*?
7 Oxford bags were a type of what?
8 Which Dylan song starts, 'Come gather round people wherever you roam'?
9 A black mamba is what type of creature?
10 In the proverb what do drowning men clutch?
11. Who wrote *Franny and Zooey*?
12 What is the main language of North America's two main countries?
13 Against which conflict is *Dances With Wolves* set?
14 In Edward Lear's poem, what was remarkable about the Pobble?
15 What game is played at Roland Garros?

(Answers on Overleaf)

Answers

1 Will Smith. 2 Sweet corn. 3 Destiny's Child. 4 Computer languages. 5 Guns N' Roses. 6 Oliver Reed. 7 Trousers. 8 *The Times They Are A-Changin'*. 9 Snake. 10 Straws. 11 J.D. Salinger 12 English. 13 American Civil War. 14 It had no toes. 15 Tennis.

How did you do?

12-15
Saviour of the Universe

8-11
Intergalactic Hero

4-7
Middle of the Road

1-3
Alien Abductee?

More UFO Sightings and Stories

An Egg-Shaped Craft. On 2nd November 1957, several motorists in Levelland, Texas reported seeing a strange, glowing, object shaped like an egg which caused their vehicle's engines to shut off. When the object departed, they were able to restart their engines again.

In Front of the Moon

On 1st December 1965, the Adhara Observatory UFO Lunar Transit in San Miguel, Argentina, received a number of calls from members of the public saying that something strange seemed to be happening on the moon. The observatory staff photographed the moon at regular intervals and the series of images showed disk-shaped objects moving in front of the moon. Later that night three strange glowing objects were seen flying over La Plata.

The Kecksburg Incident

On 9th December 1965, a massive fireball was seen in the sky by thousands across a large area of the United States and Canada. It lit up the sky over Michigan and headed over into the Ontario area. It was widely assumed to be a meteor, and this was how it was reported in the press. However, eyewitnesses in Kecksburg, a small village to the southeast of Pittsburgh, saw something crash into a wooded area. A young boy claimed to have seen the object land and his mother saw blue smoke billowing from the woods and contacted the local police. Other local observers, including volunteers from the fire department, described an object shaped like an acorn and about as large as a car. In a band around the base of the object they observed strange writing, resembling hieroglyphics. A large military force arrived rapidly and sealed off the area, ordering all civilians and local emergency services to leave. The object was loaded onto a truck and removed. Various explanations have been suggested for the Kecksburg incident, including a crashed satellite or military experiment, but many people believe the craft may have been of alien origin.

Glowing Lights

On 12th August 1953, it is claimed that a UFO appearing as a red glowing light was witnessed by forty-five people in Bismarck, North Dakota. The sighting took place over two consecutive nights.

Thought For the Day

I've observed that there are more lines formed than things worth waiting for.

Robert Brault

Superior Disappearance
A US Air Force pilot disappeared near Lake Superior on the US/Canadian border. It is claimed that he was chasing a UFO when he disappeared.

Wannaque UFO
On 11th January 1966 at the Wanaque Reservoir, Wanaque, New Jersey, people claimed to have seen a UFO in the form of a bright light. The sighting led to traffic jams and choked the police communications networks to a standstill. The UFO apparently kept changing color, although it was mainly white. It shot a beam of light down towards the ice on the reservoir close to the dam. After about half an hour it flew off to the southeast, where it was seen by other spectators. Another similar UFO sighting of a similar nature occurred the following night in Wanaque. The mayor, Warren Hagstrom, Police Chief Floyd Elston and Captain Joe Sisco all claimed to have had a clear sighting of the craft. Two reservoir police, Sgt.Ben Thompson and patrolman Edward Wester, also claimed to have witnessed the craft along with other Wanaque residents.

Alien Sex Fiend
In 1957, a Brazilian man called Antonio Villas Boas claimed to have been abducted from his home in São Francisco de Sales and subjected to alien experiments. He also made the lurid claim that he had had sex with an alien woman during his time on the UFO.

Strange Happenings
On 20th May 1957, US Air Force pilot Milton Torres reported that he had been ordered to intercept and fire on a UFO which

was exhibiting 'very unusual flight patterns' over East Anglia in the United Kingdom. Apparently, ground radar operators had been tracking the object for some time before Torres' plane was scrambled to the area.

Shag Harbor Crash

On 4th October 1967 in Novia Scotia, Canada, a UFO was reported as having crashed into Shag Harbor. An official Canadian naval search was dispatched and the incident is still today referred to as a UFO crash.

The Cash-Landrum Incident

On 29th December 1980, there was a strange incident which, uniquely among UFO incidents, led to American citizens suing the USA for damages. In Piney Woods, Texas Betty Cash, Vickie Landrum, and Colby Landrum were driving through a wooded area on their way to an evening of bingo.

Through the trees they saw a diamond-shaped UFO over the road ahead. Betty and Vickie, the two adults, assumed it was a helicopter or airplane. This was not uncommon as there were several airfields in the area. However, this object was unlike anything they were familiar with. The UFO was shooting out intermittent reddish-orange flames toward the road below. Betty got out of her car, and watched the UFO hover ahead of them. At this stage, a large number of helicopters were heard, and they quickly started to arrive in the skies over the woods.

The helicopters seeemed likely to be from one of the local airbases. When Betty returned to the car, she was astonished to find that the door handle was so hot it burnt her hand. The three drove home, but all of them became ill within a couple of hours. Betty, who had left the safety of the car, was in the worst shape. There was blistering on her head and neck, her eyes swelled up so she couldn't see, and she felt extremely sick.

She was admitted to the hospital as a burns patient, even though no-one knew how the burns could have originated. Over fifteen days she was treated, she lost her hair, and she couldn't open her eyes to see for a week. Seven-year-old Colby also had eye problems while Vickie also suffered hair loss. As the treatment progressed, they were all treated for potential radiation poisoning of a life-threatening nature. Betty lost weight, and developed sores over her body. Finally her condition was diagnosed as skin cancer.

Local police tried to locate the origin of the helicopters, in order to investigate the witnesses' story. None of the military air bases in the area would acknowledge having anything flying in Piney Woods on that night. The road near the site showed fire damage that tallied with their story of down bursts from the UFO. Without knowing where the helicopters were from, a military exercise could not be assumed to be the explanation.

The Fame Name Game

What did Richard Starkey change his name to?

Answer: Ringo Starr

In spite of this uncertainty, Betty Cash, Vickie Landrum, and Colby Landrum sued the US government for medical damages resulting from their encounter with the unidentified object. At a congressional hearing, the Department of the Army Inspector General denied any military involvement and no compensation was awarded. Betty Cash died 18 years later, having suffered from bad health ever since the encounter.

Sugarloaf
In the 1970s, Sheriff Barry A. DeLong of Somerset County, Maine, claimed to have witnessed a UFO. He described it as hovering about 15ft (4.6m) from his police cruiser, late at night. It had fixed lights that were spinning, was huge, and oval-shaped. He then watched it slowly starting to back off toward Sugarloaf, then leaving at a high speed.

Tunnels in Mongolia
There was a serious border incident between Russia and China in April 1970, 1000km north of Ulan Bator, Mongolia. Both Chinese and Russian air traffic controllers claimed to have observed a number of unidentified objects. Both sides mistook the objects for spy planes and assumed that the other side was lying and invading their airspace. On 24th April 1970, a Russian bomber disappeared without a trace during its flight from Moscow to Vladivostok. On the same day a lot of these strange flying objects were observed in the area. Each attempt to shoot them down failed. It was discovered that the UFOs came from an area in Mongolia. A major force of Russian planes bombed the area, revealing a secret underground tunnel system, which was

Weird And Crazy Laws

Louisiana law not only prohibits couples shopping for a new bed from putting it to the 'ultimate test' by trying out making love on it. It even forbids any simulation of this activity, suggesting that too much suspicious jiggling and bouncing whilst bed-hunting may lead to a brush with the law.

In Kentucky, anyone who has been drinking is defined as 'sober' until they 'cannot hold onto the ground.' In the same state, it is illegal to carry an ice cream cone in your pocket, which is a strange thing to do, unless you are so 'sober' you forgot you put it there in the first place.

Cats and dogs in Ventura County, California, are not allowed to have sex in public without a permit. Presumably this law does also refer to cats and dogs separately.

In Oblong, Illinois it is illegal to have sexual relations while fishing or hunting on your wedding day. It is not specified whether this is legal if you are at least with your new bride rather than another party, but one imagines that any man who overstepped that particular mark would be in plenty of trouble without the intervention of the law.

In Texas it is legal for a chicken to attempt to have sex with a human, but not the other way round – it's illegal for the human to reciprocate.

If a police officer in Coeur d'Alene, Idaho, suspects a vehicle is being used for sexual purposes they are required to honk their horn three times, then wait for two minutes before they are allowed to approach the car and check what is really going on.

largely destroyed by their action. It has been widely rumoured that a nuclear weapon was used in this maneuver.

A Ball of Light

On 30th October 2007, there were numerous reports of a UFO near Eastern Metropolitan Bypass, Calcutta, India. It was also captured on video camera by an amateur film-maker. It was shaped like a ball of light which alternately hovered, then darted away, with the shape and size of the craft varying as it moved. The video was subsequently broadcast on Indian news channels.

UFO Balloons

On 12th May 2007, several orange-colored UFOs were spotted in Bangor in Northern Ireland. They were reported by a man called Clifford Rossbottom who reported that he had seen three orange globes travelling through the sky. Belfast International Airport's air traffic control received several calls from people (including the Coastguard) who had spotted the same objects, but there were no reports of aircraft in the area during the time of the sightings. In this case a company called UFO Balloons later claimed that their product had been responsible for the events. However, the mystery deepened when, a month later, two similar aircraft were sighted over Buela in Colorado.

The Richter Scale

There was an alleged UFO crash in Llandrillo, North Wales on 23rd January 1974. Witnesses described the crash as involving lights in the sky and a big impact shock that was felt throughout the whole area. However, this was an instance where the initial suspicions of UFO involvement were definitively proven wrong, as scientists identified the cause as an earthquake measuring 3.5 on the Richter Scale – an unusual event in the area, to say the least.

Spikes in the Forest

On 9th November 1979, an English forester called Robert Taylor claimed that he was pulled by two spiked globes towards a strange craft on a clearing near Livingstone in the UK. He passed out and afterwards had trouble walking and speaking. He was also dehydrated and felt thirsty for days afterwards. In the forest at the site, unidentified track marks were found and the incident has never been explained.

Obscure English Language Facts

Singles Night

Dermatoglyphics, misconjugatedly, *and* ***uncopyrightable****, are the longest English words in which no letter appears more than once (15 letters each). The 14 letter runners up include* ***ambidextrously, benzhydroxamic, hydromagnetics, hydropneumatic, pseudomythical, schizotrypanum, sulphogermanic, troublemakings, undiscoverably,*** *and* ***vesiculography****.*

The Unseen Image

On 4th September 1971, a photograph was taken at Lake Cote in Arenal, Alajuela, Costa Rica, that is often referred to as the finest UFO picture of all time. The UFO was photographed during an official mapping mission from an airborne camera, over Lake Cote. None of the crew actually observed anything out of the ordinary, but an image appeared later on the developed film that clearly showed a flying craft unlike any seen before on Earth.

Empty Black

In August 1993, 27-year-old Australian Kelly Cahill, her husband and three children were driving home shortly after midnight, having visited friends. They noticed the lights of a curved craft with windows. It appeared to hover noiselessly above the road. The UFO was so close to the car that Kelly believed she could see humanoid figures through some of the windows. Shortly afterwards, a light surrounded them, so bright that they couldn't see anything. When they finally reached home there was a foul smell surrounding the car, like vomit. Kelly was convinced that something had happened on the way home. She also realised that

The Fame Name Game

What did Nathaniel Adams Coles change his name to?

Answer: Nat King Cole

it was later than she had thought and that an hour or more of their time had gone missing.

When she undressed, she saw a strange triangular mark on her stomach – this was a mark she had never seen before. She suffered from general illness for the next two weeks. When she thought back on the events of that strange night, there were discontinuities in her recollection of where exactly the craft had been. Memories eventually came back to her – they had stopped the car, and she and her husband had got out and walked to the large craft. There they saw a peculiar creature that she described as being black, not a black color but 'empty black'. She later described it as 'not having a soul,' being 'void of color,' and about seven feet tall. Both Kelly and her husband remembered there being another car on the road at the same time.

As she recalled these events she realized she had lost consciousness, and then found herself back in her car. The occupants in the other car later came forward. They had a very similar story, claiming to have suffered amnesia, having been abducted and also subjected to medical procedures, which might explain the mark on Kelly's stomach.

Minot Attacked

In 1967, servicemen at Minot Air Force Base, North Dakota, claimed to have seen an unidentifiable craft attack the air base, and the missile silos in particular. The craft was sending out two fierce beams of light, which appeared to observers to be weapons. The base was home to a stockpile of nuclear weapons, and was the scene of other alleged UFO incidents. On 6th June 1968, another UFO hovered over a silo, then departed. After the UFO left, it was discovered that one of the missiles was armed and unlocked, ready to launch – swift action was taken to remove the immediate danger.

New Year's Day
On 1st January 1969, three separate witnesses in Prince George, British Columbia, Canada, reported seeing a peculiar sphere in the sky in the early evening. The object was emitting yellow or orange light and rose rapidly from low in the sky to about 10,000 feet before disappearing.

Fire In The Sky
On 5th November 1975, logger Travis Walton disppeared for five days and, on his reappearance, reported that he had been abducted by aliens. Six of Walton's workmates claimed to have witnessed a UFO at the start of their shift and before Walton's subsequent disappearance. Walton described the event and its aftermath in *The Walton Experience*, which was later dramatized in the film *Fire in the Sky*. On the day in question, Walton's colleagues finished their shift shortly after 6pm. During the drive home the crew say they saw saw a bright light shining over the horizon of a nearby hill. Driving closer, they saw a large metallic disc hovering above a clearing, and emitting bright lights. It was around 8ft (2.4m) high and 20ft (6.1m) across. Walton jumped off the truck and started to run towards the disc which was shaking and giving off a loud vibration or hum. Walton appeared to levitate towards the craft, but then dropped heavily to the ground. The crew were terrified, and believed Walton to be dead. They drove away as fast as they could, but when they went back to search the next day for the body

there was no sign of Travis or the silver disk. A police-led search was organized but nothing of interest was found.

Late at night on Monday, 10th November, Grant Neff, Walton's brother-in-law, received a phone call from Travis Walton. Walton said he was injured and needed him to come and get him. He gave the address of a nearby gas station where he was discovered, having collapsed in the phone booth. He was in a bad way, and kept muttering inexplicable things. At his mother's house, Walton found that eating even the mildest foods made him vomit. As a medical precaution, he kept a urine sample after his first visit to the bathroom. When Walton was examined by doctors, he was found to be in good physical condition, but there were a couple of unexplained anomalies. There was a small red spot in the crease of his elbow consistent with having been given an injection and his urine sample was very low on acetone. This would be a natural result of five days without food as his body would have begun using stored fat deposits leading to high levels of acetone. He had no cuts or bruises.

He reported that after he ran towards the UFO, his last memory was being struck by the beam of light. He subsequently

Natural Thoughts

A wise man can see more from the bottom of a well than a fool can from a mountain top.

Author Unknown

woke up on a reclined bed. There was a bright light above him, and the air was humid and heavy. He had breathing difficulties and was in pain, but he believed initially that he was in an ordinary hospital. As he regained consciousness, he realized he was being attended by three strange figures, wearing garments that looked like orange jumpsuits. They were not human; he described them in terms that are familiar from many abduction accounts – as short gray creatures with large dark eyes. He said that he shouted at them to stay away from him and they left the room. After that he was questioned in English by another creature, which looked nearly human except for its large gold-colored eyes. He was then taken into another room with three more beings with golden eyes, a female and two males. The female placed a mask on his face and he lost consciousness. He woke up by the gas station and immediately phoned Neff. No one has been able to prove whether or not this tale was a genuine experience of aliens or a complicated hoax.

When The Sun Falls

During August, September and October in Portugal, 1917, thousands of people saw what they thought was the sun spin and descend. Some time later, Jacques Vallee, Joaquim Fernandes and Fina d'Armada insisted that it was a possible UFO sighting that was not originally recognized as such due to cultural differences.

Watch the Skies

In Los Angeles, California, on 24th February 1942 unidentified objects in the sky caused the military to fire thousands of anti-aircraft rounds into the sky. There has never been an explanation for this incident.

Bright Lights In Iran

In Tehran, Iran on the 19th September 1976, it is claimed that a UFO appeared on radar and was sighted over Tehran, the capital of Iran, during the early hours of the morning. Electrical equipment onboard two F-4 interceptor aircraft ceased to work as they flew close to it and ground control equipment was also affected by the UFO.

At approximately half past midnight (local time), the Imperial Iranian Air Force command post at Tehran received four telephone reports of unusual activity in the night sky. The calls came from civilians in the Shemiran city district. Some reported seeing a object shaped like a bird; others reported a helicopter with an unusually bright light. The command post knew that no helicopters were airborne that could account for the reports, so they called General Yousefi, assistant deputy commander of operations. Yousefi's first guess was that the object was a meteorite. He conferred with flight control at Mehrabad International Airport, then looked for himself and saw an extremely bright object, larger than a star. At this point he decided to scramble a F-4 Phantom II jet fighter from the nearby Shahrokhi Air Force Base.

An F-4 piloted by Captain Mohammad Reza Azizkhani flew to approximately 25 nautical miles from the object. At this point the aircraft suddenly lost all communication and flightdeck instruments stopped working. Azizkhani decided to turn back toward Shahrohki. Within a few miles all the flightdeck systems started to work again.

A second F-4 was scrambled, this time piloted by Lieutenant Parviz Jafari. Jafari's jet managed to get a radar lock on the object at a distance of 27 nautical miles. The radar signature of the mysterious craft resembled that of a Boeing 707. As Jafari flew closer, the object began to move away from him, staying a constant 25 nautical miles from the F-4. It was hard for him to establish the object's size due to the intense lights it gave off, a flashing sequence of blue, green, red, and orange arranged in a square pattern. The lights flashed in sequence, but changing so quickly that they all could be seen simultaneously.

While the object and the aircraft continued flying south, a smaller second object seemed to break off from the first and flew towards Jafari's jet at high speed. Lieutenant Jafari thought he was being attacked, and tried to launch a missile, but at this point he too lost control of the instruments on his flight deck. He wisely chose to take evasive action and once again his instruments started to function once he was beyond a certain range

This incident was recorded in a detailed US Defense Intelligence Agency (DIA) report given to the White House,

---

 # Memorable Movie Quotes

Amanda: Why are you dressed like somebody died?
Wednesday: Wait...
Addams Family Values

Dark Helmet: If there's one thing I despise, it is a fair fight.
Spaceballs

the Secretary of State, Joint Chiefs of Staff, National Security Agency (NSA) and Central Intelligence Agency (CIA). It remains one of the most well-documented and convincing encounters with UFOs in history. The Iranian generals involved in the incident went on the record to say that they believed the object involved was of extraterrestrial origin.

The World's Oddest Animals

Hag fish *Hag fish are marine cranials. Their unusual feeding habits and slime-producing capabilities have led to them being dubbed the most 'disgusting' of all sea creatures. Hag fish are long, worm shaped and can exude large quantities of a sticky slime or mucus. When captured and held by the tail, they escape by secreting a fibrous slime, which turns into a thick and sticky gel when combined with water. Their odd characteristics continue with their ability to then clean themselves by tying themselves into a knot which works its way from the head to the tail of the animal, squeezing off the slime as it goes. Some also suggest that this singular behavior may also assist them in removing themselves from the jaws of predatory fish. However, the 'sliming' also seems to act as a distraction to predators, and hag fish are sometimes seen to 'slime' when agitated and later clear the mucus off by way of the same travelling-knot behavior.*

Hilarious Misprints

Ernie Pyle Died 50 Years Ago
AP

Family Can Be Close While
Apart
Richardson News

Fatal Mudslide Blamed On Hill
Associated Press

Double-Hand Transplant
Patient Applauds Operation
Reuters

Couple Slain; Police Suspect
Homicide
Monterey Herald Sun

Federal Agents Raid Gun
Shop, Find Weapons
Tulsa World

Divorces Are Fewer Among
Single People, Chicago
Figures Show
Chicago Tribune

Doctor Execution Policy
Debated
AP

Fireworks To Be Aired On
Radio
Orlando Sentinel

For Now, There's No End
Insight
Dallas Morning News

Head of Anti-Violence
Group Arrested for Hitting
Referee
AP

Florida May Need Disabled
Voter Machines
AP

Fitness Club Closes, Going
Belly Up
St. Louis Post-Dispatch

For Sale . . .
Four-poster bed, 101 years
old. Perfect for antique
lover.
Advertisement

Drunks Get Nine Months In
Violin Case
Monterey Herald Sun

163

Peculiar Inventions

Amazing amounts of human ingenuity are constantly expended on devising new inventions, most of which turn out to be no use to anyone.

Patent offices around the world are marvellous storehouses for this constant stream of fatuous inventiveness. Below is a list of some of the stranger patents that have been taken out for devices that strangely enough never caught on.

Flying Chicken Plane

As the name suggests, this is a giant airplane in the shape of a chicken. It doesn't seem to have occurred to the inventor that chickens are famous for their taste, and their egglaying, and for many other things. Just not for their ability to fly.

The Dad Saddle

Many small children like to pretend their father is a bear or a horse and ride him around the house. If only the dad saddle had caught on they would have had a foolproof way of staying on.

Fart Collecting Device

This strange idea is made up of an air-tight collecting tube which can be inserted into the rectum in order to capture farts before they pollute the atmosphere. Presumably you can store them up for a later date.

Scented Doll With the Appearance of an Aged Person

Sometimes the idea behind a patent is so staggeringly odd that all one needs to know is the name of the intended device.

Dining Table Dishwasher

From the great line of 'combo' inventions comes the dining table that doubles as a dishwasher. When your meal is finished, just open up the table and put the dirty dishes inside!

User-Operated Amusement Apparatus for Kicking the User's Buttocks

This is a rather elaborate machine made up of cranks and paddles. The user can operate various controls and handles to control the parts of the machine which will then give them a kick in the buttocks. Why this didn't become the must-have Xmas present of 2002 is anyone's guess.

The Spider Ladder

This is a ladder which would allow spiders to climb out of a bath. It is made from a thin flexible latex rubber strip which moulds to the contours of the bath. A suction pad holds it in place.

Thought For the Day

Men are probably nearer the central truth in their superstitions than in their science.

Henry David Thoreau

This would be the perfect gift for those who are too kind to simply run water on the poor spider, but too squeamish to rescue the spider by other means. No spiders were available to comment on this device.

Device For Producing Dimples
An 1894 patent which consisted of a cunningly designed clamp which could be applied to the cheeks in order to fold the flesh into dimples. It looks rather painful and doesn't seem to have set the world on fire, though it could in a sense be seen as a precursor of today's plastic surgery revolution.

Poodle Earrings
Another invention for which the name really does say it all, these are special earrings designed for poodles. Piercing is required.

Brassiere Having Integrated Inflatable Bladders For the Holding of Comestible Liquids
Here is another irresistible name, describing a device that more or less does what it says on the tin.

Apparatus for Facilitating the Birth of a Child by Centrifugal Force
This 1965 patent described a rotating table on which the mother to be would be whirled around as though on a fairground ride. It may have failed for two different reasons. Firstly, most mothers might not be too keen to be spun around in such an undignified manner. Secondly there may not be enough nurses trained in the advanced art of babycatching whilst running in circles. Other than that it was a quite brilliant idea.

Talking Dog Collar

This is a patent for a dog collar with recorded messages which makes it sound a little bit like your dog is talking. Most pet owners talk to their pets anyway, regardless of whether they get a response, so maybe there just wasn't the market for this gizmo.

The Santa Detector

This is a stocking fitted out with a special alarm which will sound when the stocking is filled. The ideal present for children who want to meet Santa Claus, or for parents who are tired of keeping up the pretence.

A Horse-Powered Minibus

A horse walks on a conveyor belt treadmill inside of the bus. This connects to the wheels via a gearbox. There is a thermometer under the horse's chest and this connects to the vehicle instrument panel. The driver can use a handle to prod the horse and send him signals to start and stop.

The Fame Name Game

What did Margarita Cansino change her name to?

Answer: Rita Hayworth

The Bird Diaper
For those who love to let their parakeets and budgerigars roam free but who don't want their house to smell of a bird cage at the zoo, this is the ideal solution. Or would have been if it had ever gone into mass market circulation.

An Underwater Golf Swing Training Device
This is a hydrodynamically adjustable paddle that can be used to practice golf swings whilst standing in the ocean or in a lake or swimming pool. The controls set a variable resistance as you swing the device through the water.

The Self-Spreading Toilet Seat
This rather odd toilet seat was invented in Germany. Two side pieces spread outwards as the user sits down, thus spreading the buttocks apart. This is intended to make defecation easier and more comfortable. An additional benefit, according to the patent, is an improvement in personal hygiene as soiling in the area around the anus is reduced. It has the disadvantage of seeming rather uncomfortable and weird.

Meat Goldfish
This is a meat-jerky snack that doubles up. You can eat it yourself or you can attach it to a fishing rod and use it as bait.

Abraham Lincoln's Large Boat Flotation Device
The famous president wasn't just a politician but also a part-time inventor and he believed he had made a significant contribution to the age old problem of keeping boats afloat.

Dolls Formed in the Likeness of the Lord Jesus With a Movable Head and Extremities

What is it with dollmakers and patents? Some of the strangest patents of all time seem to revolve around odd doll ideas. Presumably one could use the movable extremities to make Jesus point out the sinners in the neighborhood.

Hat Simulating a Fried Egg

This one could be a big hit in areas with a lot of chicken farmers. It is a white hat with a large yellow circle, with the entirety of the hat giving the 'visual impression of a fried egg'.

Pat On The Back Apparatus

This was described in the patent as a self congratulatory apparatus. And what could be more useful in those moments when you are feeling underappreciated than a simulation of a human arm with which you can actually pat your own back. Very useful for solitary workers and those whose bosses don't appreciate all their hard work.

Birthday Cake Candle Extinguisher

This 1964 patent aimed to create the perfect device for blowing out birthday candles. An unidentifiable animal, looking rather like a sphinx, concealed an air-expulsion tube which would direct a stream of air in the direction of the candles. People preferred to blow out candles the old-fashioned way, so the device never got off the ground in marketing terms.

Apparatus For Signaling From Graves
The two men who invented this 1904 patent had presumably woken up a few too many times in the small hours from a nightmare of being buried alive. The device consisted of a tube running from the coffin up into a signal tower to be placed on top of the grave. A button or lever would be placed close to the hand of the supposed 'corpse'. In turn this triggered a bell in the tower above and could be used to alert the graveyard operators if someone had been wrongfully buried and wanted to be rescued from six feet below.

The World's Oddest Animals

Hawaiian Hoary Bat This bat is commonly seen on the islands of Hawaii, Kauai, and Maui, inhabiting particularly the wet and dry areas, and from sea level up to 13,000ft. It has short and rounded ears with black and naked rims. Its strangest feature is its yellow buff throat and puffed up throat which makes it look quite scary. It emits ultrasonic calls at frequencies as high as 30 KHz to detect its flying prey.

Weird And Crazy Laws

Bikini car washes (where topless women wash cars) are prohibited in many states of the US. However, since fines are only $50 per incident, some car washes simply charge an extra $50 to cover the legal costs.

In Connorsville, Wisconsin it is illegal for a man to fire a gun while his female partner is having a sexual orgasm. As they say in northern England, there's nowt as strange as folks.

In Bozeman, Montana, there is a prohibition on any sexual acts in the front yard of any home, taking place after sundown, and also if you are nude.

In Helena, Montana, a woman may not dance on a saloon table unless her clothing weighs more than three pounds, two ounces. Rumour has it that the inventor of the lead-weighted bikini was a Helena resident.

Sex in cars is a frequent preoccupation of lawmakers. In Massachusetts, taxi drivers aren't allowed to make love in the front seat of their taxi during their shifts. In Carlsbad, New Mexico, couples may engage in a sexual act while parked in their vehicle during a lunch break, but only if their car has curtains. While in Liberty Corner, New Jersey any couple engaging in sexual relations inside a vehicle, and accidentally sounding the horn may be imprisoned.

Hotels in Sioux Falls, South Dakota can only legally furnish their rooms with twin beds. These should be a minimum two feet apart. And to further frustrate amorous couples, it is illegal to make love on the floor between the beds.

In the town of Willowdale in Oregon, it is illegal for a man to curse while having sex with his wife.

Grisly Tales

Old Bones. Dynasties of Ancient China
Fortune telling has always been
popular with the Chinese. During the
days of the Shang Dynasty (1122 BC to 256
BC) they did this by cracking the bone from a
dead animal and reading the fracture lines (like
reading tea leaves). They were known as oracle bones. When they
were found many years later people then thought they were
'magic' dragon bones and crushed them to use in medicinal
potions.

Writers Block Dynasties of Ancient China
The first Emperor of China was called Qin Shi Huangdi (260 BC
– 210 BC or the 3rd Century BC). He took the throne at the age
of nine and was by all accounts a terrible tyrant. He had all the
books and papers of the past destroyed because he wanted things
done his way. He also buried alive all the writers to make sure
they didn't write any more!

Walled In Dynasties of Ancient China
In 400 BC the Chinese began building the Grand Canal and the
Great Wall. The Great Wall is 4000 miles long and took 2000
years to build as each Emperor added a bit more. However, it is
not visible from space as is popularly thought. Each Emperor
would build more because they wanted to take the credit for
'finishing it'. In fact, several walls, referred to as the Great Wall

of China, were built since the 5th Century BC. The most famous one is the one built between 220 BC and 200 BC by the first Emperor of China, Qin Shi Huang; this wall was located much further north than the current wall as we know it, built during the Ming Dynasty, and little of it remains.

The Great Wall is the world's longest man-made structure, stretching over approximately 6400km (4000 miles) from Shanhai Pass in the east to Lop Nur in the west. It runs along an arc that roughly delineates the southernmost edge of Inner Mongolia.

Caesar's Ransom Ancient Rome
Julius Caesar was imprisoned by pirates who took him hostage, demanding a large amount of money. The ransom was paid for his release and he subsequently hunted down the pirates who did it and had all of them killed.

The Female Pharaoh Ancient Egypt
The civilization of Ancient Egypt lasted for more than 3000 years and made Egypt one of the richest countries in the world. The people were ruled by Pharaohs who were believed to be

---

 The Fame Name Game

What did Lucille LeSueur change her name to?

Answer: Joan Crawford

descendants of gods and if they didn't obey them then bad fortune would fall upon them. There was once a female Pharaoh called Hatshepsut who is always depicted in Ancient Egyptian drawings as wearing men's clothes because a woman wasn't really allowed to be Pharaoh but she happened to be the only child of the previous Pharaoh able to take up the job!

Egyptian Cats Ancient Egypt
In Egyptian mythology, Bastet (also spelled Bast, Ubasti, and Pasht) was an ancient goddess, worshipped at least since the Second Dynasty (from around 2575 BC). Originally she was viewed as the protector goddess of Lower Egypt, and consequently depicted as a fierce lion. Indeed, her name means (female) devourer. As a protector, she was seen as defender of the pharaohs, and consequently of the chief god, Ra. Bastet was originally a goddess of the sun, but later changed by the Greeks to a goddess of the moon. In Greek mythology, Bast is also known as Aelurus (Greek for cat).

By the Middle Kingdom (roughly between 2030 BC and 1640 BC), she was generally regarded as a domestic cat rather than a lioness. Occasionally, however, she was depicted holding a lioness mask, which hinted at suppressed ferocity. Because domestic cats tend to be tender and protective toward their offspring, Bast was also regarded as a good mother, and she was sometimes depicted with numerous kittens. Consequently, a woman who wanted children sometimes wore an amulet showing the goddess with kittens, the number of which indicated her own desired number of children.

Due to the threat to the food supply caused by vermin such as mice and rats, cats in Egypt were revered heavily, sometimes being given golden jewelry to wear, and being allowed to eat from the same plates as their owners. They were also prized for their ability to fight and kill snakes, especially cobras, Consequently, as the main cat (rather than lion) deity, Bast was strongly revered as the patron of cats, and thus it was in the temple at Per-Bast that dead (and mummified) cats were brought for burial. Over 300,000 mummified cats were discovered when Bast's temple at Per-Bast was excavated.

Cut Up in Greece Ancient Greece
The Ptolemaic period was a time of the emergence of new thoughts and ideas in the arts and sciences in the two major civilizations, the Egyptian and the Greek. Ptolemy the third let a physician called Erasistratus practice his surgery skills on criminals who had been given the death sentence. No anaesthetic was used! The fourth Ptolemy killed his father because he couldn't wait to become King and the most famous Queen of Egypt, Cleopatra, killed her brother so that she could take the throne. After she married the Roman Mark Anthony in 31 BC she lost a war with the Roman army and Egypt subsequently became a Roman state. Cleopatra was so upset she killed herself with a bite from an asp.

The Minoan Goddess Ancient Greece
The Minoans were the first civilization of ancient Greece and they lived on the island of Crete around 2100 BC to 1500 BC. They were apparently a rich and peaceful people. However, they were taken over by the Myceneans around 1500 BC. The Mycenaeans worshipped goddesses instead of gods and would

deal with famine or earthquake disasters by attacking neighboring countries to steal what they needed.

Tales of Troy Ancient Greece

According to mythology, around 1250 BC the Trojan War started and was to last for ten years. Apparently Helen of Sparta was so beautiful that all the Greek kings wanted to marry her. She eventually married Menelaus but then fell in love with Paris of Troy and went to live with him in the walled city leaving her husband behind. Her ex-husband's brother was so angry at what she'd done to his brother that he and the Greek army tried for ten years to get into the walled city to get her back without much luck. Eventually they came up with the idea of the now famous wooden horse.

The Trojans found the wooden horse outside their gates one day and wheeled it inside. The horse was full of soldiers who leapt out after dark to open the city gates to let in the rest of the army. They attacked the sleeping city, killing all the men and making the women and children into slaves. Although the Greek poet Homer wrote the story, a German explorer in the 19th Century believed it to be true and set out to find Troy. He is said

Thought For the Day

Think like a man of action, act like a man of thought.

Henri Louis Bergson

to have found the remains of a city which might be Troy in what is now Turkey.

The Persians and the Greeks Ancient Greece
Around 490 BC, the Persians (now Iran) were persistently trying to take the Greeks' land. They built a bridge of boats to cross the Hellespont, a stretch of water between Greece and Asia Minor. They had such a huge army that it took them seven days to walk to Greece across the boats. When the Greeks beat the Persian army at Marathon in 490 BC, the Greeks suffered only 192 dead soldiers but the Persians lost 6400 men. The tactics of the Greeks were far superior to those of the Persians.

No More Words Ancient Greece
Did you know that the Greeks forgot how to write during the Dark Ages? It was only when they started trading with the Phoenicians (from what we now know as Lebanon) around 800 BC that they started to write things down again. However, the Phoenician alphabet contained no vowels so the Greeks added extra signs for the vowels and so started the alphabet as we know it today. The Greeks gave the Phoenicians their name from the Greek word for purple ('Phoinikes') because they made purple dye.

Sparta Ancient Greece
Sparta was a state in the south of Greece known for producing very tough people. In school boys who didn't do well enough or pay enough attention to the teacher were badly beaten. Girls were not allowed to go to school but were encouraged to run and be athletic and active. It is rumoured that Spartan girls wore their

skirts much shorter than the rest of Greece to help with all the running. The Spartans were a fierce military nation, widely feared in the Aegean area.

Party On Ancient Greece
Festivals and drinking parties were very popular with the Ancient Greeks. They played a game called cottabos. This seems to have involved throwing what was left in your wine cup at a chosen target. The person with the most direct hit was the winner. Knucklebones was a game played mostly by girls. The bones were the ankle bones of goats which were thrown into the air and then caught on the back of the hand. They even had a version of snakes and ladders!

Last of the Greeks Ancient Greece
Ever wondered what happened to the great Greek civilization? After Alexander the Great defeated Persia at the Battle of Gaugamela in 331 BC he became known as the King of Asia and the Greek Empire became huge and very wealthy. However, when Alexander died in 323 BC his greedy generals fought over the bits

Natural Thoughts

If a man who cannot count finds a four-leaf clover, is he lucky?

Stanislaw J. Lec

of the empire and the army became so weakened that it was easy for the Romans to come and take over.

Sacrificial Beasts Roman Empire

The Romans had different gods for different things and tried to keep all the gods happy all of the time lest things go bad for them. Many animals were killed on temple altars as sacrifices to the gods, especially cockerels and rams that were considered holy creatures and therefore killed most often. When cows and other large animals were sacrificed they would be killed and their insides would be taken out for the priest to examine the liver. If it wasn't deemed to be healthy or was in some way badly formed it was considered a bad omen. In these cases, they sometimes found a human to sacrifice as well.

Loud Roman Geese Roman Empire

In 390 BC, the Gauls were trying to attack Rome's Capitoline Hill. Apparently, the Romans' holy geese made such loud squawking noises that the Romans woke up and so evaded capture. Thanks to those sacred geese of Juno, the Romans went on to win the subsequent battle.

The Fame Name Game

What did Declan Patrick McManus change his name to?

Answer: Elvis Costello

The Fascinating Body

The stomach produces a new layer of mucus every two weeks; without this it would digest itself.

Our eyes remain the same size from birth, but our nose and ears grow throughout our lives.

The ancient Sumerians (from the 5th millennium BC) believed that the liver made blood and the heart was where thought happened.

Out of the 206 bones in the average human body, over half are in the hands and feet. (There are 54 in the hands and 52 in the feet.)

Men have a larger amount of blood than women. Men have 1.5 gallons while women have 0.875 gallons.

Each year about 98% of molecules in your body are replaced.

Your thumb is almost always the exact same length as your nose.

The right lung generally takes in more air than the left lung.

The substance that human blood is most similar to in terms of chemical composition is sea water.

Dogs and humans are the only two animals with prostates.

The brain is the recipient of a quarter of all the oxygen the body uses.

During a kiss up to 278 bacteria colonies may be exchanged between the kissers. On the bright side, kisses can be slimming. A kiss uses up 6.4 calories per minute.

There are over 10 trillion living cells in the human body.

The World Series – Rome vs Carthage Roman Empire
The first Roman war with Carthage was in 264 BC and battles
between the two raged for the next twenty three years. Eventually,
the Romans won and by 146 BC Rome was the greatest power in
the Mediterranean.

Roman Plumbing Roman Empire
The Romans gave us the beginning of plumbing. Their system of
waterways and drainage was so impressive that it wasn't bettered
until the Victorian era. They used sponges on sticks instead of
toilet tissue and this gave rise to the term 'getting the wrong end
of the stick'. They loved to go to the public baths to bathe and
exercise with their friends and family. Oh, and they used olive oil
instead of soap and scraped dirt off them with a special tool!

We Who Are About To Die Roman Empire
The Romans loved their bloodsports. They watched gladiators
fight in special arenas called amphitheaters. Gladiators always
began their routine by calling 'We who are about to die salute
you' to the Emperor. Most gladiators were slaves or criminals
forced to take up the role. If they were really good they could
earn their freedom.

Unlucky Christians Roman Empire
Whenever the Romans encountered a Christian they thought the
Christians would bring them danger because it was against their
religion to sacrifice things to the gods or to worship more than one
god (the Christian god). The Romans would throw Christians to
the lions to try and persuade them to change their minds.

Purple Patch Roman Empire
Only the Roman Emperor was allowed to wear the color purple.
If any ordinary person was seen wearing purple they were
executed as a traitor.

Up Pompeii Roman Empire
In AD 79, Mount Vesuvius erupted burying the citizens of
Pompei. The hot dust and lava buried everything several meters
deep and 'froze' the bodies in the position of whatever they were
doing at the time.

Life in Rome Roman Empire
Life expectancy in ancient Rome was not much over fifty. Many
died very young because of disease. The poor often left new-born
babies outside to die if they couldn't afford to feed them. It was
also not uncommon to sell children as slaves. Although the
Romans had some knowledge about the workings of the human
body they had no such things as painkillers or anaesthetic and
operations were performed whilst the patient was still conscious.
They did however, know the healing power of garlic and herbs
and ate a lot of them along with large quantities of olive oil thus
establishing the basic ingredients of modern Italian cuisine.

Thought For the Day

*Losing an illusion makes you wiser than
finding a truth.*

Ludwig Börne

The Nazca Plain 100 BC–AD 600

In Peru, between the Andes and the Pacific, lies the Nazca Plain. It is a vast, flat expanse of sunbaked stones; and from the ground extremely boring. Fly over it however, and what seemed like abstract markings from ground level resolve themselves into complex drawings of a bird, a lizard, a monkey, a spider and many other stylized images. They were created by moving the dark stones that litter the surface of the desert to reveal the lighter earth beneath. This has been done on a grand scale; some of the 'drawings' are over a hundred feet long.

These markings are believed to have been made by the Nazcan Indians, a pre-Inca race, between 100 BC and AD 600. It has been suggested that they correspond to some astronomical alignment, but study has shown that the small extent to which they do could very easily be coincidental. Erich von Däniken, the God-as-Astronaut theorist, believes the lines to be landing strips from alien spacecraft. In his book *Chariots of the Gods?* he shows two parallel lines with a widened area halfway along one of them. This, he puts forward, is a runway with a flying saucer parking area. The picture is in fact one of the Nazcan birds' legs. The wide area is its knee, a space hardly large enough to park a bicycle in.

Von Däniken does raise an interesting question however. Short of building hot-air balloons, the Nazcan Indians could never have been sure that they looked as they intended. One can only conclude that the pictures were designed to be seen by the gods. Whether these gods drove spaceships or not is a matter for conjecture.

Germ Warfare in Ancient Times Middle Ages
There is evidence that germ warfare was used as early as the 14th
Century, when a band of Tartars surrounded a group of Genoese
merchants who had taken refuge in the walled town of Caffa in the
Crimea. After a three year siege, the Tartars finally achieved victory
by catapulting into the village the bodies of soldiers who had died of
the bubonic plague. The entire town was infected. Even worse, when
the Tartars departed, the survivors returned to their homes, infecting
their families and contributing to the spread of the Black Death. The
bubonic plague that swept through the civilized world between
AD 542 and AD 543 was reported by the historian Procopius to
have killed as many as 10,000 people each day. Emperor Justinian
was among those who recovered.

At Sea with the Vikings Middle Ages
The Vikings were around for about 300 years from the 8th to the
11th Century and were excellent at building ships. The ships
were called longships and were specially shaped to sail in very
shallow water. They had both sails and oars so that when it was
too shallow or narrow to use the sails they could row the rest of
the way. By this method they could land their ships right up to
the beach. They wore chainmail and padded leather tunics,
helmets and nose guards and often metal goggles to protect their
eyes. They carried huge double-edged swords, wooden shields and
spears and ferociously attacked anyone who tried to fight them.

The Abbey of Lindisfarne Middle Ages
One of the Vikings' earliest attacks on Britain was in AD 793.
They arrived at the island of Lindisfarne near Scotland. The

island had a castle and an abbey but the only inhabitants were monks. The Vikings killed most of the monks. The rest they beat and captured to be sold as slaves. After that they kicked the buildings to bits and stole all the treasure from the abbey at a time when religious places were seen as sacred.

That Viking Thing Middle Ages
The Vikings socialised at a gathering called the Thing. Here they could all have the chance to get off their chest anything that was bothering them. They also sorted out their arguments there as well. If a disagreement couldn't be sorted out at the Thing they had something else they called Ordeals. At Ordeals both parties of the argument would try to prove they were right. They proved their righteousness by walking over hot coals or boiling themselves alive because they believed that the gods would look after them if they were innocent.

The Ice Pick Method Middle Ages
In the 13th Century, priests in Europe treated mad people with beatings and force-feedings of blood and sheep dung to exorcise

---

Natural Thoughts

In a mist the heights can for the most part see each other; but the valleys cannot.

Augustus William Hare
and Julius Charles Hare

185

evil spirits. Between 1790 and 1813, American physician
Benjamin Rush whirled clinically depressed patients around at
high speeds before submerging them in water. In the late 1940s,
Walter Freeman developed a 10-minute procedure to scramble
the frontal lobes of the insane – by jamming an ice pick through
their eye sockets.

Shopping for Teeth Middle Ages
In the 13th Century, if you had toothache you were taken to the
market place where the offending tooth was pulled out with a
pair of pliers, without anaesthetic or painkillers.

What's Your Poison? Middle Ages
A medieval poisoner had a variety of choices: deadly herbs
(henbane), toxic mushrooms (death angel) and other deadly
foodstuffs, animal venom or fluids (snake venom, rabid dog
saliva), heavy metals and minerals (such as mercury), and other
plant-derived poisons (ergot fungus growing on rye and other
grains). A person intent upon poisoning another person in the
Middle Ages had a good variety of poisons at hand to draw upon.
Common poisons could be obtained from monkshood or
wolfsbane, hemlock and black hyoscyamus from the herb
henbane. These could be relied upon by any poisoner, as could
thorn apple, arsenic, mercury, and antimony sulfide that could be
sprinkled or diluted or spread with dependably efficacious results.
The simplest method of poisoning someone was to add a single
or compound poison to a highly spiced and/or chopped dish or
in a victim's glass of wine. The strong flavors and uneven texture
would mask the bitter taste and consistency of the poison.

In a Stew Middle Ages

Apparently, medieval man loved having baths, contrary to what is
popular legend. Many historians believe that people most likely
bathed more than they did in the 19th Century. Ladies often
bathed sociably in bathing parties at important castles that had a
special room beside the kitchen where hot water could be
brought in easily along with a choice of herbs, perfume or rose
leaves. Lords bathed in their bedchamber in tubs shaped like a
half-barrel and containing a stool, so that the occupant could sit
and soak long. Cities had public baths, known as 'stews', for the
populace.

Burying the Bones Middle Ages

In medieval China, at appointed times of the year, officials buried
abandoned corpses, and in order to banish agents of death and
disease, communities held rites for 'hungry ghosts.' For the
medieval Chinese, death turned the living into bones, ghosts, and
memories. It was important to reconcile and attempt to harness
the volatile schism between these states and even more so when
the corpses were unaccounted for or abandoned. Strategies often
involved exorcism.

To Hell and Back Middle Ages

It seems that people had near-death experiences during the
Middle Ages too. In one story a hermit was revived from death
and testified that he had been to hell. Apparently he saw several
powerful men dangling in fire. He says that just as he too was
being dragged into the flames, an angel in a shining garment

came to his rescue and sent him back to life with the words
'leave, and consider carefully how you will live from now on.'
According to folklore, after his return to life, the hermit took to
fasting and praying, He was convinced that he had indeed seen
the terrors of hell.

Burn Middle Ages
In medieval warfare, the siege predominated: for every battle,
there were hundreds of sieges. This is one of the reasons that
there is so little documentation of the period. Sieges often
involved burning everything to the ground.

Baptism Before Birth Middle Ages
In cities, villages and noble houses, babies were born at home and
midwives attended the birth. Men were excluded from the room
whilst their wives were in labour. Many historians believe that
the woman in labor assumed a sitting or crouching position.
However, childbirth was dangerous for both mother and child.
The newborn infant was immediately prepared for baptism, in
case it died in a state of original sin. If a priest could not be
located in time, someone else must perform the ceremony and at

The Fame Name Game
What did Frank James Cooper change his name to?

Answer: Gary Cooper

all times water must be kept ready for this purpose. If the baptizer did not know the formula in Latin, he must say it in English or French: 'I christen thee in the name of the Father and the Son and the Holy Ghost. Amen.'

The words must be said in the right order. For example, if the baptizer said, 'In the name of the Son and the Father and the Holy Ghost,' the sacrament was invalid. Many babies were baptized as soon as their head and shoulders appeared during the birth process with the rest of their bodies still inside the mother.

The World's Oddest Animals

Alpaca Part of the camel family, the alpaca is a domesticated species developed from wild alpacas. It looks somewhat like a sheep, but is larger and has a long slim neck and its fur can be many different colors. They are found in herds that graze in the Andes of Ecuador, southern Peru, northern Bolivia, and northern Chile at an altitude of 3500-5000m. Alpacas are considerably smaller than llamas, but are used only for their hair to make a wide range of products including blankets, sweaters, hats, gloves, scarves, a wide variety of textiles and ponchos in South America, and also in other parts of the world. Their hair fiber comes in more than 52 natural colors.

It was deemed to be too dangerous to risk waiting until the birth was complete.

Spanish Soap Middle Ages
Soap was most likely invented in the Orient and brought to the Western world early in the Middle Ages. It was made in workshops, of accumulated mutton fat, wood ash or potash, and natural soda and had a soft texture like grease. Hard soaps appeared in the 12th Century. They were luxury articles, made of olive oil, soda, and a little lime, often with aromatic herbs. They were manufactured in the olive-growing south, especially Spain; hence the modern Castile soap. Only the very wealthy could afford such soap.

Fighting Girls Middle Ages
It is a little known fact that women fought in battles from the 10th Century to the 17th Century. It has always been assumed that the women who did fight were only doing so in defense of homes during desperate circumstances or for religious reasons (like Joan of Arc). In the European Middle Ages, war was the main activity in which masculinity was demonstrated. However,

The Fame Name Game

What did Herbert George change his name to?

Answer: H.G. Wells

by the end of the 11th Century, women fighters are mentioned in the chronicles. In the later Middle Ages women fighters were written about as wondrous oddities.

There is documented evidence that women fought in defense of homes, of aggressive women and women who made a lifestyle of warfare for personal or religious reasons, warrior queens or great women leaders. Usually peasant women or minor nobility, aggressive women were often frowned upon as they were seen to be out of place, and presumptuous. In 1640, several young ladies in Provence and in Paris fought duels out of spite and jealousy. They fought in the streets and aimed their blows at each other's faces and breasts!

Choose Your Punishment Middle Ages
There were many kinds of inventive punishment during the Middle Ages. People were dragged behind a galloping horse, stretched out on a rack, whipped, put in the stocks or hanged. The crimes were often arbitrary and at the whim of the feudal lord or baron. Many people were burned alive. This became a popular punishment for witches. Accused women were dunked into a lake or pond; if they drowned they were innocent but if they survived they were burnt at the stake.

Thought For the Day

You never know what is enough, until you know what is more than enough.

William Blake, *Proverbs of Hell*

Clean Shave Middle Ages

Shaving in the Middle Ages was difficult, painful, and infrequent because the soap was inefficient and the razors, which looked like carving knives, were likely to be old and dull. Even haircutting was a disagreeable experience. Scissors were similar to grass trimming shears; they must have pulled mightily. By the 13th Century some aristocrats had toothbrushes although cleaning the teeth was generally accomplished by rubbing with a green hazel twig and wiping with a woolen cloth.

Drunk and Disorderly in the 13th Century Middle Ages

In medieval times, the favorite English adult recreation was undoubtedly drinking. Both men and women gathered in the 'tavern,' although the term often meant the house of a neighbor who had recently brewed a batch of ale, going cheap at the price of three gallons for a penny. Apparently, accidents, quarrels, and acts of violence often followed a session of drinking, in the 13th Century as well as subsequent ones. The rolls of the royal coroners, reporting fatal accidents, have many such incidents.

In 1276 in Elstow, Osbert le Wuayl, son of William Cristmasse, was coming home sometime around midnight. He is described as being 'Drunk and disgustingly over-fed,' after an evening out in Bedford. He fell and fatally struck his head on a stone 'breaking the whole of his head.' In another account, a man stumbled off his horse riding home from the tavern and it trampled him to death.

Another man fell into a well in the marketplace and was drowned. Other tales include a report of a man who relieved himself in the local pond, fell in, and drowned whilst another was bitten by a dog whilst carrying a pot of ale down the village street. He is said to have tripped while picking up a stone to throw at the dog, and fatally struck his head against a wall. There is also an account of a child who slipped from her drunken mother's lap into a pan of hot milk on the hearth.

Black Death Middle Ages
In the years 1346 to 1350 twenty-five million people in Europe (approximately one third of the population) died from the Black Death now known as the bubonic plague, more than twice as many as the number killed in the First World War. It was spread by the fleas from infected rats. If the fleas bit a human he or she developed lumps called buboes and developed black marks on their skin.

Living on the Land Middle Ages
In the Middle Ages most people worked on the land and they were very poor. The average life span of a peasant was only twenty five years. The Lord of the manor owned the land and the peasants worked the land for him. As payment the peasants received a small plot of land on which they could grow their own food, even so a portion of this had to be given to the lord as 'taxes'. He was the only one with a mill able to grind corn for flour. Many banned the peasants from using hand mills so that they had to use the lord's mill and pay for using it. Mostly, the lord would use the money for large feasts.

Trial by Combat Middle Ages
In medieval times, if the court couldn't sort out a quarrel between two people, the judge would allow what was called 'Trial

by Combat'. This meant that the two arguing parties would arm themselves with a sword or axe and fight to the death. Sometimes they simply killed each other but if one survived then he was deemed to have won the argument.

The Cargo Cult

The inhabitants of the Melanesian islands in the Pacific have, since their first contact with Western travellers, developed the so-called 'cargo cults'. Cargo refers in the islanders' pidgin to goods of any kind given by visitors. First contact occurred with the arrival of the Russian Count Nikolai Mikiouho-Maclay in 1871. He was received as a god, due to the incredible nature of his transport, a Russian frigate, and his gifts, which were amazing to a culture that was still in the Stone Age. German traders and Christian missionaries only served to reinforce the natives' awe and faith. The basic tenets of the religion became set: visitors who give 'cargo' are good, those who do not are evil, as they withhold what are seen as spiritual gifts.

In 1940 the Americans built a military base on the Melanesian island of Tanna in the southern Hebrides. Cargo planes zoomed in and out leaving radios, canned beer and other Western necessities. The natives observed the American service men in uniform; and wishing to bring more planes and enjoy similar luxuries they improvised uniforms and spoke into empty beer cans, as they had seen the Americans speak into microphones. What began as adoration and emulation soon turned to dissatisfaction as their rituals failed to get the desired response. The faith changed its nature, becoming a conviction that the present Western presence on the island was of the wrong kind.

Soon a messiah would come to give the natives what the Americans refused to give them. John Frum or Jonfrum was the name that the natives gave this messiah, although the reason is not clear. Some say that Frum is a corruption of broom, to sweep away the white man. Others put forward the simpler explanation that the name is derived from 'John from America'. He is described as a small man with bleached hair, a high-pitched voice and a coat with shiny buttons.

The cult persists in many different forms on each of the remote Melanesian islands. What began as simple worship of Westerners has developed into an entire liberation theology in a very short time: John Frum will one day arrive and hand over all of the 'cargo' to the natives, while getting rid of the Westerners. After that the islanders will live on as normal, only richer and happier than before.

The Mind Bending Quiz

1   What is significant about bonsai plants?

2   What was the movie sequel to *Silence Of The Lambs* called?

3   Were Honda cars originally manufactured in Canada, Honduras or Japan?

4   In the Old Testament which of David's sons was famous for his wisdom?

5   Maoris were the first settlers in which country?

6   Cardinal, ordinal and prime are all types of what?

7   Which actor Jeff did Geena Davis marry?

8   Where in Germany is a passion play staged once every ten years?

9   In the traditional song, the House Of The Rising Sun is in which US city?

10 Which country marks the most westerly point of mainland Europe?

11 On the third day of 1959 which area became a state of the USA?

12 The Anschluss concerned Nazi Germany and which other state?

13 A perennial is a plant which lives longer than how long?

14 Ellis Island is in which harbor?

15 In which series are Marge and Homer the stars?

(Answers on Overleaf)

Answers

1 Small. 2 *Hannibal*. 3 Japan. 4 Solomon. 5 New Zealand.
6 Number. 7 Goldblum. 8 Oberammergau.
9 New Orleans. 10 Portugal. 11 Alaska. 12 Austria.
13 Two years. 14 New York. 15 *The Simpsons*.

How did you do?

12-15
Top of the range jacuzzi

8-11
Luxury steam room

4-7
Standard hotel bathroom

1-3
Backyard bathtub

Breakfasts Of The Ancient World

Breakfast in Ancient Greece. The Ancient Greek diet consisted of foods that were readily available in Greece's rocky landscape. The typical breakfast, eaten soon after sunrise, was made up of bread dipped in wine and possibly honey cakes. Sugar was unknown to the Ancient Greeks, so natural honey was their main sweetener. Wealthier Greeks would add some olives, figs, cheese or dried fish. How they coped with all that alcohol in the hot Grecian climate is anybody's guess but they managed to create some magnificent buildings in spite of their breakfast drinking, so it can't have been that bad for them. To be fair, the wine that was drunk with every meal including breakfast was watered down – to drink it straight was considered barbaric, a lower-class habit. Interestingly this is the opposite of the modern world where the poor often water down their alcohol to make it last longer while the rich are all in rehab.

The Aegean Sea was teeming with marine life, as it is to this day. Fish was the main source of protein in the Greek diet and was occasionally eaten for breakfast. Beef was extremely expensive because very few people kept cattle, so it was rarely eaten. Beef and pork would only be available to poor people during religious festivals, when cows or pigs were sacrificed to the gods, and the meat was cooked and handed out. The best bits for the rich, trotters and ears for animals and the rest for the poor. Even then 'benevolent' employers who wanted to give their skivvies a treat probably picked it out of the dog bowl.

The Ancient Greeks did not have any eating utensils, so they ate all their meals with their fingers. Bread was often used to scoop out thick soups. Bread also served as a napkin for cleaning hands. After being used this way, the bread would be thrown on the floor for the dogs or slaves to eat up at a later time.

Breakfast in Ancient Rome

Emperor Hadrian is best known for constructing a long wall across Britain because he was afraid of the Scots who lived beyond. During his reign the Roman Empire reached its peak size, but breakfast habits were fairly uniform amongst the Romans, if not amongst their subjects. At dawn, the slaves got up to prepare food for their masters, and to start on the household chores. The first meal of the day was the ientaculum. Wealthy Romans would eat bread, honey and fruit in the morning. To drink they might have a nice glass of Italian red or, if they had overindulged the night before, perhaps plain water. The rich also ate cheese, olives and raisins for breakfast depending on the season and how agriculturally productive their slaves were.

However, for the vast majority of ordinary Romans, breakfast would have been just plain water and, maybe, a piece of bread. The poor got very little by the way of luxury food. There was a custom whereby free bread was distributed every morning for the poor. Presumably this act of charity made the rich feel better about themselves, although it was often just last night's table crumbs. The distribution could turn into a free-for-all as Romans on their way to work grabbed bread for their breakfast from a rich man's slave.

Breakfast Chocolate for the Aztecs:
Ancient Aztec and Maya civilizations were the first to discover the power of chocolate. They primarily used it to celebrate the harvest of the cacao beans, brewing it into a hot, spicy drink. They believed that drinking cacao would grant them wisdom, enlightenment and sexual prowess. Only the dominant men of the ruling and religious classes were allowed to drink the chocolate. However, over time, it became a breakfast staple for the rich and powerful. It would often be drunk mixed with sugar, cinnamon, or even dried and ground chili peppers (an early forerunner of today's craze for chilli chocolate). Women were not permitted to drink the cacao for fear of its effects (see above).

Breakfast in the Stone Age
Evidence from a site in Israel suggests that Stone Age humans ate toasted wheat and barley cereal for breakfast 23,000 years ago. Stone Age humans also ate wild grains as part of their staple

The Fame Name Game

What did Harry Lillis Crosby change his name to?

Answer: Bing Crosby

everyday diet, their toasted wheat and barley were probably quite similar to the breakfast cereals we eat today. A large grinding stone found at the site by an intrepid anthropologist, looking like a giant mortar and pestle, suggested that the cereals were ground prior to being prepared either as porridge or as an ingredient in a type of flat bread.

As well as cereal for breakfast, Stone Age people ate small hoofed animals such as goats or hogs. A typical day's breakfast might consist of cereal, followed by a meat-based 'fry-up' and a selection of nuts and berries including acorns, almonds, pistachios, wild olives, Christ's thorn, raspberry, wild fig and wild grape. It sounds a bit like the breakfast buffet at the Holiday Inn!

Bronze Age Breakfast

By the Bronze Age humans had developed a sweet tooth and used a lot of honey in their cooking, especially for the first meal of the day. Crop seeds would be ground into flour to make unleavened bread. A wide variety of nuts and seeds would be added, including hazelnuts, sweet chestnuts, beech, acorns and walnuts. Thus they were creating what could be described as the first breakfast bar cookies.

Thought For the Day

What you see, yet can not see over, is as good as infinite.

Thomas Carlyle, *Sartor Resartus*,
Book II, chapter 1

Evidence from Northern Europe shows that beer had already become an important part of people's lives, young and old alike, just as it is there today. In the Bronze Age beer was even seen as a health food. Barley beer seems to have been brewed to drink as a safer alternative to water, because the alcohol killed off a proportion of river water parasites. The more beer that was drunk, the more people believed in its magical life-giving powers – and the drink is still enormously popular in the British Isles, Germany, Denmark and elsewhere today. Nuts and beer with a bit of bread and honey was an essential way to start the day, although nodding off whilst on the job in a field was not uncommon either. In modern times Northern Europeans tend to enjoy nuts and beer after work rather than before.

Breakfast in Ancient China
It is no surprise to discover that rice was the first grain to be widely farmed in China. There is evidence of rice farming along the Yang-tse River from as early as about 5000 BC. Just as today it was prepared by being boiled in water. However, not to be outdone by their fellow ancient peoples, the Chinese made wine out of the rice as well. Rice wine has been popular in China since prehistory and was almost certainly a key breakfast ingredient. By 4500 BC, people in northern China had begun farming millet and boiling it into a kind of breakfast porridge. By about 3500 BC tea was being cultivated, and it wasn't long before everybody in China drank tea with their breakfast. At this time people would be still be combining the rice wine and tea at breakfast. One has to wonder how they coped with the rest of the day – the effects of rice wine are potent, as anyone who has drunk saki will testify.

To their breakfast rice, the ancient Chinese added fruit or vegetables including oranges, lemons, peaches, apricots, soybeans and cucumbers. All of these are native to China and made for a healthier element in the breakfast. Homegrown flavorings such as ginger or anise would be used, just as they are today, to liven up the taste of the ubiquitous boiled rice.

For a special occasion breakfast, they would put little pieces of meat on their rice, usually chicken or homegrown pork. However, Buddhists (the majority religion at the time) didn't eat meat, so began to use tofu, or bean curd, as an alternative source of protein as early as 1000 BC. There are no large forests in China, so firewood was in short supply. This is the original reason why the Chinese cut their meat up into such tiny portions and cooked it for only a few minutes. They cooked in flat pans on small fires, the ancient version of the modern 'stir-fry'.

Breakfast in Ancient India

Early Indians ate food that could be readily gathered from their environment. Fruits, wild berries, meat and fish were the staples for the nomadic tribes. As they turned to agriculture, they broadened their diet to farmed crops and pulses. The most fertile regions of Ancient India were in the river valleys. As with the Chinese, rice was a staple food and would be eaten at various meals with cooked lentils, vegetables and very occasionally a small amount of meat.

The early Indus Valley Civilization (later called the Harappans) is recorded as breakfasting on wheat and rice and lentils, complemented with cows, pigs, sheep, and goats, and chicken at breakfast. At this stage of history, they had somewhat omnivorous tastes, but this changed as the Hindu religion spread, and the diet changed as a result. By around 300 BC, many Hindus felt that animal sacrifices added to your karma and kept you from breaking free from the wheel of reincarnation. While not all Hindus gave up eating meat entirely, they ate much less of it and many became vegetarians, a practice that entices the karma-concerned to visit India and wander round trying to 'mend' their karma to this day.

The vegetarian breakfast favored by the early Hindu Indians was mainly wheat flatbreads (chapati), or a kind of flatbread made out of chickpeas, with yogurt and vegetables including lots of spicy peppers. Unlike many other ancient peoples the Indians seem to have shunned alcohol for breakfast – it might be conjectured that karma doesn't sit so happily with alcoholic abandonment. They preferred to drink simple water at the start of their day.

The Fame Name Game

What did Bernard Schwartz change his name to?

Answer: Tony Curtis

Leaders Have Their Say

In the attitude of silence the soul finds the path in a clearer light, and what is elusive and deceptive resolves itself into crystal clear clearness. Our life is a long and arduous quest after truth.
Mahatma Gandhi

I am not sure exactly what heaven will be like, but I don't know that when we die and it comes time for God to judge us, he will not ask, how many good things have you done in your life? Rather He will ask, how much love did you put into what you did?
Mother Theresa

Education is the most powerful weapon which you can use to change the world.
Nelson Mandela

It is common sense to take a method and try it. If it fails, admit it frankly and try another one. But above all, try something.
Franklin D. Roosevelt

Only do what your heart tells you.
Diana Frances Spencer (Princess Diana)

Leaders aren't born they are made. And they are made just like anything else, through hard work. And that's the price we'll have to pay to achieve that goal, or any goal.
Vince Lombardi

A nation which has forgotten the quality of courage which in the past has been brought to public life is not as likely to insist upon or regard that quality in its chosen leaders today – and in fact we have forgotten.
John F. Kennedy

As we look ahead into the next century, leaders will be those who empower others.
Bill Gates

The World's Worst Jobs

Blue Cheese Factory Laborer Blue cheese and its distinctive pungent flavour and aroma is created by letting it decay, so anyone who works with it is essentially handling large amounts of rotting cheese. The smell is incredibly difficult to get rid of, and remains in clothes and hair for a long time. This scent is transferred by microscopic amounts of mould, therefore by the end of a day at work the body is covered by thousands of very small molecules of mould.

Brazilian Mosquito Researcher
The Anopheles Darlingi or Brazilian mosquito, can only be studied by using a human as bait. Quite simply, the researcher has to sit on a chair, and catch only the bugs that bite them. However, they must be prepared for a great deal of itching and a very dull work day. In just three hours, there could be up to 500 mosquitoes, and about 3000 bites. If any of them happen to be carrying malaria, the researcher could spend two or three years recovering from the disease.

Body Inspector during Bubonic Plague
The bodies of people who died from the Bubonic plague were often unrecognizable because of the symptoms of the illness: pus,

buboes (painful, swollen lymph glands), and maggots covering their half-rotted corpses. The job of the body inspector was to take the body to a victim's family for identification and burial. Because the plague was highly contagious, remaining in the body even for a while after death, the life expectancy for this job was extremely short.

Toilet Attendant in a Constipation Clinic

At a constipation clinic people who have not been able to move their bowels, sometimes for weeks, are given tablets and liquids and have things inserted physically, to help cure them. Unfortunately this leads to vile smelling, unpleasant sewage that can block up the toilets. It is then the toilet attendant's job to unblock it.

Guillemot Egg Collector

Guillemots are seabirds which live high on cliff edges, They are fiercely protective of their eggs and if you try to take them they will attack in order to drive you away. Their droppings also make the cliffs slippery and slimy, making the journey to work very dangerous. Even if you manage to collect a few eggs, they could drop out of your hands because slime from the cliffs makes hands very slippery.

Carcass Cleaner

Before a skeleton can be displayed in a museum or academic institution, the rotting carcass must be cleaned so it is fit for the general public. There are a few different ways to achieve this. Sometimes the carcass is boiled, which can release noxious fumes that potentially cause lung infections and skin ailments. Or, the carcass can be put into a large aquarium where maggots pick over the bones until clean. Alternatively the decaying flesh can be removed from the bone manually in the same way one would de-bone a turkey.

Sensory Deprivation Research Subject
This job involves being sealed into a small room designed to create a completely blank and empty environment. All the senses are deprived: sight, hearing, smell, touch and taste. The subject starts to lose their sense of time, and will usually begin to hallucinate. This occurs because the brain is simply not able to function normally in a vacuum, and will create images just to keep itself occupied. Subjects have reported seeing what look like demons, thousands of tiny ants crawling over them, and other hellish images. These experiments can last several days. Sensory deprivation becomes more effective over time, the experiments can last anything from a few hours to several days at a time.

Worm Taster
There are many varieties of worm, some of which are more attractive to fish than others. For this reason worm breeders are always searching for worms that are irresistible to fish to sell to the fishing tackle shops that then sell them to fishermen. Worm tasters have to sniff, feel and eat raw worms to try and find the new breeds that the fish will like best.

Flatulence Analyst
A gastroenterologist once attempted to find out if flatulence is related to intestinal health. He advertised for assistants to breathe in the 'gases' given off by subjects who had consumed large amounts of pinto beans.

Violin Gut String Maker

Violin gut strings are made from the intestines of dead sheep. To make them, the dead sheep must be disemboweled and its intestines stretched to around nine meters. The guts are then soaked in cold water until soft and pliable. They are then fumigated over a sulphur fire and twisted into delicate strings. Exposure to these sulphurous fumes can cause brain damage and unpleasant skin ailments.

The World's Oddest Animals

Komondor Dog *Komondors are one of the largest breeds of dogs, at a minimum of 28 inches tall at the withers with many over 30 inches tall, They are not heavy bodied animals however, and people are often surprised by how quick and nimble the dogs are. They have the heaviest fur in the dog world, with long, thick strikingly corded white coats which resemble dreadlocks or a mop. As puppies their coats are soft and fluffy but these develop into curls as the puppy grows, forming tassels, or cords as the dog fully matures. This requires grooming to separate the cords so the dog does not turn into a large matted mess. Surprisingly there is only minimal shedding with this breed (once cords are fully formed). The only substantial shedding happens when they are a puppy before the dreadlocks fully form. Komondors are born with a white coat although this can become discolored if not cleaned regularly.*

The Mind Bending Quiz

1   What was the name of John the Baptist's mother?
2   Which dance was Chubby Checker doing at the start of the 1960s?
3   Cantilever, railway, and suspension are all types of what?
4   In which country is Havana?
5   What did Antonio Stradivari specialise in making?
6   In Internet abbreviations, what does the middle w in www stand for?
7   Which brothers starred in the film *Duck Soup*?
8   The *Titanic* sank while travelling across which ocean?
9   Who was the tallest person in Robin Hood's band of Merry Men?
10   What is the line across the middle of a circle called?
11   In our solar system which planet takes the least time to orbit the sun?
12   How many angles do 12 separate triangles contain in total?
13   Which two world leaders had a meeting in the Brenner Pass in the Second World War?
14   What is an okapi?
15   In 1960s surfing songs, who was Jan's singing partner?

(Answers on Overleaf)

Answers

1 Elizabeth. 2 Twist. 3 Bridge. 4 Cuba. 5 Violins.
6 Wide. 7 Marx. 8 Atlantic. 9 Little John. 10 Diameter.
11 Mercury. 12 36. 13 Hitler and Mussolini.
14 Animal. 15 Dean.

How did you do?

12-15
Gold Ingot

8-11
Silver Spoon

4-7
Bronze Medal

1-3
Wooden Spoon

Miracle Workers Through The Ages

The Messiah 700 BC The word messiah means 'anointed' in Hebrew, and refers to the Jewish belief that King David will one day return and lead his people to victory. (Christ means the same thing in Greek.) The prophet Isaiah announced triumphantly that 'unto us a child is born', and that the Messiah would take the 'government upon his shoulders'. Isaiah was writing roughly around 700 BC, after the Assyrians had conquered Israel and led its people (including the mythical 'lost tribes') into exile. Ever since then, certain men have become possessed of the conviction that they are the promised Messiah, and ordered their disciples to follow them to victory and kingship. None has so far succeeded.

The Great Pyramid Ancient Egypt
Some groups believe that the Great Pyramid in Egypt had encoded within its measurements many great truths. Christian sects have maintained that it was not the Egyptians who built it at all but the Israelites. According to this theory the internal passageways of the Pyramid, measured in the correct units, are a three-dimensional model of the history of the world up to Christ's birth. On a more secular level, twice the length of the base of the Pyramid divided by its height, again in the correct units, is supposed to approximate to pi. It is difficult to verify

these statements as the nature of the correct units is a matter of conjecture, and the actual size of the Pyramid in any units is still problematic.

The Anglo-Israelite fundamentalist sect took the argument a stage further. Not only did the Egyptians not build the Pyramid; it was also not entirely correct to say the Israelites built it. According to the Anglo-Israelites, the Anglo-Saxon races of Britain and America were the only true tribe of Israel remaining. It was they who had built the Pyramid, as a warning that the world would end and that Christ would return on 20th August 1953. When the date passed without significant upheaval, the Anglo-Israelites began to formulate the theory that the message of the Pyramid was not literal, but a religious metaphor.

The Millennium AD 1000

In the first millennium, it was widely believed that the year AD 1000 would mark the end of the world. It failed to materialize, but there was plenty of war and bloodshed – the Crusades, for example – to encourage the believers to feel that the end was nigh. Many cults and sects were formed who spent their time preparing for the forthcoming destruction.

Thought For the Day

Don't miss the donut by looking through the hole.

Author Unknown

Off With His Head 12th Century

In 1172, an unnamed prophet from the Yemen was dragged in front of the Caliph, who demanded proof that he was a messenger from God. 'That is easy,' replied the prophet. 'Cut off my head and I shall return to life.' 'That would indeed be a sign,' said the Caliph, 'and if you can do as you say, I will become your follower.' At this point he signaled to his headsman. The head of the prophet rolled on the floor, and – predictably – the messiah failed to keep his promise.

The Flying Monk

Giuseppe Desa (Father Joseph) was born in Apulia, Italy, in 1603. He was a strange, sickly boy who became known as 'Open Mouth' because his mouth usually hung open. One commentator remarked that 'he was not far from what today we should call a state of feeblemindedness'; a bishop described him as idiota (although the word meant innocent rather than idiotic). He was subject to 'ecstasies' and, even as a teenager, given to ascetic self-torments that undermined his health.

At the age of seventeen he was accepted into the Capuchin order, but dismissed eight months later because of total inability to concentrate. Not long after, the order of Conventuals near Copertino accepted him as a stable boy, and at twenty-two he became a Franciscan priest. He continued to starve and flagellate himself, acquiring a reputation for holiness. Then one day, in the midst of his prayers after mass, he floated off the ground and landed on the altar in a state of ecstasy. He was unburned by candle flames, and flew back to his previous place.

Sent to see the Pope, he was again seized by such rapture that he rose in the air. His flying fits seem to have been always associated with the state that the Hindus called samadhi, ecstasy. His levitations ceased for two years when a hostile superior went out of his way to humiliate and persecute him; however, after a holiday in Rome and an enthusiastic reception by the people of Assisi, he regained his good spirits and sailed fifteen yards to embrace the image of the Virgin on the altar.

He seems to have been a curious but simple case; floating in the air when in a state of delight seems to have been his sole accomplishment. The ecstasy did not have to be religious; on one occasion, when shepherds were playing their pipes in church on Christmas Eve, he began to dance for sheer joy, then flew on to the high altar, without knocking over any of the burning candles. Oddly enough, Father Joseph could control his flights. On one occasion, when he had flown past lamps and ornaments that blocked the way to the altar, his superior called him back, and he flew back to the place he had vacated.

When a fellow monk remarked on the beauty of the sky, he shrieked and flew to the top of a nearby tree. He was also able to lift heavy weights; one story tells of how he raised a wooden cross that ten workmen were struggling to place in position, and flew with it to the hole that had been prepared for it. He was also able to make others float. He cured a demented nobleman by seizing his hair and flying into the air with him, remaining there a quarter of an hour, according to his biographer; on another occasion, he seized a local priest by the hand, and after dancing around with him, they both flew, hand in hand. When on his deathbed, at the age of sixty, the doctor in attendance observed,

Hilarious Misprints

Alton Attorney Accidently
Sues Himself
The Madison St Claire Record

Heat Wave Claims Frostbite
Victim
Reuters

Ford Contour Sales Slow To
Accelerate
GM *International Newsline*

Funeral Home Head Finds
Live Body
AP

Iraqi Head Seeks Arms
Monterey Herald Sun

Hooked On Internet? Help Is
Just A Click Away!
Reuters

Gays in Roanoke Recover
After Slaying
AP

Lost Portrait Of Czar Shown
AP

Herndon Area – Your
Cardiac Risk
GM *News*

Illiteracy Is Still A Poblem (sic)
Among Mississippi Adults
Hendersonville (NC) Times-News

French Police Suspect Nudist
Site Has Something To Hide
AFP

Health Department Wants
Mayor's Ear
Deseret Morning News

Inmate Missing After
Escaping Via Mail Slot
Lexington Herald

Invisible Man Disappears
From View
Reuters

County Invited To Waste Day
Planning Meeting
Oceana's Herald-Journal

Maybe Error Led To Crash
AP

as he cauterized a septic leg, that Father Joseph was floating in the air six inches above the chair. He died saying that he could hear the sounds and smell the scents of paradise.

Kings, dukes and philosophers witnessed his feats. When his canonization was suggested, the Church started an investigation into his flights, and hundreds of depositions were taken. He became a saint 104 years after his death.

The Day of Judgment According to William Miller 12th Century
On 22nd October 1843, crowds of men and women gathered on a hilltop in Massachusetts, led by their prophet William Miller. In the previous year, Miller, a farmer and an ardent student of the Book of Daniel, had arrived at the conclusion that the end of the world was at hand, and that Christ was about to return to earth. One man tied a pair of turkey wings to his shoulders and climbed a tree to be ready for his ascent into heaven; unfortunately, he fell down and broke his arm. Other disciples carried umbrellas to aid the flight. One woman had tied herself to her trunk so that it would accompany her as she sailed upward.

When midnight passed with no sign of Armageddon, the disciples ruefully went home. One farmer had given his farm to

The Fame Name Game

What did Joe Yule, Jr. change his name to?

Answer: Mickey Rooney

his son – who was a non-believer, and who now declined to give it back. Most of the others had sold all they had. In this moment of depression, Miller suddenly had an inspiration: his calculations had been based on the Christian year, and no doubt he should have used the Jewish year. That would make the date of Armageddon the following 22nd March. On that date, his followers once more gathered for the last Trumpet. Still nothing happened.

One man wrote sadly: 'Still in the cold world! No deliverance – the Lord did not come.' Miller's 50,000 followers soon dwindled to a small band of 'true believers'. Miller himself was not among them; he admitted sorrowfully that he had made his mistake through pride and fanaticism. Another follower made an even more penetrating comment, which might be regarded as the epitaph of any number of 'messiahs': 'We were deluded by mere human influence, which we mistook for the Spirit of God.'

The Death of Joanna Southcott 19th Century
Sometimes, the prophet – or prophetess – loses faith at the last moment, but even when that happens, the disciples remain immune to doubt. When the English prophetess Joanna Southcott lay on her deathbed in 1814, she suddenly announced to her dismayed followers that her life's work now appeared a delusion. Although Joanna was a virgin, she had been convinced that she was about to give birth to the 'child' foretold by Isaiah. And when one of her followers reminded her that she was carrying the Messiah (called Shiloh) in her womb, Joanna's tears suddenly changed to smiles.

After her death a few days later, her followers kept her body warm for three days as she had instructed them – then summoned a small army of medical men to remove the Christ child from her womb. The smell of putrefying flesh filled the room as the surgeon made the first incision, and some of the disciples hastily lit pipes to cover the smell. But when the womb was opened there was obviously no baby there.

'Damn me', said a doctor, 'if the child is not gone.' These words filled the disciples with new hope. Obviously, he meant that the child had been there, but had now been transferred to heaven. And even today, there are a small number of followers of Joanna Southcott – they call themselves the Panacea Society – who believe that when her mysterious box is opened – a box supposed to contain her secret writings – all sin and wickedness in the world will suddenly disappear.

The Crucifixion of Margaret Peter 19th Century
Women have also been among these prophets of the new millennium, and a few have shown even greater fanaticism than their male counterparts. Perhaps the most gruesome example is the German prophetess Margaret Peter. In the week after Easter 1823, a horrible ceremony took place in a house in Wildisbuch, on the German-Swiss border. A twenty-nine-year-old woman named Margaret Peter, who was regarded as a holy woman by her disciples, announced that she had decided that she had to be crucified if Satan was to be defeated. Her sister Elizabeth immediately begged to be allowed to take her place. To demonstrate her sincerity, she picked up a mallet and struck herself on the head with it. Margaret then shouted: 'It has been revealed to me that Elizabeth shall sacrifice herself,' and she hit her sister on the head with a hammer. Then the remaining ten people in the room – including Margaret's other brothers and

sisters – proceeded to beat Elizabeth with crowbars, hammers and wedges. 'Don't worry,' Margaret shouted, 'I will raise her from the dead.' One tremendous blow finally shattered Elizabeth's skull.

'Now I must die,' Margaret told them. 'You must crucify me.' Following her sister's example, she picked up a hammer and hit herself on the head, then ordered the others to make a cross out of loose floorboards. When it was ready, she sent her sister Susanna downstairs to fetch nails.

When Susanna returned, Margaret was lying on the floor on the cross. 'Nail me to it,' she ordered. 'Don't be afraid. I will rise in three days.' Two followers obediently nailed her elbows to the cross. The sight of the blood made them hesitate, and one was sick. Margaret encouraged them. 'I feel no pain. Go on. Drive a nail through my heart.' They drove nails through both her breasts, and a girl called Ursula tried to drive a knife through her heart. It bent against one of her ribs. Her brother Conrad, unable to stand the sight any longer, picked up a hammer and smashed in her skull.

The ten remaining disciples then went to eat their midday meal. They were exhausted but had no doubt that Margaret and Elizabeth would be among them again in three days' time. The

Thought For the Day

Beware lest you lose the substance by grasping at the shadow.

Aesop

deaths had taken place on Saturday; that meant Margaret and Elizabeth were due to arise on Tuesday.

But as the disciples sat around the battered corpses on Tuesday morning, no sign of life answered their prayers. Meanwhile, the local pastor, who had heard about the 'sacrifice' from another disciple, called in the police. (He had known about the deaths for two days, but felt he had to give Margaret time to make good her promise.) The disciples were arrested, and taken to prison. They were tried in Zurich that December, and were all sentenced to varying prison terms.

A Miraculous Cure 20th Century
Josephine Hoare, a healthy girl of twenty-one, had been married for only six months when she developed chronic nephritis, a

 # Memorable Movie Quotes

I'd rather have thirty minutes of wonderful than a lifetime of nothing special...
Steel Magnolias

You get what you settle for...
Thelma & Louise

Why torture yourself when life will do it for you? Who said that? I did! Go ahead and quote me.
Big Girls Don't Cry . . . They Get Even

serious inflammation of the kidneys. Her family was told that she had no more than two years to live. At her mother's suggestion, she was taken to Lourdes. At the famous French shrine, Josephine braved the icy waters of the spring. Although she felt peaceful, she was not conscious of any change. When she went home, however, her doctor said in amazement that the disorder seemed to have cleared. Her swollen legs returned to normal size, her blood pressure became normal, and her energy increased. But she was warned that pregnancy would certainly cause a relapse.

Several years passed. Then Josephine and her husband had the opportunity to revisit Lourdes; and Josephine lit a candle of thanksgiving. Soon after they got home she felt a sharp pain in her back. Fearful that nephritis was recurring, she went to her doctor. His diagnosis was simply that she was six months pregnant – and she had had no relapse. Josephine Hoare had her baby, a son, and remained in good health. For her and her family, the spring of Lourdes had produced a double miracle.

A Hairy Tale 20th Century
Does a place of worship have more intense thought fields than ordinary buildings? Can this explain the incredible case of the doll with human hair that keeps on growing? The story comes from northern Japan and started in 1938. In that year Eikichi Suzuki took a ceramic doll to the temple in the village of Monji-Saiwai Cho for safekeeping. It had been a treasured possession of his beloved sister Kiku, who had died nineteen years before at the age of three. Suzuki kept it carefully in a box with the ashes of his dead sister.

Suzuki went off to World War II and didn't return for the doll until 1947. When he opened the box in the presence of the priest, they discovered that the doll's hair had grown down to its shoulders. A skin specialist from the Hokkaido University medical faculty said it was human hair. The doll was placed on the altar, and its hair continued to grow. It is still growing, and is now almost waist length. The temple has become a place of pilgrimage for worshippers who believe the doll is a spiritual link with Buddha. The priest of Monji-Saiwai Cho claims that the little girl's soul somehow continues to live through the doll she loved so much.

Search for a Missing Boy 20th Century
In 1933 a six-year-old boy vanished from his home in Miège in the Swiss Alps. After an unsuccessful search for the boy, the town's mayor wrote to Abbé Mermet, who had often assisted police in locating missing people. The Abbé needed an article used by the missing person, a description of the last place he or she was seen, and a map of the surrounding area to do his work. He used a pendulum and a form of dowsing to find the missing person. After the Abbé applied his pendulum to the problem of the missing boy, he reported that the child had been carried away into the mountains by a large bird of prey, probably an eagle. He also said that the bird – although enormous – had dropped its load twice to rest and regain its strength.

There was no trace of the boy at the first place the Abbé indicated. A recent heavy snowfall prevented a thorough search at the second place, but the conclusion was that Abbé Mermet had made a mistake. When the snow melted two weeks later, however; a gang of woodcutters found the torn and mangled body of a small boy. It was the missing child. The bird had apparently been prevented from completely savaging the child's body by the sudden heavy storm that had also hidden the forlorn evidence. Scientific investigation established that the boy's shoes and clothes had not come into contact with the ground where the body was found. He could only have reached the remote spot by air – the pitiful victim of the bird of prey. Later the boy's father apologized to the Abbé for having doubted him.

Obscure English Language Facts

Twins and Triplets

*Esophagographers is the longest English word in which each of the letters occurs exactly twice (16 letters). Shorter words with the same pattern of twin letters include **scintillescent** (14 letters), **happenchance** and **shanghaiings** (12 letters), **arraigning**, **concisions**, **intestines**, and **horseshoer** (10 letters).*

*In the word **sestettes** each of the letters occurs thrice.*

Scientific Snippets

Of the salt mined in the world each year, 95% is used on the roads in America for de-icing.

The only rock that floats in water is pumice.

Absolutely pure gold is so soft it can be molded and bent in your hands.

A lump of pure gold the size of a golfball can be flattened into a thin sheet the size of a tennis court.

In 1982, doctors at the University of Utah Medical Center implanted a permanent artificial heart in the chest of retired dentist Dr. Barney Clark, who lived 112 days with the device. This was the first time such an operation had been successfully undertaken.

The largest hailstone ever recorded was a massive 17.5 inches in diameter.

The Cullinan Diamond is the largest gem-quality diamond ever discovered. Found in 1905, the original 3100 carats were cut to make jewels for the British Crown Jewels and the British Royal family's collection.

A single ounce of gold is capable of being stretched into a wire 50 miles long.

In Nazi Germany's gas chambers, prussic acid, in a crystalline powder called Zyklon B, was used to kill. The gas paralyzed the lungs of the victims, and death by suffocation resulted.

On a very hard surface a glass ball will bounce higher than a rubber one. When the rubber is squashed, energy is lost.

Diamonds do not dissolve in acid. The only thing that destroys a diamond is intense heat.

Further UFO Sightings and Stories

The Allagash Mystery. On 20th August 1976 four campers in the Allagash wilderness, Maine, USA, claimed they had been abducted by aliens. They were all art students in their early twenties and they were on a canoeing and camping trip in the wilderness. According to their reports, one night in the early hours of the morning a large oval glowing object appeared above the trees. They were then completely covered in a bright white light and lifted up into the craft. The experience is said to have left them shocked and disorientated. Many years later, two of the party, the twins Jack and Jim Weiner, recounted their strange dreams and flashbacks of events on the alien craft. Under hypnosis, they revealed identical tales of physical examinations which had been carried out on them by aliens in the craft.

A Massive Object

During the night of 5th January 2000, six people, including four police officers, saw a large, triangular object only a few hundred feet over St Clair County, Illinois. It glided silently and slowly towards the south-west, passing over a number of towns before vanishing. The last sighting was near the town of Dupo close to dawn. The object was reported to have several bright lights, and was massive, being reportedly as tall as a two-story house and as long as a football field.

The UFO Memorial

In Scandinavia in 1946 objects were sighted repeatedly in the sky. Swedish Defense Staff even expressed concern in writing to the government. A Swedish man from Ängelholm, Gösta Karlsson, reported seeing a UFO land and alien beings emerge from the craft. A model of a flying saucer is now erected at the site known as the UFO-Memorial Ängelholm.

The Val Johnson UFO Incident

This occurred in Minnesota USA on 27th August 1979. Val Johnson, a Marshall County Deputy Sheriff, was driving his patrol car in the early morning close the North Dakota border when he saw bright lights in a thicket of trees. As he approached he realized that the light was not illuminating the rest of the area. At this point the light suddenly shot towards him at terrific speed coming to rest just over his car.

At this point he lost consciousness and awoke with his head against the steering wheel. He had skidded into the opposite lane of the highway and he was having severe visual disturbance. He called his colleague Greg Winskowski, who arrived to give

The Fame Name Game

What did Richard Jenkins change his name to?

Answer: Richard Burton

assistance. He reported that Johnson had a red bump on his forehead. He thought that he'd probably banged his head on the steering wheel and been knocked out. At the county hospital in Warren, Dr. W.A. Pinsonneault examined Johnson's eyes. He found that shining a light onto them caused him extreme pain. He also noted a 'pinkish irritation' around Johnson's eyes. He compared Johnson's eye injury to 'mild welder's burns', and gave him some salve and bandages.

On examination, Johnson's car was found to be damaged in peculiar ways. The inside driver's side headlight was smashed, but only on the right hand side. On the hood, close to the windshield, was a circular dent about an inch in diameter. The windshield was cracked from top to bottom; the crack showed four impact points which could have been caused by 'small objects, stones perhaps.' The dashboard clock, which had been set correctly at 7pm when Johnson reported for duty, was running 14 minutes late. This was of particular significance as Johnson's wristwatch was also 14 minutes late. The red plastic over the roof light had a triangular puncture, and the lens had been knocked loose. The radio antenna shaft had been bent back at a 60-degree angle, five inches over the hood. The rear radio antenna had been bent at a 90-degree angle, but only at the top three inches. In general the driver's side of the car had suffered the bulk of the damage.

Skid marks at the site of the incident showed that his car had skidded for 850 feet before the brakes locked, and for another 100 feet before it came to a halt. A Ford engineer suggested that the windshield damage couldn't be explained by the car swerving and coming to a halt. Weirdly, the damage seemed to have been

caused by outward forces as well as inward ones. His conclusion
was that the cracks were from mechanical forces of unknown origin.

The incident received widespread publicity, becoming one of
best-publicized UFO events of the 1970s. Johnson only appeared
on television one time, on ABC-TV's *Good Morning America*
program. He refused to take any hypnosis or polygraph tests but
insisted he was not a hoaxer. As with so many incidents, the truth
will never be known for certain.

Strange Cigar

On 21st April 1990, Alitalia pilot Achille Zaghetti reported
having seen a cigar-shaped UFO flying past his plane at high
speed as he was descending into Heathrow Airport on a flight
from Milan to London. Straight after the near-miss, Zaghetti
contacted a Heathrow control center radar operator. The
operator confirmed that an unidentified object had been
observed 10 nautical miles behind Zaghetti's plane. British
defence officials strongly asserted that this had not been a missile,
but no other explanation has been offered.

Night Siege

In the 1980s, Hudson Valley, one hour north of Manhattan,
became the sight of hundreds of claimed UFO sightings. They
began just before midnight, on 31st December 1981. A retired
police officer was in his backyard when he saw peculiar bright
lights to the south. They were colored red, green and white. He
assumed they belonged to a commercial aircraft. However, as they
came closer he realised that they couldn't be. They were flying far
too low, they were arranged in a triangular formation, and there

was a solid object connecting them. There was also a loud vibration or hum coming from them.

Following this initial sighting, there were many many more similar incidents around the Hudson Valley over the next few years. Hundreds of witnesses claimed to see the same triangular set of bright lights. As the sighting came to wider attention, an investigation group set up a UFO hotline to investigate. They took hundreds of calls from people on one night alone, 24th March 1983, all making the same claims. This led to a book *Night Siege: The Hudson Valley UFO Sightings*. The lights were always visible at night, never during the day. On that same March night, the city of Yorktown was swamped with reports of a giant flying craft. The police switchboard had so many calls about the UFO that they were concerned they might not being able to deal with real emergencies. Cars on the Taconic Parkway came to a standstill as drivers watched the large object drift slowly across the skies. About 5,000 reports were made over the five-year period, from 1982 through 1986.

One of the most extraordinary reports came from guards at the Indian Point Nuclear Plant. They saw the massive UFO hovering

Natural Thoughts

Knock on the sky and listen to the sound

Zen Saying

over the plant for an extended period, sometimes only 30 feet above the plant. Security supervisors even once discussed calling in the air force to have it shot down, as it appeared to present a danger to the reactors. The object over Indian Point was said by some of the guards to be a thousand feet long. The craft was also seen hovering over the Croton Falls Reservoir, apparently using a red beam to scan the surface of the water. Given all of the information available, the only terrestrial object that might have been getting mistaken for an alien craft of this description was some kind of blimp. Investigators talked to blimp manufacturers and pilots across the country, without finding any explanation. The Hudson Valley sightings are unexplained to this day.

UFO Cover-Up

On 7th November 2006, United Airlines employees and pilots saw a saucer-shaped, unlit craft over Chicago O'Hare Airport. The craft hovered briefly before shooting up in a vertical direction. At first the FAA denied having received any reports of this incident. However, researchers later used the Freedom of Information Act to force disclosure and it became apparent that a

---

Thought For the Day

It is better to know some of the questions than all of the answers.

James Thurber

number of reports had indeed been made. No explanation has ever been given.

Bangalore Lights
In Bangalore, India on 28th May 2007, Afzal Khan told American news journalists that he had photographed a UFO. He was with his brothers when they saw a bright, slow-moving object like a triangular set of lights moving across the sky towards the north-west. They had been certain that this was not an airplane because of the unnaturally slow motion of the lights which made it appear to be a hovering craft rather than a man-made flying object.

The Face on Mars
In July 1976, when the Viking 1 orbiter began sending back photographs of the surface of Mars, a NASA researcher named Toby Owens observed what looked like an enormous face in the Plain of Cydonia. Mentioned at a NASA press conference as a kind of joke, the 'Face on Mars' was soon exciting widespread attention. Richard Hoagland, a former NASA adviser, argued that the face, and what look like other 'man-made' (or Martian-made) structures in the same area, prove that Mars was once the home of a technically accomplished civilization. Sceptics replied that the face, and other such structures, are natural features, and that they were no more significant than the face of the man in the moon. In 1998 the NASA probe Mars Global Surveyor photographed the object again. This more finely grained image of the object revealed that the object was far more scarred and asymmetrical than the Viking photo had portrayed. Supporters of Hoagland

pointed out that NASA had taken their new picture on a day when Cydonia was partly masked in cloud. Perhaps, they argued, the intervening mist had disguised the features of the 'Face'. Finally in 2001 NASA took a third picture of the object, again using the Mars Global Surveyor probe. This time the sky over Cydonia was clear, and the object appeared even less like a face and more like a ravaged and worn mountain. Some still argue that the object shows signs of intelligent design, although most now accept that the 1976 Viking image of the face was a fluke caused by singular lighting conditions and low-resolution photography.

Yellow Disks on Guernsey

On 23rd April 2007, a commercial airline pilot spotted two UFOs in the sky over Guernsey. The yellow flat disk shapes were estimated to be twice the size of a Boeing 737. Captain Ray Bowyer was flying from Alderney to Southampton when he observed the stationary objects through binoculars. His initial impression was that it was the sun reflecting from greenhouses on the island of Guernsey. Apparently the objects were bright like the sun, but looking at them didn't damage his eyes or give him discomfort. The same objects were also observed by other aircraft and the passengers on the plane.

Men In Black

On 21st June 1947 Harold A. Dahl from Washington reported an alleged UFO incident in which his dog was killed and his son wounded. It was also claimed that a witness had been threatened by strange 'men in black.'

Watching a Crop Circle Form

In August 1991, a British couple were present when a circle was formed. They were Gary and Vivienne Tomlinson, and they were taking an evening walk in a cornfield near Hambledon, Surrey, when the corn began to move, and a mist hovered around them. They reported a high-pitched sound. Then a whirlwind swirled around them, and Gary Tomlinson's hair began to stand up from a build-up of static. Suddenly, the whirlwind split in two and vanished across the field, and, in the silence that followed, they realized they were in the middle of a crop circle, with the corn neatly flattened.

Animal Mutilation

On 9th September 1967, a three-year-old horse named Lady was found lying on her side on a ranch in the San Luis Valley of Colorado, her head and neck completely stripped of flesh. Her hoof tracks stopped a hundred yards from the place she was found. Strange lights had been seen in the sky in the past few days, and newspaper reports of the mystery mentioned UFOs.

By the 1970s, there was a wave of animal mutilations all over America. Inner organs had been neatly and bloodlessly removed;

The Fame Name Game

What did Richard Wayne Penniman change his name to?

Answer: Little Richard

so, often, had the genitals. Newspapers spoke of 'Satanic rituals', but few Satanists were likely to be found out on the open ranges. The cuts looked as if they had been done with some kind of laser, which seemed to explain the lack of blood. (Surgical lasers were not in use in 1967.) An investigator who went to look at the site of Lady's death months later noted that nothing would grow on the place where the carcass had lain.

The World's Oddest Animals

Shoebill The Shoebill (also known as Whalehead) was only recently added to ornithological lists and is a very large bird related to the stork. It derives its name from its massive shoe-shaped bill. The species was only discovered in the 19th Century when some skins were brought to Europe. Many years later live specimens reached the scientific community. However, the bird was known to both ancient Egyptians and Arabs and ancient Egyptian images exist depicting the Shoebill. The Arabs referred to the bird as 'abu markub', which means 'one with a shoe'. The Shoebill is a very large bird, averaging 1.2m (4ft) tall, 5.6 kg (12.3 lbs) with a 2.33m (7.7ft) wingspan. The adult is mainly gray, the younger ones are browner. It is found in tropical east Africa, in large swamps from Sudan to Zambia.

Mexico City

On 6th June 1997, an amateur cameraman with a digital camera captured footage of a UFO passing behind and above several buildings in Mexico City. The reason for suspicion about this object is that air traffic was restricted that day. Only two helicopters had been allowed to fly over the city all day, and no one has been able to say what the UFO was.

The Belgium Triangles

On 3rd March 1990, one of the oddest UFO incidents ever took place in Belgium. There had been a previous UFO sighting in November 1989 when two policemen noticed an array of strange lights in the sky. The lights looked to be bigger than stars and seemed as though they might be attached to a large aircraft, in a triangular shape. The lights came closer and hovered above the road. At this stage two laser beams appeared to come down from it to scan the area below. A ball of light emerged from the vehicle, floated towards the ground, then went back to the craft. After this another giant triangular craft, exactly like the first, emerged from beyond the horizon and came closer before both craft flew away together.

Over the next two years, there were thousands of sightings of similar triangular-shaped lights in the sky over Belgium. Many of those who saw these UFOs were respectable professionals with no reason to tell anything other than the truth. At one stage the Belgian government contacted the American embassy to see if they had been making secret test flights over Belgium. The American embassy assured the government that there were no unauthorized flights of American airplanes taking place in

Belgian airspace. Following this intervention, the Belgian Air Force made it policy that whenever a UFO was observed and confirmed by radar, they would scramble jets to the area.

As a result of this a strange incident took place in March 1990. Following reports of a UFO and confirmation from multiple radar stations, two F-16s were scrambled to the location to investigate. Radar controllers guided them towards their target by radio. On approach pilots observed two of the mysterious triangular craft, with lights shifting in color. Similar to the Hudson Valley sightings, the lights were changing irregularly from white to red, yellow, blue and green. The pilots tried to get a targeting lock on the UFOs and came close to success, but the UFOs kept responding by immediately accelerating away at huge speeds, in unpredictable directions. The UFOs also exhibited rapid altitude changes. For instance one of the craft dropped from 10,000 feet to just above ground level in only five seconds. All of these quick maneuvers would have been entirely impossible for a terrestrial craft piloted by a human. Finally the pilots lost sight of the craft and radar contact and returned to base. Footage filmed from the cockpit of one of the F-16s was later shown at a press conference, showing the mysterious craft making those sharp changes in speed and altitude.

Over Kodiak Island
In the early hours of the morning on 25th September 2007, a bright red light appeared travelling rapidly over the Kenai Peninsula in Alaska. Within seconds, it had reached Kodiak Island air space, which is over 300 miles from the peninsula. At this stage there were numerous eye-witness reports saying that

they had seen it land behind a mountain. However, local troopers and Coast Guards didn't find any trace of the alleged UFO.

Face in the Sky
In Sutton, to the south of London, on 2nd May 2007, John Gregory spotted a UFO late in the evening. He noticed a very bright object in the sky, which he first thought was a star. However, as he continued to observe the object, he became doubtful. The strange phenomenon, which was clearly visible for miles around, seemed to be shaped like a face, nose and mouth. This peculiar object remained for about 20 minutes before vanishing.

 # Memorable Movie Quotes

On a long enough timeline, the survival rate for everyone drops to zero.
Fight Club

Scarecrow: I haven't got a brain... only straw.
Dorothy: How can you talk if you haven't got a brain?
Scarecrow: I don't know... But some people without brains do an awful lot of talking... don't they?
Dorothy: Yes, I guess you're right.
Wizard of Oz

Betty: Wilma, how did you get rid of ring around the collar?
Wilma: I just started washing Fred's neck.
The Flintstones

The Fascinating Body

The fully grown human heart only weighs about ten ounces.

When compared to a computer, the storage capacity of the human brain is between four and five terabytes.

The heart of a woman generally beats faster than that of a man.

Those who believe women to be more highly evolved than men may be interested to hear that females have 500 genes more than males – the extra genes explain their immunity to problems such as color blindness and haemophilia.

While it may not be as convenient to use for identification purposes as fingerprints, every person has a unique tongue print.

In certain cases, gold salts can be injected into the muscles to relieve arthritis.

Brain surgery is generally done with the patient awake. The brain doesn't have any nerves so it has no sensation. The patient is put to sleep while the skull is opened up, but after that the person is allowed to wake up for the remainder of the operation.

If you combined all the muscles in an average human into a single huge muscle, it would be able to produce 2000 tons of force.

A new-born baby breathes up to five times faster than a grown man.

From the age of thirty onwards, people's bodies gradually begin to shrink in size.

Curly hair results from hair follicles that are oval in shape, when cut in section. Round follicles result in straight hair.

Messiahs, Fanatics and Cults

Was Jesus a Messiah?
The answer to that question may seem obvious, for his followers certainly regarded him as the Messiah. But did Jesus agree with them? The answer is probably not. When his disciple Peter told him: 'They call you the Christ, the Messiah,' Jesus advised him to be silent. The claim obviously embarrassed him. The Jewish craving for a messiah arose out of the longing for someone to lead them to victory. After the Assyrian invasion, the Jews became a conquered people, oppressed by a series of more powerful nations: the Seleucids (descendants of Alexander the Great), the Babylonians, the Egyptians, the Romans. For the same reason, the British of a thousand years later came to believe firmly that King Arthur would return to throw off the foreign yoke. Jesus had no desire to be regarded as a military commander, which is what the word messiah originally implied.

Jesus was only one of many Hebrew prophets who were believed to be the Messiah; the historian Josephus mentions several of them. He regarded them all as charlatans and agitators. Christians later changed Josephus's text, in which Jesus is described as a small man with a hunched back and a half-bald head, to read: 'six feet tall, well grown, with a venerable face, handsome nose . . . curly hair the color of unripe hazel nuts . . .', along with various other details that transform the unprepossessing little man into the early Christian equivalent of a film star. But if Jesus declined to be regarded as a military leader, why did anyone pay any attention to him? The answer is that he announced that the end of the world was about to take place, and that this would happen within the lifetime of people then alive. This is why he told them to take no thought for the morrow, and that God would provide. The world would soon be ending.

It was the Jews, not their Roman conquerors, who disliked Jesus. The Sadducees, who loved Greek culture and disbelieved in life after death, thought him an uncultivated fanatic. The Pharisees, who regarded themselves as the guardians of the Law, reacted angrily to Jesus's attacks on them as narrow-minded and old-fashioned. The Zealots wanted to see the Romans conquered and thrown out of Palestine, and had no patience with a messiah who preached peace and love. While Jesus was wandering around the countryside preaching in the open air, no one worried about him. But when he rode into Jerusalem on a donkey (fulfilling the prophecy of Isaiah) and was greeted with enthusiasm by the people, the Jewish establishment became alarmed. And when Jesus threw the money changers out of the temple, they saw the

The Fame Name Game

What did Steveland Judkins change his name to?

Answer: Stevie Wonder

writing on the wall and had him arrested. The arrest had to take place in a garden at night to avoid causing trouble.

The Jews demanded Jesus' execution, declining to allow him to be pardoned in honour of Passover. Jesus died, like so many other messiahs and political agitators, by crucifixion. How, then, did Christianity go on to conquer the world? The answer lies partly in

The World's Oddest Animals

Emperor Tamarin *Tamarins are squirrel-sized New World monkeys. The Emperor Tamarin primate was allegedly named for its physical similarity to the German emperor Wilhelm II. This name was probably originally intended as a joke, but has since become the official scientific name. This tamarin is found in the southwest Amazon Basin, in east Peru, north Bolivia and in the west Brazilian states of Acre and Amazonas. Its fur is mainly gray, with yellowish speckles on its chest. The hands and feet are black and its tail is brown. Its most distinctive feature is the long, white moustache, which extends to beyond the shoulders. The animal reaches a length of 24-26cm, plus a 35cm long tail and weighs approximately 300-400g. It inhabits tropical rain forests, living both deep in the forest and also in open tree-covered areas. It spends most of its days in the trees with quick movements and broad jumps between the branches.*

the many stories of miracles that circulated about Jesus – including the story that he had risen from the dead. A Jewish sect called the Messianists (or Nasoraeans) believed that Jesus would return and lead them against the Romans. At this point, a convert to Christianity named Paul produced a strange and mystical new version of Jesus's teaching that seemed to have very little to do with anything Jesus had actually said. Paul declared that Jesus was the Son of God (which Jesus had denied) who had been sent to redeem Man from the sin of Adam, and that anyone who believed in Jesus was 'saved'. In fact, Jesus had preached salvation through the efforts of the individual, and insisted that the Kingdom of God is within everybody. But since there was still a widespread belief that the End of the World would occur within a year or so, Paul's version of the Christian message was a powerful incentive to belief.

The Messianists regarded such a notion as absurd and blasphemous, and since they were politically stronger than Paul's Christians, it looked as if their version would triumph. However, as it happened, the Messianists were among those wiped out by Titus, the son of the Roman emperor Vespasian, who was sent to put down the latest rebellion. He did more than that; he destroyed the Temple and carried its treasures back to Rome. Paul's 'Christians' were so widely scattered that they were relatively immune from massacre. And so, by a historical accident, Paul's version of Christianity became the official version, and the 'vicarious atonement' – the notion that Jesus died on the cross to redeem man from the sin of Adam – became the basis of the religion that went on to conquer the world.

By the year AD 100 it was obvious that the world was not going to end within the lifetime of Jesus's contemporaries, and that Jesus, like so many other messiahs, had quite simply been wrong. But by that time, Christianity was too powerful to die out. It was now a political force, the focus of all the dissatisfaction of the underdogs and victims of Roman brutality. The belief now spread that the end of the world would occur in the year AD 1000. And, as we have seen, there was so much violence, pestilence and bloodshed around that time that the believers had no doubt that the end was just around the corner.

Simon Bar Kochba

Even before the millennium, there were plenty of messiahs. In AD 132, a Jewish revolutionary named Simon Bar Kochba led a revolt against the Romans in Judaea when he learned that the Emperor Hadrian intended to build a temple dedicated to Jupiter on the site of the temple that had been destroyed by Titus. A celebrated student of the Talmud (the Jewish book of law), Rabbi Akiva, told Simon Bar Kochba: 'You are the messiah.' And Bar Kochba behaved exactly as a Jewish messiah was expected to behave (and as Jesus had failed to behave); he seized towns and villages from the Romans, had his own head stamped on the

Natural Thoughts

If you chase two rabbits, you will not catch either one.

Russian Proverb

coinage, and built fortresses. But he stood no real chance against the Romans, with their highly trained troops.

It took Julius Severus three and a half years to destroy the rebels, and in that time he destroyed fifty fortresses and 985 villages, and killed over half a million people. Since Bar Kochba's men were guerrillas, and guerrillas survive by being supported by sympathizers, Severus set out to kill all the sympathizers. He finally killed Bar Kochba himself in the fortress of Bethar, and renamed Jerusalem Aelia Capitolana. So one more messiah was proved to be mortal after all. The Jews were so shattered by this defeat that there were no more Jewish messiahs for many centuries.

Moses of Crete

In about AD 435, an unnamed messiah from Crete, who called himself Moses, announced that, like his predecessor, he would lead his followers back to the Promised Land, causing the sea to part for them so they could walk on the bottom. Hundreds of followers gathered on the seashore, and Moses raised his arms and ordered the sea to separate. Then he shouted the order to march into the waves. They obeyed him, but the sea ignored his

Thought For the Day

To learn something new, take the path that you took yesterday.

John Burroughs

order, and many of his followers were drowned. Moses may have been drowned with them; at all events, he disappeared.

The Christ of Gevaudon

In AD 591, an unnamed messiah began to wander around France. This man had apparently had a nervous breakdown after being surrounded by a swarm of flies in a forest. He recovered after two years and became a preacher, clad himself in animal skins, and wandered down through Arles to the district of Gevaudon in the Cevennes (noted later for a famous case of a werewolf). He declared he was Christ, had a companion called Mary, and healed the sick by touching them. His followers were mostly the very poor, and they often waylaid travellers (most of whom would be rich) and seized their money. The messiah redistributed it to the poor. His army of 3,000 became so powerful that most towns lost no time in acknowledging him as the Christ.

Aldebert

In AD 742, a messiah called Aldebert, who came from Soissons, announced that he was a saint; his followers built chapels for him which he named after himself. He claimed to own a letter from Jesus himself. Pope Zachary was so worried about 'Saint' Aldebert's influence that he tried hard to capture him, and, when that failed, excommunicated him. Aldebert went on for at least two more years, and seems to have died of natural causes.

Eudo de Stella

In the 12th Century another messiah called Eon or Eudo de Stella was less lucky. He gathered hordes of disciples in Brittany, and organized his followers into a Church with archbishops and bishops. Unlike Jesus of Nazareth, he had no hesitation in declaring that he was the son of God. 1144 was a good year for a messiah to acquire followers, for an appalling winter caused multitudes to starve. Eon's followers lived in the forest, and ravaged the countryside, living mainly by plunder. But in 1148, he was taken prisoner by soldiers of the Archbishop of Rouen and imprisoned in a tower, where he was starved to death. His followers refused to renounce him, and the 'bishops' and 'archbishops' were burned alive in the now traditional Christian spirit.

Tanchelm

One of the most remarkable messiahs of the 12th Century, Tanchelm of Antwerp, was already dead by then. He seems to have started his career as a monk, then become a diplomat working for Count Robert of Flanders, trying to persuade the Pope to hand over some of Utrecht to Count Robert. The Pope refused, and when Count Robert died, Tanchelm's career as a diplomat came to an end. He became a wandering preacher, making his headquarters in Antwerp.

Tanchelm seems to have possessed what all messiahs possess: tremendous powers as a preacher and orator. We also have to remember that a large part of his audience would be ignorant peasants who had never heard a really good preacher. As Tanchelm addressed them in the open fields, dressed as a monk, the audiences reacted like modern teenagers to a pop idol. He denounced the Church for its corruption, and told them that if the sacraments were administered by sinful priests they would fail to work. So many were convinced that the churches were soon

Amazing Animals

A cat has four rows of whiskers.

The milk of a camel does not curdle.

Porcupines can float in water.

Due to their incredible wingspeeds and flexibility, hummingbirds are the only animals that can fly backwards.

Armadillos have four babies at a time, always all the same sex. They are perfect quad-ruplets because the fertilized cell splits into quarters. The result is four identical armadillos.

A chimpanzee can learn to recognize itself in a mirror, but most other monkeys can't.

Giraffes do not have vocal cords.

Mice, whales, elephants, giraffes and man all have seven neck vertebras.

It is not only cats that like catnip – lions and tigers do as well. It contains a chemical similar to a dominant female's urine, which is why they are affected by it.

A polecat is not technically a cat. It is a nocturnal European weasel.

A zebra is white with black stripes, not black with white stripes.

Emus lay emerald or forest green eggs.

A penguin usually only has sex twice a year.

Cheetahs make a chirping sound that is like a bird's chirp. The sound is so loud, it can be heard a mile away.

empty. And when Tanchelm told his followers not to pay taxes to the Church (called tithes), they were delighted to follow his advice.

Was Tanchelm a charlatan, or did he really believe he was a messiah? He certainly felt that he had a right to live like a king. He dressed magnificently, and was always surrounded by a large retinue, including twelve men who were supposed to be the twelve disciples. One day he announced that he would become betrothed to the Virgin Mary, and held a ceremony in which he and a sacred statue were joined together in front of a vast crowd who offered their jewelry as an engagement present. With so many followers, the Church could do nothing about him; he held Utrecht, Antwerp and large areas of the countryside. Finally, about AD 1115, he was killed by treachery, being stabbed by a priest who had been allowed to approach him. But his influence remained as powerful as ever, and it took another 'miracle worker', Norbert of Xanten (who was regarded with favor by the Church), to finally 'de-convert' his followers in Antwerp and restore power to the Church.

The Fame Name Game

What did George Alan O'Dowd change his name to?

Answer: Boy George

The Free Spirit Movement – The Wife Who Lost her Ring
12th Century
One popular story of the Middle Ages was about a rich merchant
whose wife began to spend a great deal of time in church. When
her husband heard rumours that the church consisted of believers
in the Free Spirit, he decided to follow her one day. Wearing a
disguise, he walked behind her into an underground cavern where –
to his surprise – the service began with a dance, in which everyone
chose his or her partner. After that, the congregation ate food and
drank wine. The husband began to understand why his wife
preferred this to the local Catholic church; the service was better.

When the priest stood up, he announced that all human
beings are free, and that provided they lived in the spirit of the
Lord, they could do what they liked. 'We must become one with
God.' Then he took a young girl and led her to the altar. The two
of them removed their clothes. Then the priest turned to the
congregation and told them to do the same. 'This is the Virgin
Mary and I am Jesus. Now do as we do.' The girl lay down on the
altar, and the priest lay on top of her and, in full view of the
congregation, commenced an act of intercourse. Then the
congregation each seized his dancing partner, and lay down on
the floor. In the chaos that followed, the wife did not notice as
her husband took hold of her hand and pulled off her wedding
ring; she was totally absorbed in her partner. Realizing that no
one was paying any attention to him, the husband slipped away.

When his wife returned home, he asked her angrily how she
dared to give herself to another man, even in the name of
religion. She indignantly denied everything, demanding whether,
as the wife of a wealthy merchant, he thought she would behave

like a prostitute. But when the husband asked her what had happened to her wedding ring, she went pale. Then, as he held it out to her, she realized that he had seen everything, and burst into tears. The wife was beaten until she bled, but she was more fortunate than the others, who were arrested by inquisitors and burnt at the stake.

The Assassins

In the year 1273, the Venetian traveller Marco Polo passed through the valley of Alamut, in Persia, and saw there the castle of the Old Man of the Mountain, the head of the Persian branch of the sect of Ismailis, or Assassins. By that time, the sect was two hundred years old, and was on the point of being destroyed by the Mongols, who had invaded the Middle East under the leadership of Genghis Khan. According to Marco Polo, the Old Man of the Mountain, whose name was Aloadin, had created a Garden of Paradise in a green valley behind the castle, and filled it with 'pavilions and palaces the most elegant that can be imagined', fountains flowing with wine, milk and honey, and beautiful houris who could sing and dance seductively. The purpose of this Garden was to give his followers a foretaste of Paradise, so that they might be eager to sacrifice their lives for their leader.

When the Old Man wanted an enemy murdered, he would ask for volunteers. These men would be drugged and carried into the secret garden – which, under normal circumstances, was strictly forbidden to all males. They would awake to find themselves apparently in Paradise, with wine, food and damsels at their disposal. After a few days of this, they were again drugged and taken back to the Old Man's fortress. 'So when the Old Man would have any prince slain, he would say to such a youth: "Go thou and slay so-and-so; and when thou returnest, my angels shall bear thee to Paradise . . ."'

There is evidence that the story may have a foundation in fact. Behind the remains of the castle, which still exists in the valley of Alamut, there is a green enclosed valley with a spring. But it is hardly large enough to have contained 'pavilions and palaces'. The Ismailis were a breakaway sect from the orthodox Muslims; they were the Mohammedan equivalent of Protestants. After the death of the Prophet Mahomet in 632, his disciple Abu Bakr was chosen to succeed him, thus becoming the first Caliph of Islam.

Obscure English Language Facts

The Vowel Olympics
Eunoia is the shortest English word that contains all five principal vowels (excluding y). Longer words that achieve the same feat include **adoulie, douleia, eucosia, eulogia, eunomia, eutopia, miaoued, moineau, sequoia**, and **suoidea** (7 letters each).

Caesious is the shortest English word containing all five principal vowels in alphabetical order. Tied for second place with 9 letters each are **acheilous, acheirous, aerobious, arsenious, arterious, autecious, facetious**, and **parecious**.

It is a pity that Mahomet, unlike Jesus, never made clear which of his disciples – or relatives – was to be the rock upon which his church was to be built. For other Muslims felt that the Prophet's cousin Ali was a more suitable candidate: the result was a dissension that split the Muslim world for centuries. The Sunni – the orthodox Muslims – persecuted and slaughtered Ali's followers, who were known as the Shi'a. In 680, they almost succeeded in wiping out their rivals, when seventy of them – including the Prophet's daughter Fatima – were surprised and massacred. But the killers overlooked a sick boy – the son of Fatima; so the rebel tradition lived on.

All this murder and suffering produced powerful religious emotions among the Shi'a. They set up their own Caliph – known as the Imam – and they looked forward to the coming of a messiah (or Mahdi) who would lead them to final victory. Strange sects proliferated, led by holy men who came out of the desert. Some believed in reincarnation, others in total moral and sexual freedom. One sect believed in murder as a religious duty, strangling their victims with cords; these may be regarded as the true predecessors of the Assassins.

Thought For the Day

The moment a little boy is concerned with which is a jay and which is a sparrow, he can no longer see the birds or hear them sing.

Eric Berne

The Ismailis were a breakaway sect from the original breakaway sect. When the sixth Imam died, his eldest son Ismail was passed over for some reason, and his younger brother Musa appointed. The Ismailis were Muslims who declared that Ismail was the true Imam: they were also known as Seveners, because they believed that Ismail was the seventh and last Imam. The rest of the Shi'a became known as the Twelvers, for they accepted Musa and his five successors as true Imams. (The line came to an end after the twelfth.)

The Twelvers became the respectable branch of the heretics, differing from orthodox Sunni only on a few points of doctrine. It was the Ismailis who became the true opposition, creating a brilliant and powerful organization with its own philosophy, ritual and literature. They were intellectuals and mystics and fanatics. With such drive and idealism they were bound to come to power eventually. It was some time around the middle of the 11th Century that the greatest of the Ismaili leaders was born – Hasan bin Sabbah, a man who combined the religious fervour of Saint Augustine with the political astuteness of Lenin. He founded the Order of Assassins, and became the first Old Man of the Mountain.By AD 1300, the Assassins had ceased to exist in the Middle East, at least as a political force.

The Flagellants

If there is one thing that history teaches us it is that when bad things happen, man will look around at his fellow man and wonder whose fault it is. For some this is far as the process will go, but sadly it is often the case that zealots and those who despise those of other religions, races or nations will choose to reinforce their prejudice by attacking those who they regard as being responsible. As the Black Death began to spread from the corpses of earthquake and flood victims in China, and was carried by rats along the caravan trails to Europe it brought with it a relentless search for scapegoats. It reached the Crimea, in southern Russia, in 1346. In a manner that seems sadly typical of human nature, the Tartars looked around for a scapegoat, and decided that the Christians must be to blame. This led to the famous bombardment of Genoese merchants in the town of Caffa. And this in turn led to the spread of the terrible disease to Europe.

Here the search for scapegoats continued along some predictable roads. It was at Chillon that Jews were seized and tortured after it was alleged that they had spread the disease by tampering with the water supply. In the Middle Ages it was regarded as acceptable to torture suspects to obtain confessions and this was no exception. Under torture, they confessed to the charge. They were executed, and there were massacres of Jews in Provence, at Narbonne and Carcassone, then all over Germany: Strasbourg, Frankfurt, Mainz and the trading towns of the north belonging to the Hanseatic League. Here Jews were walled in their houses and left to starve; others were burnt alive.

One of the stranger phenomena that flourished under the Black Death was the movement known as Flagellants. These had originated about a century earlier in Italy, when various plagues and famines convinced the Italians that God wanted them to show repentance, and took the form of pilgrimages in which people walked naked to the waist, beating themselves with whips or scourges tipped with metal studs. On that occasion it had seemed to work and had been tried periodically since then. Now the Black Death convinced increasing numbers of people that desperate remedies were necessary.

A letter, supposed to have fallen down from heaven, declaring that only Flagellants would be saved, was first published around 1260, but reappeared in 1343 in the Holy Land – it was supposed to have been delivered by an angel to the Church of St Peter in Jerusalem. Now waves of flagellation swept across Europe with all the hysteria of religious revivals. The Flagellants – mostly fairly respectable 'pilgrims' of both sexes – would arrive in a town and hold their ceremony in the main square.

They would strip to the waist, then flog themselves into an increasing state of hysteria until blood ran down to their feet, staining the white linen which was the traditional dress on the lower half of the body. The pilgrimage would last for thirty-three days, and each Flagellant would have taken a vow to flog himself, or herself, three times a day for the whole of that time. A Master also moved among them, thrashing those who had failed in their vows. As Flagellants themselves carried the plague from city to city, public opinion suddenly turned against them. The magistrates of Erfurt refused them entry, and no one objected. It was best not to wait until the Flagellants were within a town to

The Fame Name Game

What did Frances Gumm change her name to?

Answer: Judy Garland

raise objections, for their own frenzy made them violent, and they were likely to attack the objectors – one Dominican friar in Tournai was stoned to death.

Human beings seem to be glad of an excuse to change their opinions, and only a year after they had been generally regarded with respect and admiration, the Flagellants were suddenly attacked as outcasts and cranks. The Pope issued a bull against them, and the hysteria vanished as abruptly as it had begun.

The Bloodfriends

Around 1550, a man named Klaus Ludwig, who lived in Mulhausen in Germany, formed a church in which members were initiated by having sex with a stranger. Like so many messiahs, Ludwig said he was Christ, the son of God, and that these things had been revealed to him. The sacrament was another name for sex. Man was bread and woman was wine, and when they made love, this was Holy Communion. Children born out of such communion were holy. And the members of his congregation could not be killed. His sermons ended with the words 'Be fruitful and multiply', and the congregation made haste to undress and do their best to obey.

Ludwig taught that sexual desire is the prompting of the Holy Spirit, so that if a man feels desire for any woman, he should regard it as a message from God. If, of course, the woman happened to be a member of Ludwig's 'Chriesterung' (or Bloodfriends), then it was her duty to help him obey the will of the Lord, even if she was another man's wife. Ludwig told the Bloodfriends to observe great secrecy and to behave like other people. But no doubt some of his congregation was eager to make converts of husbands with attractive wives. Like the congregation in the medieval story, the Bloodfriends were found out and put on trial, although Ludwig himself escaped. One member of the Council of Twelve Judges admitted that he had celebrated Holy Communion with sixteen different women. Three Bloodfriends were executed, and the others were re-converted to a more conventional form of Christianity.

 # Memorable Movie Quotes

I was impressed to see that she made proper use of the word 'myriad' in her suicide note.
Heathers

And then one time I ate some rotten berries. Man! There were some gases leaking outta my butt that day!
Shrek

Lloyd: What's the soup du jour?
Waiter: It's the soup of the day.
Lloyd: Mmm . . . that does sound good.
Dumb & Dumber

Leaders Have Their Say

I dream of the realization of the unity of Africa, whereby its leaders combine in their efforts to solve the problems of this continent. I dream of our vast deserts, of our forests, of all our great wildernesses.
Nelson Mandela

Great leaders are almost always great simplifiers, who can cut through argument, debate and doubt, to offer a solution everybody can understand.
Colin Powell

It doesn't take a majority to make a rebellion; it takes only a few determined leaders and a sound cause.
H.L. Mencken

Leaders must be close enough to relate to others, but far enough ahead to motivate them.
John C. Maxwell

The people of the world genuinely want peace. Some day the leaders of the world are going to have to give in and give it to them.
Dwight D. Eisenhower

You are priests, not social or political leaders. Let us not be under the illusion that we are serving the Gospel through an exaggerated interest in the wide field of temporal problems.
Pope John Paul II

Men make history and not the other way around. In periods where there is no leadership, society stands still. Progress occurs when courageous, skillful leaders seize the opportunity to change things for the better.
Harry S. Truman

The great leaders have always stage-managed their effects.
Charles de Gaulle

More Mad Scientists

Aviation Terror. Paperwork in the army is often inconsistent in its information so an experiment was undertaken to see if soldiers responded differently to paperwork under stress. In the 1960s, ten soldiers on a training flight were told by the pilot that the aircraft had developed a technical fault and they had to ditch the plane in the ocean. The soldiers were then required to fill in insurance forms before the crash (ostensibly so the army was not financially liable for any deaths or injuries). They were actually unwitting participants in an experiment; the plane was not faulty at all. It unsurprisingly revealed that fear of imminent death did cause soldiers to make more mistakes than usual when filling in forms.

Two-headed Dogs

In 1954 Vladimir Demikhov, a Soviet surgeon, revealed that he had surgically created a two-headed dog. He had managed to graft the head of a puppy onto the neck of a fully grown German shepherd. The second head would instinctively lap at milk, even though it did not need to eat and had a disconnected oesophagus. The result was that the milk then dribbled down the neck. The result of this experiment was that both animals died of tissue rejection. However, in true mad scientist style, this didn't discourage Demikhov. He went on create nineteen more two-headed animals over a fifteen year period.

Subliminal Messages

Over one long summer in 1942 at the College of William and Mary in Williamsburg, Lawrence LeShan, Virginia, tried to subliminally influence boys into giving up the bad habit of biting their fingernails. While they were sleeping, he repeatedly played them a recording of a voice saying: 'My fingernails taste terribly bitter.' Eventually the record player broke down, but LeShan was not to be thwarted. He simply stood in the dormitory repeating the phrase over and over himself. This is one experiment that did have a successful outcome. By the end of the experiment, nearly half of the boys had stopped biting their nails.

Tickling

In the 1930s Clarence Yeuba, a Psychology Professor at Ohio's Antioch College, decided to test the hypothesis that people's laughter in response to tickling is a learned response rather than an innate one. Like all the strangest scientists he decided that the best subject for an experiment would be his own family. He chose his young son for the experiment. In his presence, the family were not allowed to laugh if tickled or if the boy was tickled. Over a period of time this seemed to be working, but sadly the experiment was sabotaged by Leuba's own wife. One day he discovered her red-handed bouncing the boy on her knee while laughing and saying 'Bouncy, bouncy.' At the age of seven, the boy was laughing when tickled, but Leuba couldn't be sure if this was due to innate qualities or the learned response he had tried to ban. So he tried the experiment one more time – this time on the boy's younger sister.

How To Excite A Turkey

Martin Schein and Edgar Hale, of Pennsylvania State University, were studying the sexual behavior of turkeys in the 1960s. Their great discovery was that turkeys are not particularly choosy when it comes to mating. They started with a model of a female turkey, and then progressively dismembered it, taking away body parts until the males lost interest. However, even when the only thing left was a head on a stick, the male turkeys continued to display mating behavior and court the head on a stick.

The World's Oddest Animals

Warthog *The Warthog is an unusual black or brown pig commonly found in Africa. It is frequently seen in both moist and arid savannas. Whilst identifiable by its barrel-like body, and its huge, wide head decorated with six facial warts, its most distinctive feature is the pair of huge curved canine tusks which are used to fight against predators. The Warthog size ranges from 0.9-1.5m (2.9-4.9ft) in length, 25-33 inches in height and 50-150kg (110-330 lbs) in weight. It holds its tufted tail erect whilst running to scare off predators by suggesting that it taller than it actually is.*

Weird And Crazy Laws

In Florida, topless walking or running is prohibited within a 150-foot zone adjacent to the beach. In the same state, it is also illegal to sing in any public place while attired in a swimsuit.

In Kentucky, legislators were historically sufficiently concerned about the state of public hygiene to make it mandatory for every citizen to take a bath once a year.

In the state of Indiana, it is illegal to go to a movie house or theater or to ride on a public streetcar within four hours of having eaten a meal including garlic.

Cattle branding was not originally a practice in the Wild West. In fact it began in Connecticut during the 19th Century. Farmers there were legally required to mark all their pigs to make their ownership of the animal clear.

Dropping chewing gum in the street is illegal in Singapore because it is a way of 'tainting an environment free of dirt.'

Historically Louisana law had some strange allowances for criminal behavior. For instance, it was illegal to shoot at a bank teller with a water pistol, especially if you had just robbed the bank. Meanwhile biting someone with your teeth was deemed 'simple assault,' while biting someone with false teeth was regarded as 'aggravated assault,' presumably because the false teeth were regarded as a weapon.

In Texas, it is against the law for sixteen-year-old divorced girls to discuss sex during extracurricular high school activities.

In Ames, Iowa, a husband should not take more than three sips of beer while in bed with his wife.

Culinary Treats From Iceland

If you ever plan to visit Iceland, it might be useful to know about a few of the traditional delicacies that the country has to offer. Here are a few of the strange and delicious meals you can expect to encounter during a visit to this remote northern land.

Slátur – the traditional Icelandic dish

Slátur means 'slaughter' and is similar to Scottish haggis. Slátur is traditionally made in the autumn and the main ingredient is the innards of a sheep. The slátur is served boiled, and can be eaten either hot or cold. Traditionally, Icelandic housewives would make slátur each autumn following a family party during which the sheep would be slaughtered. Thankfully, they usually now make do with meat from the supermarket. Killing a sheep is a messy process, and after the innards have been boiled there are a lot of leftovers to deal with, so the supermarket version is a more convenient option for the modern family.

Hákarl (rotten shark) is an alternative method of preserving marine food for the long, dark winter months when livestock cannot survive outside. The shark is cured by being buried in the garden during the summer. After being dug up during the winter months, it can be washed down with a shot of schnapps. Again, this is not for the faint hearted, and locals recommend consuming about a quarter of a litre of Black Death schnapps before attempting to eat this special rotting fish dish for the first time. It is usually served at a Þorrablót – an ancient midwinter feast where pickled, sour meats and rotten shark are among the preserved dishes served.

Kyr is a milk product. It is thicker than yoghurt, more cheese-like in consistency and is usually consumed with a bit of extra milk. Most restaurants offer it as a dessert, often with berries, but it can also be bought in most grocery stores and makes a tasty snack.

Svið is a burned sheep-head, another slightly bizarre Icelandic speciality. It is hugely popular but very, very ugly. As in the making of Slátur, families would traditionally behead a sheep and throw it on the fire to burn. But in today's age of convenience food, they simply buy the heads ready chopped off in the supermarket and leave them in the oven a bit too long to achieve the burnt effect.

The Icelandic Pancake Frying Pan. In the 1950s, Gudmundur Haraldsson invented a new kind of frying pan, specifically for making pancakes in the Icelandic style. Mr Haraldsson, working for the Malmsmidja Ámunda Sigurdssonar company, came up with the new pan in a moment of boredom. The company took up the idea and has been manufacturing them ever since. These special pancakes cannot be purchased in the bakeries of Reykjavik, being a staple of home cooking, popular at family gatherings. Fortunately Iceland is a friendly place, so there is a reasonable chance that the determined pancake seeker will be invited to a family occasion and be able to experience the fruits of Mr Haraldsson's ingenuity.

Snúðar, vínarbrauð and kleinur are delicious traditional pastries which are best washed down with gooseberry vodka or the famous Black Death schnapps.

Shrove Monday in February is celebrated by the Icelandic people with buns. It is traditional to bake a huge pile of buns which are eaten with whipped cream, jam or chocolate. The bun-making is a special time when families come together in good times and bad to cook together.

Harðfiskur (dried fish) is a common Icelandic snack. It is delicious but has a pungent smell. Locals advise that the best way for beginners to enjoy the snack is to hold their nose whilst chewing, in order to avoid the smell reaching the nostrils.

 The Fame Name Game

What did Issur Danielovitch Demsky change his name to?

Answer: Kirk Douglas

Hilarious Misprints

Lawyers Weigh O.J. Witnesses
AP

Japan, Russia Still Far Apart
On Islands
Reuters

Lack Of Brains Hinders
Research
Columbus Dispatch

One-Armed Man Applauds
The Kindness Of Strangers
Tulsa World

Illiterate? Write today for free
help.
Advertisement

Italian Plane Passengers See
Flames, Vote to Land
Reuters

Spaniard Dies After Fall From
Ferry To Britain
Reuters

Male Infertility Can Be Passed
On To Children
Reuters

Moron Arrested After Driving
Truck Into House
Fox 4 News

New Yorker Finds Roommate
Dead, Second Time In A Year
AP

Officials Consider Bridge
Suicide
UPI

Indian Plane Reported
Hijacked By Authorities
Reuters

Prostitutes Appeal To Pope
Monterey Herald Sun

Life Goes On Year After
Deaths
Richardson News

Man Struck By Lightning
Faces Battery Charge
Monterey Herald Sun

Paleontologist Wants Students
To Dig Up Dirt On Prehistory
Washington Post

Gruesome History

No One Under 30. The Aztecs lived in Mexico from around AD 1345 to AD 1520. They had some very strict rules. Alcohol was banned unless you were over thirty years old and even then you had to be ill to drink it. If someone did something considered wrong, the King would have them knocked down and if they committed a second crime they were killed. They had funny superstitions too. If a warrior was feeling a bit uncertain about a battle he had to dig up the body of a woman who died in childbirth. He was then supposed to cut off her hair and fingers and stick them onto his shield. It was supposed to bring him luck.

Slaves to the Pope 15th Century

Pope Innocent VIII (1432-1492), famed for his worldliness, once received a gift of 100 matching items. The kind pope generously distributed them as gratuities to various cardinals and friends. The items were actually Moorish slaves. It was Innocent who later appointed the Spanish Dominican friar Tomás de Torquemada to serve as the grand inquisitor (in 1487) under whose authority thousands of Jews, suspected witches, and miscellaneous heretics were killed or tortured during the Spanish Inquisition.

The Velvet Potty The Tudors (15th – early 17th Century)

During King Henry VIII's reign people in general were still

indulging into some nasty habits left over from medieval times. People defecated into chamber pots and then threw the contents out of their windows into the streets, regardless of who was walking outside! However, apparently, Henry VIII used a velvet, padded box which had a potty concealed inside. He had a servant with him to clean him and the potty up afterwards too, called Yeoman of the Stool.

Babies were often kept in tightly bound bundles for the first few months of their life, to make their bones grow straight. The remedy for teething was to rub a mixture of hare's brains, goose fat and honey on their gums or a good chew on a horse's tooth. Not surprisingly infant mortality was high. Only one in three babies grew into adulthood.

High Church 16th Century
Henry VIII created the Church of England in order to divorce his first wife Catherine of Aragon (she was Catholic and divorce for her was forbidden). This was a time when the Church in Europe was being torn apart by the battle between Protestant and Catholic ideology, although Henry was more concerned about fathering a male heir. He married Anne Boleyn soon after his divorce and

Thought For the Day

No matter where you go or what you do, you live your entire life within the confines of your head.

Terry Josephson

she gave birth to a baby girl, Elizabeth, who would grow up to become Queen Elizabeth I. Henry wasn't happy in this marriage either and had Anne Boleyn beheaded. He brought in a special French executioner (who used a sword rather than an axe) to do the deed. His next wife Jane Seymour died in childbirth giving birth to a son, Edward. The next Queen of England was Anne of Cleves whom he married in 1540. He divorced this one after claiming he was disappointed that she was not as pretty in real life as her portrait, which until the marriage was all he had seen of her. He then went on to marry Catherine Howard. Catherine Howard however, started seeing someone else in secret and when he found out Henry had her beheaded too. Henry VIII's final wife was Catherine Parr who outlived her husband by a year.

English Rose 16th Century
The most famous warship during the reign of the Tudors was the Mary Rose, built in 1510. In 1545, the Mary Rose flipped onto her side off the coast of Portsmouth. All the sailors fell into the sea and 750 drowned. The ship was salvaged in 1982.

The Disposable Castle 16th Century
After becoming Queen in 1558, Elizabeth I moved her court and courtiers around the country a lot, staying in large noble houses and castles. This is now thought to be due to lack of personal hygiene, fleas and disease. The place would eventually become very smelly and need a good clean which was why the Royal party moved on... the cleaners then moved in to get rid of all the accumulated dirt and rubbish.

Blood and Bandages 16th Century
Barber's shops traditionally had red and white poles outside their
shops. This was supposedly to represent blood and bandages. It
dates from the 15th and 16th Centuries. They used razors and
didn't only cut hair with them. They were also used to cut off
other things such as gangrenous toes or other appendages and
also to lance boils to let the pus out.

Liz and John 16th Century
Elizabeth I is credited with being responsible for the world's first
flushing toilet. She was so offended by the palace toilets that she had
a flushing one invented for her by Sir John Harington. This could be
why it's still sometimes referred to as 'the John' to this day.

Greedy Pig 17th–18th Century
Louis XVI of France fell out of favor with his courtiers and public
over his huge appetite. He was nicknamed Loius the Pig by the
French and rumours were rife about the amount of food that the
king of France ate. At a time when most of France was poor and
starving, the king is said to have eaten four lamb cutlets, a whole
chicken, a plateful of ham, six eggs in sauce and a bottle and a
half of champagne...and that was just breakfast.

Things got so bad that in July 1789, an angry mob attacked the
infamous Bastille jail in Paris and let out all the prisoners. The
leaders of what is now known as the French Revolution quickly
arrested all members of the royal court and sentenced them to
death. They executed them using a guillotine, a tall weighted axe
that dropped onto the neck of the accused, chopping off their
head. The head then fell into a basket. The executioner would

hold up the head and the gathered crowd of spectators would cheer on the executions. After the king and his wife Marie-Antoinette were executed beheadings became a major French pastime. Anyone who looked like they might be getting a bit too much power was likewise sent to the guillotine. As angry mobs rioted through the streets, heads were cut off and carried aloft on pikes. The instigators of the revolution were almost all eventually accused and beheaded themselves.

In the French town of Nantes, the citizens all refused to accept the new Revolutionary government and were all sentenced to death. To guillotine them all would take too long so they were taken on a barge into the middle of the river and the barge was sunk, drowning them all.

Russia Under Siege 17th Century

In 1664, Tzar Dmitri was allegedly told that a comet seen over Russia was an indication of a plague the same autumn, albeit one less dangerous to Russia than to other countries. Dmitri promptly set up a sanitary cordon at his borders and banned foreign ships in general (and English ships in particular) from entering Russian

The Fame Name Game

What did Susan Weaver change her name to?

Answer: Sigourney Weaver

ports. Interestingly, Russia did in fact escape the Great Plague that devastated the rest of Europe in 1666.

Betting on the Gallows 17th Century
In the 17th Century, Oliver Cromwell, Lord Protector of England, passed an edict to curtail the savage practices of some of his troops (ranging from rape to pillage and murder). The offending soldier and his entire company would assemble underneath the local gallows and hold a meeting.

The meeting consisted of a rolling of dice. Everyone would participate. The man who lost would be hanged. The man who lost was not necessarily the instigator of the crime. The results were fewer crimes, fewer troops – and fewer meetings.

A Traveler's Tale 18th Century
In the late 18th Century a traveler's tale was passed around London. It told of two Welsh missionaries who, having been captured by American Indians and sentenced to death, began lamenting to each other in Welsh. The tribe of Indians were

Natural Thoughts

You cannot step into the same river twice.

Heraclitus, in *Diogenes Laertius, Lives*

astounded: they too spoke Welsh. The missionaries were freed
and received the Indians' heartfelt apologies.

The great Welsh Druid Edward Williams, or lolo Morganwg,
took the story so seriously that he raised backing for an
expedition to investigate the Welsh Indians. The theory put
forward for their existence traced their roots to the expedition of
the Prince Madoc, who set sail westwards in the 12th Century
and was never heard of again. Williams was eventually prevented
from going on the expedition by failing health, but one of his
followers, John Evans, did attempt the journey. He eventually
died in New Orleans after many adventures, having been unable
to locate the Welsh Indians.

Child Labour 19th Century
During Victorian times it was common to send children as young
as five to work, sweeping chimneys and working down coal
mines. This left some children in the dark for up to thirteen
hours a day. In the mines the youngest child workers were known
as 'trappers' which meant that they had to be in the dark in a tiny
cramped and cold space and open or close ventilators called
'traps' to allow a little air into the mines.

The Original Iron Maiden 19th Century
Did you know that an iron maiden is an iron cabinet allegedly
built to torture or kill a person by piercing the body with sharp
objects (such as knives, spikes, or nails), while he or she is forced
to remain standing? The condemned bleeds profusely and is
weakened slowly, eventually dying because of blood loss, or
perhaps asphyxiation. In addition, the condemned were starved

for a period of 7-20 days to maximize their suffering and weakness. They were then struck on the back repeatedly with a large metal rod, stripped, then forced to walk through the streets, at which point all civilians were permitted to whip them from any angle, including the face.

The most famous device was the iron maiden of Nuremberg. The Nuremberg iron maiden was actually built in the 19th Century as a misinterpretation of a medieval 'Schandmantel' ('cloak of shame'), which was made of wood and tin but without spikes. The 'cloak of shame' did not harm the body, but was used as a chastisement for poachers and prostitutes, who were made to wear it in public for a certain time. The iron maiden of Nuremberg was anthropomorphic. It was probably styled after Mary, the mother of Jesus, with a carved likeness of her on the face. The maiden was about 7 feet (2.1m) tall and 3 feet (0.9m) wide, had double doors, and was big enough to contain an adult man. Inside the tomb-sized container, the iron maiden was fitted with dozens of sharp spikes. Supposedly, they were designed so that when the doors were shut, the spikes skewered the subject, yet missed vital organs, permitting him to remain alive and upright. The spikes were also movable in order to accommodate each person.

The condemned person was kept in an extremely confined space to maximize his level of suffering by claustrophobia. Mobility was nearly impossible, and as the condemned was weakened by the ordeal, the piercing objects would remain in place and tear into the body even further, causing even more intense pain. The doors of the maiden could be opened and closed one at a time, without giving the victim opportunity to escape. Supposedly, this was helpful when checking on the victim.

The Fascinating Body

It takes only seven pounds of pressure to rip off a human ear.

Human thigh bones are measurably stronger than concrete.

During a lifetime, one human being generates more than 1000 pounds of red blood cells.

If you lock your knees in position while standing still for long enough, you will eventually pass out as this restricts bloodflow.

Drinking water shortly after eating reduces the amount of acid in your mouth by up to two thirds.

The brain burns as much as a fifth of our daily calorie intake.

By the age of sixty, most people have lost about half of their taste buds – which is one reason why stronger tastes become more acceptable as we age.

The liquid that lubricates the eyes is called lacrimal fluid.

The iris membrane controls the amount of light that comes into your eye.

The most widespread non-contagious disease in the world is tooth decay.

Corpses don't decompose as rapidly as they did in the past. This is because modern humans consume far more chemicals, including ones that preserve the body from decay.

Human blood travels over 50,000 miles a day as it travels through the arteries, arterioles and capillaries and back through the veins.

The pupil of your eye expands by between a third and a half when you look at something pleasing.

Victoria and Bertie 19th Century

It is said that initially Queen Victoria wasn't too keen on marrying her cousin Albert but she asked him to marry her anyway. (No man can propose to a queen!) He said 'yes', apparently because he had been told he had to. However, when Prince Albert died of typhoid in 1861, Queen Victoria was reportedly so upset that she was not seen in public afterwards for ten years. Even after that she wore black until she died to show she was still in mourning.

The World's Oddest Animals

Leafy Seadragon This animal is named after the dragons of Chinese mythology, and is often mistaken for a piece of leafy seaweed. This is because the Leafy Seadragon, is green, orange and gold and covered with leaf-like appendages to camouflage it from birds and other predators. It also has an independently swivelling eye. Like the seahorse, the male Seadragon can carry as many as 150-200 eggs. After being laid by the female, the eggs remain in a honeycomb-shaped area (known as the brood patch), under the male's tail for approximately two months. Seadragons have no teeth or stomach and feed only on mysidopsis shrimp. In Australia, Seadragons are known as Australian Seahorses, and are only found in calm, cold water of approximately 50-54°F (10-12°C).

In the Factories 19th Century
The Industrial Revolution in the 19th Century was a time when machines were first invented to do things that before had been hand made like spinning yarn and weaving cloth. Most of the machines were originally powered by steam and were sometimes kept going all day and night so a lot of coal had to be burned to make enough steam to power them. Apparently the air became so smoky that all the surrounding buildings turned black and there was a huge increase in breathing problems due to the polluted air. Even worse, there were many accidents with people getting themselves caught in the new machines. The doctors would amputate arms and legs without any anaesthetic.

The Great Stink 19th Century
In 1886 the River Thames got so filled with sewage and rubbish that MPs had to leave the Houses of Parliament because the stench was so bad. People were still quite ignorant about hygiene and cholera and typhoid were very common.

Hitler's Real Name 20th Century
Did you know Adolf Hitler's father was originally called Adolf Schicklgrüber but he changed his name to Hitler before Adolf was born? One wonders if he would have gone as far as he did if he'd had to use his father's original name. It's hard being a dictator when your name makes people giggle.

Hollywood Mobster 20th Century
In the early 20th Century a mobster known as Benjamin 'Bugsy' Siegel charmed most everyone that he met, especially in

Hollywood, operating as a mob killer at the same time that he was seducing nubile young starlets. Although sent to California to watch over mob interests, many believed that what he really wanted from Hollywood was to be an actor. This mobster has long said to be haunting two places that he knew in life... one of them is a place that he loved and the other is a spot where he left a terrified presence behind.

He grew up on New York's Lower East Side and by the age of 14 was already running his own criminal gang. He formed an early alliance with a youth named Meyer Lansky, who was already a criminal genius in his teens. By 1920, they had formed a gang specializing in bootleg liquor, gambling and auto theft. The emerging national crime syndicate assigned Spiegel to carry out numerous murders that were aimed at gaining control of various criminal operations. He became an excellent killer and was so enthused by it that he was called 'Bugsy', but never to his face.

In the 1930s Siegel was sent to California to run the syndicate's West Coast operations, including the lucrative racing wire service for bookmakers and a casino club called the Flamingo Hotel. He was suave and entertaining and became friends with Hollywood celebrities like Jean Harlow, George Raft, Clark Gable, Gary Cooper and Cary Grant. Many of them even put money into his enterprises. On one hand, he was the life of the party and on the other, a cold-blooded killer. On occasion, Siegel could be at a party with his 'high class friends' and then slip away for a gangland execution, all in the same night. The syndicate became upset about the $6 million they had invested, as the Flamingo, when it opened, was a financial disaster. Reportedly, the mob demanded that Siegel make good on their losses but what they didn't know was that Bugsy had also been skimming from the construction funds and from the gambling profits. Virginia Hill had been busy hiding the money in Swiss bank accounts. The syndicate passed a death sentence on Siegel at the famous Havana conference in December 1946.

On 20th June, Siegel was sitting in the living room of Virginia Hill's Beverly Hills mansion. She was away in Europe at the time. He was reading the newspaper when two steel-jacketed slugs tore through the front window. One of them shattered the bridge of his nose and exited through his left eye, while the other entered his right cheek and blew out the back of his neck. Authorities later found his right eye on the dining room floor, more than 15 feet from his body. Bugsy Siegel was dead before he hit the floor.

Virginia Hill's former home is reportedly still haunted by the panicking presence of Bugsy Siegel as he scrambled for cover from the bullets that killed him. According to reports, witnesses have been surprised for years by the apparition of a man running and ducking across the living room of the house, only to disappear as suddenly as he came.

After Siegel was assassinated, the mob continued to support the Flamingo Hotel and eventually saw it grow and prosper. And it is at the Flamingo where the spirit of Ben Siegel is said to reside today.

The Fame Name Game

What did Edward Kennedy Ellington change his name to?

Answer: Duke Ellington

He is believed to haunt the Presidential Suite of the hotel, where he lived for many years. Guests in this room have apparently reported a number of strange encounters with his ghost, from eerie, moving cold spots to items that vanish and move about the suite. They have also seen him in the bathroom and near the pool table. Those who have supposedly seen him say his spirit doesn't seem unhappy or distressed. They report him as seeming very content.

Training the Spies 20th Century
During the Second World War training for spies and special agents was done at secret London addresses and large country houses. The agents were taught things like how to get in and out of places without anyone finding out, picking locks and breaking safes. They had mock interrogations where they had to pretend that they had been captured by the enemy so that they could learn how to avoid giving away any information. They were also taught how to dress in disguise and were given clothing right down to the last detail. Special clothes were made in workshops for whatever 'character' the agents had to become so the style of clothing was exactly right. They were given new weapons such as silent pistols and guns that looked like pens. Female spies might have hidden cameras in their handbags. One way of sending a secret message was to write on the agent's body in invisible ink that could only be seen by putting a special chemical onto the skin. They had forged papers and left secret messages in walls.

The Mind Bending Quiz

1   Which American city is named after a British Prime Minister?

2   In baseball, which team bats first?

3   What London suburb is the G in GMT?

4   On how many stone tablets were the Ten Commandments engraved?

5   In which Shakespeare play does a ghost walk on the battlements?

6   What would a mural be painted on?

7   Which golfer was responsible for founding the US Masters in Augusta?

8   Whose real name is Steveland Judkins?

9   Which is the largest Greek island?

10 In Greek tragedy, which king married his own mother?

11 E, G and O – which of these is not the name of a note in music?

12 Which mega star sang his own song at Princess Diana's funeral?

13 How many colors appear on the Australian flag?

14 Which country was first to host both the Summer and Winter Olympics in the same year?

15 Under what name is cosmetics queen Florence Nightingale Graham better known?

(Answers on Overleaf)

Answers

1 Pittsburgh. 2 The visiting team. 3 Greenwich.
4 Two. 5 *Hamlet*. 6 Wall. 7 Bobby Jones.
8 Stevie Wonder. 9 Crete. 10 Oedipus. 11 O.
12 Elton John. 13 Three. 14 France.
15 Elizabeth Arden.

How did you do?

12-15

Champagne in a crystal goblet

8-11

Fine wine in a delicate glass

4-7

Beer in a pitcher

1-3

Moonshine in an old clay jug

More Weird News Stories

Grammatical Error. The misplacing of a comma cost the United States treasury over a million dollars. In the Tariff Act of 1872, 'fruit plants, tropical and semi-tropical' were exempted from tax. A clerk miscopied it: 'fruit, plants tropical and semi-tropical.' Importers contended that this meant that tropical and semitropical fruits should be exempted. The treasury disagreed and collected the tax, but finally gave way and refunded over a million dollars. The wording was then changed.

Giant Snow
In Montana, snowflakes fifteen inches across and eight inches thick fell during a record snowstorm in the winter of 1887.

Senior Fisticuffs
In 1822, Thomas Dawson, ninety-one, and Michael O'Toole, eighty-five, engaged in fisticuffs to settle an argument and 'fought to a finish' in Garford, Berks. O'Toole collapsed first, but ninety-one-year-old Dawson died a few hours later.

Doped Americans
There were more opium addicts in America – per head of population – in 1865 than there are today. During the Civil War,

opium was used as an anaesthetic during operations, and created 100,000 addicts in a population of 40 million. Today, with a population of 200 million, there are about 300,000 addicts.

Dr. Frankenstein

Mary Shelley's novel *Frankenstein*, written in 1816, was based on a real scientist, Andrew Crosse, whose lectures on electricity were attended by the poet Shelley and his wife in 1814. But twenty-one years after the novel was written, Crosse suddenly achieved notoriety when he announced that he had actually created life in his laboratory. In 1837, he decided to try and make crystals of natural glass; he made glass out of ground flint and potassium carbonate, and dissolved it in sulphuric acid. He then allowed the mixture to drip through a piece of porous iron oxide from Mount Vesuvius which was 'electrified' by a battery. After two weeks, tiny white nipples began to grow out of the stone, and these turned into hairy legs. When he noticed that they were moving he examined them through a microscope and saw what appeared to be tiny bugs. He thought there might be tiny insect eggs in the porous stone, so he sealed his caefully sterilized mixture into an airtight retort and passed electricity through it. In a few months,

---

The Fame Name Game

What did William Claude Dukenfield change his name to?

Answer: W.C. Fields

he again had tiny 'bugs'. A paper on his 'discovery', read to the London Electrical Society, caused him to be violently denounced by clergymen as a blasphemer. Meanwhile the great Michael Faraday repeated Crosse's experiments and obtained the same 'bugs'. Crosse withdrew and led a hermit-like existence until his death in 1855. The mystery of the 'bugs' has never been solved.

Giant Buddha
The largest statue of the Buddha in the world is in Pegu, Burma – it is 180 feet long and is in a reclining position. The statue was lost for 400 years: all records of it vanish around the middle of the 15th Century, and it was not found again until 1881, when a railway was being built. The statue was covered with earth and vegetation.

A Magic Divorce
Eliphas Lévi, the 19th-Century writer on theories of magic, seldom practiced what he wrote about. But when he was offered a complete magical chamber, he decided to try to evoke Apollonius of Tyana. Lévi made his circle, kindled the ritual fires, and began reading the evocations of the ritual.

A ghostly figure appeared before the altar. Lévi found himself seized with a great chill. He placed his hand on the pentagram, the five-pointed symbol used to protect magicians against harm. He also pointed his sword at the figure, commanding it mentally to obey and not to alarm him. Something touched the hand holding the sword, and his arm became numb from the elbow down. Lévi realized that the figure objected to the sword, and he lowered it to the ground. At this, a great weakness came over him, and he fainted without having asked his questions.

After his swoon, however, he seemed to have the answers to his unasked questions. He had meant to ask one about the possibility of forgiveness and reconciliation between 'two persons who occupied my thought.' The answer was, 'Dead.' It was his marriage that was dead. His wife, who had recently left him, never returned.

Congressional Idiocy in History
Abraham Lincoln remarked of a congressman: 'He can compress the most words into the fewest ideas of anyone I've ever known.'

Skid Row
The term 'skid row' was first used in the lumberjacking days in Seattle. The logs were sent from a hilltop down a long chute and into the sea. Around the lower end of this chute there was a slum area where drunks and down-and-outs often slept in the gutter. This area became known as 'skid row' after the logs that skidded down the chute.

Gats
The word 'gat' – American slang for a gun – was derived from the Gatling gun, the world's first machine-gun, which was invented during the American Civil War by Richard Jordan Gatling.

Wasted Ingenuity
The invention of transparent sticky tape was delayed for a long time because of unsuccessful attempts to find a way of preventing the rubber-based gum from sticking to the back of the tape when it was wound into a roll. Finally, it was discovered that the experiments had been unnecessary: the gum has a natural tendency to remain only on one side of the tape.

Singing Siamese

Siamese twins named Millie and Christina were famous singers, Millie a soprano and Christina a contralto. Born in Wilmington, North Carolina, in 1851, the twins had four legs but only one body. Either head could control the other's feet, so Millie could sing while beating time with Christina's foot, and Christina could sing while beating time with Millie's foot. They sang throughout America and Europe, and died in Wilmington in 1911, aged sixty.

Lincoln's Dream

On an April night in 1865 – with the trials of the Civil War still heavy on his mind – President Abraham Lincoln lay asleep and dreaming. In his dream, he was asleep in his huge bed in the White House. Suddenly he was wakened by sobbing. Getting up and following the sound of the weeping, Lincoln found himself in the East Room. There he saw people filing past a catafalque guarded by soldiers. The men and women were paying their last respects to a body laid in state.

The face of the corpse was covered from Lincoln's view, but he could see that those present were deeply affected by the person's

Thought For the Day

It is easy to stand a pain, but difficult to stand an itch.

Chang Ch'ao

death. Finally, he went to one of the soldiers and asked who was dead. 'The President,' was the answer. 'He was killed by an assassin.' With that horrifying reply came a loud outcry of grief from the group near the catafalque – and Lincoln woke up.

This troubling dream, which Lincoln told his wife Mary and several of their friends, turned out to be a prophetic one. In that very month, Lincoln went to the theater for a rare night away from his pressing responsibilities. Awaiting him there instead of a night of pleasure was a fatal bullet from an assassm's gun.

Burying the Yogi
In 1837 in Lahore, India [in now Pakistan] the yogi Haridas was buried alive for forty days. British Colonel Sir Claude Wade, Dr. Janos Honiborger, and the British Consul at Lahore all solemnly corroborated that he was locked in a box, placed in a sealed pavilion with doors and windows tightly blocked shut, and guarded day and night. After forty days, the box was opened.

Haridas had not gone into the tomb unprepared. For days before his burial he had no food but milk. On the burial day itself he ate nothing, but performed dhauti – a yoga purification practice that involves swallowing a long strip of cloth, leaving it in the

---

The Fame Name Game

What did Alicia Christian Foster change her name to?

Answer: Jodie Foster

stomach to soak up bile and other impurities, and then withdrawing it. Haridas then did another cleansing ritual. All the openings of his body were then sealed up with wax, and his tongue was rolled back to seal the entrance to his throat. Then he was buried.

When the box was opened the yogi's assistant washed him with warm water, removed the wax, and rubbed his scalp with warm yeast. He forced his teeth open with a knife, unfolded his tongue, and massaged his body with butter. After half an hour Haridas was up and about.

Séance for a President

During the presidency of Abraham Lincoln the vogue for the new Spiritualism was at its height among fashionable people. Even the President – a far from fashionable man – was drawn into it. Colonel Simon F. Kase, a lobbyist who had several times met Lincoln to discuss a railroad project with him, tells of encountering the President at a séance in the home of Mrs Laurie and daughter Mrs Miller. She was known for making a piano beat time on the floor as she played while in trance. Kase said of the occasion that Mrs Miller began to play, and the front of the piano in truth rose off the floor and beat the time of the tune with heavy thuds. Kase asked if he could sit on the instrument so that he could 'verify to the world that it moved.' The medium composedly answered that he and as many others as wished could sit on the piano. Four men did: Kase, a judge, and two of the soldiers who were accompanying Lincoln. Mrs Miller again began to play and the piano – heedless of its load – began to rise and thump, lifting at least four inches off the floor. Kase concluded ruefully: 'It was too rough riding; we got off while the instrument beat the time until the tune was played out.'

Zombie Workers

William Seabrook avidly studied the spirit religions of the West Indies in the 1920s. In his book *The Magic Island* he relates a strange tale told to him by a Haitian farmer. It seems that there was a bumper sugar cane crop in 1918, and labourers were in short supply. One day Joseph, an old headman, appeared leading 'a band of ragged creatures who shuffled along behind him, staring dumbly, like people in a daze.' They were not ordinary labourers. They were zombies – dead men whom Joseph had brought back to life by magic to slave for him in the fields.

Zombies must never taste salt according to the farmer's tale, so Joseph's wife fed them special unseasoned food. But one day she took pity on them and bought them some candy, not knowing it was made of peanuts. As soon as the zombies tasted the salty nuts, they realized they were dead. With a terrible cry they set off for their own village. Stumbling past living relatives who recognized them in horror, they 'approached the graveyard . . . and rushed among the graves, and each before his own empty grave so that everyone could see that the man was truly dead.'

Man Under Train

It was November 1971 in London on a day like any other. In one of the city's underground stations, a train was approaching the platform. Suddenly a young man hurled himself directly into the path of the moving train. The horrified driver slammed on the brakes, certain that there was no way to stop the train before the man was crushed under the wheels. But miraculously the train did stop. The first carriage had to be jacked up to remove the badly injured man, but the wheels had not passed over him and he survived.

The young man turned out to be a gifted architect who was recovering from a nervous breakdown. His amazing rescue from death was based on coincidence. For the investigation of the accident revealed that the train had not stopped because of the driver's hasty braking. Seconds before, acting on an impulse and completely unaware of the man about to throw himself on the tracks, a passenger had pulled down the emergency handle, which automatically applies the brakes of the train. The passenger had no particular reason for doing so. In fact, the Transport Authority considered prosecuting him on the grounds that he had had no reasonable cause for using the emergency system!

Lost in Space
In 1952 Ronald Reagan was in Brazil at a political function and, towards the end of the meal, he was asked to make a speech. 'Now would you join me in a toast to President Figueiredo,' he said, 'and to all the people of Bolivia . . . oh no, that's wrong, that's where I'm going next . . . erm . . . to the people of Brazil, yes that's right, Brazil.' His voice trailed off as one of his aides drew his attention to the fact that his next destination was in fact Bogota, the capital of Colombia.

Why Does The Sun Shine
Until the 1930s, no one knew why the sun shines. It was only then that it was understood that it is a vast nuclear furnace.

Weird And Crazy Laws

It is hard to imagine the historic events that led to the creation of a special Florida law prohibiting unmarried women from parachuting on Sunday – a crime that is to be punished by arrest, fines, or even jail. It is equally hard to imagine why the same state makes it mandatory that men should not be seen publicly in any kind of strapless gown.

Hotel owners in Hastings, Nebraska are legally obliged to provide a clean, white cotton nightshirt to each guest. Couples should not have sex unless they are wearing the nightshirts provided.

One can sympathize with the wives of Alexandria, Minnesota, where a historic law makes it illegal for a husband to have sexual relations with his wife if his breath smells like sardines, garlic, or onions.

If you are a pilot in Alaska, be careful where you direct your gaze, because it is against the law to look at a moose from the window of an airplane or any other flying vehicle.

Was it prudery or simple hygiene that led to an ordinance in Newcastle, Wyoming, banning couples from making love inside any store's meat freezer?

In Winnipeg, you can go naked in your own home, but not if you leave the blinds up, in which case it is illegal.

Are members of Congress aware that in Washington D.C., any sexual position other than the missionary position is considered illegal? Perhaps they should be told.

Twenty-four states in the United States allow divorce on the basis of impotence.

The World's Heaviest People

Carol Yager (1960–1994). Carol Yager was born in 1960 in Flint, Michigan. At her heaviest she is estimated to have weighed more than 1600 lbs. She became overweight as a child, and weighed 1189 lbs (at a height of 5 foot 7 inches) in 1993 at which point she was admitted to Hurley Medical Center, having been diagnosed with cellulitis. In hospital she lost nearly 500 lbs on a calorie-controlled diet, but after she left the hospital she put the weight back on and more. Her teenage daughter, a boyfriend, and a group of volunteers looked after her as she was unable to do so herself. Yager received media exposure from diet guru Richard Simmons and talk-show host Jerry Springer, but after her first hospital visit she didn't get much practical help. In 1994, she was refused further hospital treatment on the grounds because her condition was not deemed to be life critical. However, she died a few weeks later from a combination of massive water retention and kidney failure.

Michael Edelman (1964–1992)
Michael Edelham from Pomona, New York weighed either 994 lbs or 1200 lbs at his heaviest, depending on whether one trusts the Guinness Book of Records or his mother for the information. He weighed 154 lbs at the age of seven, and left school before his

eleventh birthday as he had become too big to sit at the schoolroom desks. He spent much of his time in bed or eating with his mother, who herself weighed in at around 700 lbs. His daily intake was extraordinary. For breakfast he would eat toast, waffles, cake, four bowls of cereal, and an entire quart of soda. At bedtime, he would 'snack' on a whole pizza. His mother did try to impose diets on both of them from time to time, but they tended to relapse into junk food habits. When they were evicted from their home in 1988, Michael had to be shifted by forklift truck. At this stage he became the center of media attention and a variety of hospitals and diet gurus attempted to co-opt him into their weight-loss programs, but Michael chose to diet on his own. He publicly vowed to lose enough weight to consummate his relationship with his girlfriend, 420 lb Brenda Burdle. Whatever kind of diet they were on didn't work – both gained weight instead of becoming thinner. The end of Michael's story was a rather sad one. He had become friendly (in a long-distance way) with Walter Hudson, who was also morbidly obese. Hudson's sudden death gave Michael a pathological fear of eating. He lost several hundred pounds very quickly, and would only eat when he was spoon fed. He died weighing 600 lbs, but the cause of death was not his obesity, but starvation.

Walter Hudson (1944–1991)

Michael Edelman's erstwhile friend, Walter Hudson, was from Hempstead, New York. He was 5ft 10in, and weighed approximately 1197 lbs; the reason his weight can't be accurately told is that the industrial scale used to gauge his weight broke in the process of weighing him. His chest measured 106 inches, his waist 110.

Hudson became a media sensation when he was discovered by the press in 1987. He had got wedged in the door of his bedroom and needed to be cut free by rescue workers. It emerged that he had spent most of the past 27 years in bed due to severe agoraphobia. Hudson lived with his family who continued to feed him whatever he asked for and seemed unconcerned by his weight and situation. Despite his huge size, *Newsday* reported that he was extraordinarily healthy with his heart, lungs, and kidneys functioning normally. Doctors who examined him found that his cholesterol and blood-sugar levels were no different from those of a healthy 21-year-old. Despite this evidence, nutritionist Dick Gregory advised Hudson that losing weight was necessary to save his life. Gregory used Hudson to get media attention for his new Bahamian Diet, and claimed that his protégé lost around 800 lbs under his care. All this was speculation however as Hudson actually only allowed himself to be weighed once. Hudson died in his sleep in 1991 after years of yo-yo starvation dieting. After his death his body was found to weigh 1125 lbs, and his outsize coffin had to be carried by twelve pallbearers.

Robert Earl Hughes (1926–1958)

Robert Earl Hughes was born in Monticello, Missouri. At just over six feet tall, he weighed 1069 lbs in February 1958. As a baby, Hughes was a healthy 11 lbs, but by the age of six he had ballooned to 203 lbs. His weight carried on rising steadily. He weighed 378 lbs at the age of ten, 546 lbs at the age of 13, 693 lbs at the age of 18, and 947 lbs aged 27 and needed specially made blue jeans as no others would fit him. He became a minor national celebrity at this age. At his heaviest, he measured

124 inches around the chest and 122 inches around the waist. A severe bout of measles led to the kidney failure from which he eventually died. When he was in need of medical attention, he couldn't fit through the door of the hospital and had to be treated in a truck trailer parked outside. He had a custom-made coffin and was many people recalled him as a good-hearted man. Strangely enough, *Life* magazine reported that he was a relatively light eater, suggesting that he may have suffered from other undiagnosed medical issues.

Johnny Alee (1853–1887)

Johnny Alee from Carbon (now Carbonton) in North Carolina is said to have weighed 1132 lbs at his heaviest. From the age of ten, Alee had a ravenous appetite and put on weight so quickly and easily that by the age of 15 he could barely support his own weight. By the age of 16, grown men couldn't get their arms around one of Alee's thighs, and he was no longer able get out of his own front door. The only movement he could manage was getting from his armchair to the dinner table, and he needed a lot of help even to manage that. He is reported to have died after falling through his cabin floor, and his post-mortem weight was taken on the local coal company scales.

Jon Brower Minnoch (1941–1983)

Minnoch was born in 1941 in Bainbridge Island, Washington. He was over six foot tall and, weighed in at over 1400 lbs in 1979. It needed thirteen people working together to roll him over in his bed. Minnoch suffered from massive water retention, a common ailment amongst those who are morbidly obese. His weight at this stage was supplemented by approximately 900 lbs of fluid. He had previously worked as a taxi driver, and had always been heavy. At the age of 22 he weighed 400 lbs. Three years later he was up to 700 lbs and by the time he was thirty five he was close to 1000 lbs. He was never especially concerned about his weight gain, although when he was put on a 500-calorie-a-day diet he was unhappy, saying it lost him his strength. He was the father of two children and had a wife who weighed only 110 lbs. He was eventually hopsitalized and slimmed down to 476 lbs in 1981, after losing significant amounts of the retained fluid. However, the weight came back extraordinarily rapidly out of hospital – in the first week alone he gained almost 200 lbs. Doctors at University Hospital in Seattle put him back on a 1200-calorie diet, but he still weighed in at close to 800 lbs when he died in 1983.

David Ron High (1953–1996)
David Ron High from Brooklyn, New York, measured 5ft 10, and weighed around 1000 lbs. Diet master Dick Gregory showed him off as one of his success stories in 1986, when he reduced from

The Fame Name Game

What did Michael Delaney Dowd, Jr. change his name to?

Answer: Mike Douglas

823 lbs to 427 lbs on a year-long fast supplemented by fruits and vegetables. (Strangely, he also lost three inches in height, shrinking from a peak of 6ft 1in.) High had been overweight since childhood, and said he used to eat just one meal each day – it's just that it lasted all day. A decade after his graduation from

The World's Oddest Animals

Platypus *Also known as the duck-billed platypus, this is a semi-aquatic mammal native to eastern Australia, including Tasmania. Unusually for a mammal, it lays eggs instead of giving birth to live young. The odd appearance of this egg-laying, duck-billed mammal baffled naturalists when it was first discovered, and some suspected an elaborate fraud. Similarly it is one of the few venomous mammals as the male has a spur on the hind foot which can deliver a poison capable of causing severe pain to humans. The platypus has become a recognizable and iconic symbol of Australia as a result of its unique features and importance to the study of evolutionary science, appearing as a mascot at national events and featuring on the reverse of the Australian 20 cent coin. Before the early 20th Century it was hunted for its fur, but is now protected throughout its habitat. Sadly captive breeding programs have had only limited success as the Platypus is vulnerable to the effects of pollution, however, it is not in any immediate danger of extinction.*

Gregory's International Health Institute, a crew of NYC firemen needed a hydraulic lift to remove the ailing High from the Brooklyn apartment where he had been confined for five years. He was taken from there to the obesity center at St. Luke's-Roosevelt Hospital, but he died after less than a month on another weight-loss program.

Carol Haffner (1936–1995)
Carol Haffner from Hollywood, Florida weighed 1023 lbs when she died. Always a large woman, Haffner loved playing bingo and had been a regular at the Seminole Tribe Bingo Parlor, where she had a special chair to accommodate her size. However, after the death of her husband, she became bedridden with depression and advancing weight problems. She spent her last five years inside the trailer where she lived, leaving only once, with help from a crew of fire fighters, during a hurricane evacuation. Friends said she had constantly been trying to get onto a weight management program through talk-shows and advertising, but had resisted being hospitalized for breathing difficulties. She died from heart failure just two weeks after her 59th birthday.

Mills Darden (1798–1857)
Mills Darden from North Carolina was 7ft 6 and 1020 lbs. Darden was diagnosed as an acromegalic giant. In contrast to him, his wife and mother of their three children weighed only 98 lbs.

Man, name unknown (c.1939–c.1986),
An anonymous man from of New York State is said to have weighed 1050 lbs with a height of just under 5ft 7in. He died due to

complications after a colossal panniculectomy (tummy tuck) to remove fat tissue. The surgery was performed at Long Island Jewish Medical Center, New Hyde Park, New York. His total weight was determined by adding the weight of the tissue removed by the operation (104 lbs) to the patient's post-mortem weight of 946 lbs. According to his medical records, he was healthy when he checked in to the hospital, and had no history of illness apart from his extraordinary weight.

Sylvanus 'Hambone' Smith (1941–1997)

Sylvanus 'Hambone' Smith was from Tifton, Georgia. He was 6ft 2in, and weighed around 1000 lbs. Smith claimed he weighed almost 16 lbs at birth and that by the time he reached the age of 11 he weighed 275 lbs. At his biggest, he measured 103in around his hips and 70in around each of his thighs. He worked as a chef, but eventually his increasing weight confined him to bed. His next job was from home where he ran a pawnshop. Smith underwent a stomach-stapling operation in 1981 when he weighed in at 602 lbs. He then served as a spokesman for Dick Gregory's Bahamian Diet in 1987 (weighing 730 lbs), then attempted yet another drastic weight loss program, sponsored by Geraldo Rivera, just before he died. Smith was the father of one son and four daughters.

G. Hopkins (late 18th Century)

G. Hopkins of Wales weighed 980 lbs. Hopkins was reported to have been brought to a London fair in a strong cart pulled by four teams of oxen, where he was displayed on a stall along with some prize hogs that were too fat to stand up. The enormous Welshman entertained paying crowds with his voracious appetite and astounded them by his remarkable bulk. He would eat one stupendous meal after another, until he was nearly stuffed to bursting, It is said that Hopkins tried to grab a piece of food that was just out of reach and tumbled off his bench whereupon he landed on a nursing sow, killing the poor beast, and flattening her piglets beneath his immense body. It took fifteen men to lift him back onto his seat, and even then only with great difficulty. Hopkins' weight (measured on a steelyard built for weighing fully-loaded wagons) is taken from a 19th-Century medical encyclopedia.

 # Memorable Movie Quotes

I got scruples too, you know. You know what that is . . . scruples? No, I don't know what it is, but if you got 'em, it's a sure bet they belong to somebody else!
Paper Moon

The worst part about being you is pretending to be so bad in bed.
The Saint

Do you know the difference between brown-nosing and ass-kissing? Depth perception.
Hijacking Hollywood

Facts From Around the World

The surface area of the Earth is 197,000,000 square miles.

The Pacific Ocean has 46% of the world's water. The Atlantic has 23.9%; the Indian, 20.3%; the Arctic, 3.7 %.

Dominica, Mexico, Zambia, Kiribati, Fiji and Egypt have birds on their flags.

There is a city named Sisters and another called Brothers in Oregon. Sisters was named for a nearby trio of peaks in the Cascade Mountains known as the Three Sisters. Brothers was then named in response to Sisters.

In the majority of countries people drive on the right hand side of the road, but there are about fifty nations in which people drive on the left. These include the United Kingdom and former British colonies such as Australia and New Zealand. There are also countries that were never British where people also drive on the left including Japan.

The only borough of New York City that isn't an island or part of an island is the Bronx.

When the Dominican Republic first gained independence, it was called Santo Domingo.

Elvis Presley was born in Tupelo, Mississippi.

The Chang Jiang River is the fourth longest river in the world.

The German Parliament (the Bundestag) has 672 members and is the world's largest elected legislative chamber.

More Brief Histories

The Ancient Greeks. The warm, dry climate of Greece always allowed people to survive through farming, fishing, and trade. One of the earliest civilizations came in the Minoan period, which started in around 3000 BC. The Minoan people on the island of Crete were successful traders, and built some remarkable palaces, which became the scenes of early myths including the Minotaur's Labrynth. This civilization ended about 1450 BC. Next came the Myceneans, soldiers from mainland Greece, before Greece entered a 'Dark Age' from around 1100 BC to around 800 BC. At this stage the Greeks started to explore their part of the world and set up colonies and trading posts, and from about 480 BC the 'golden age' began, which would eventually be known as Classical Greece and the birthplace of Western civilization. This was an age when scholars, scientists or artists flourished as well as the traditional farmers, soldiers and fishermen. Beautiful temples were built, with stone columns and statues, and people started to go to open-air theaters to watch plays. Democracy developed in Athens (although only among the citizens, not among their slaves), the first Olympic Games were held and new ideas in science, art and philosophy were established. As they were skilled sailors, the Greek civilizations spread across mainland Greece and the archipelago of islands in the Aegean Sea, as well as modern Turkey, and to colonies spread across Italy, Sicily, North Africa and even France.

The Theremin

The theremin is best known as the spooky instrument that is used on horror movie soundtracks and also in the classic Beach Boys song *Good Vibrations*. It was originally the product of Russian research into sensors which could tell how close a physical object was to them. The instrument itself was designed by a young physicist called Léon Theremin during the Russian civil war – he basically transformed the distance information into a varying electronic drone so that you could 'play' the sensor with your hands, thus controlling a tone of variable pitch. Theremin showed the device to Lenin, who saw it as a magnificent symbol of Soviet scientific progress. He learnt to play it himself and had hundreds of them made to be distributed around Communist Russia. Theremin toured the world demonstrating his invention, eventually moving to New York, and patented his invention in 1928. The first commercial theremin was the RCA Thereminvox. It wasn't a commercial success but some thereminists achieved renown, including Clara Rockmore, who often shared a bill with Paul Robeson. In 1938 Léon Theremin returned to the Soviet Union. He may have been kidnapped by Russian agents, though

Natural Thoughts

Some people walk in the rain, others just get wet.

Roger Miller

it has also been suggested he fled from personal debts and ended up being caught up in Stalin's purges by accident. He didn't return to the US until the 1990s. Meanwhile, after a hiatus in popularity, Robert Moog began to build theremins and to sell kits from which customers could make their own. Through its later use in pop and avant garde music, the theremin eventually established itself as a slightly weird but well-known niche instrument.

A Brief History of the Aztecs

The Aztecs were a nomadic tribe from the area we would now call northern Mexico. They were one of the last great Native American civilizations, dominating the region in the 14th to 16th centuries. 'Aztec' means 'person from Aztlán', but the exact location of Aztlán remains uncertain. The legend is that the Aztecs wandered for many years before they received a sign, an eagle and a serpent fighting on a cactus. This showed them where they should build their city. They also called themselves the Mehika or Meshika or Mexica, and this is the origin of the name 'Mexico'. They had an advanced system of agriculture. They cultivated the land, using irrigation and swamp drainage, and even building artificial islands in the lakes. They used a form of hieroglyphic writing, built extraordinary pyramids and temples, and also used a complex calendar system. The end of the Aztec Empire came when their enemies from Tlaxcala allied with the Spanish invaders to attack the Aztecs. This defeat combined with the arrival of diseases such as smallpox from Europe led to the collapse of the civilization, although some elements of the culture survived under Spanish rule.

A Brief History of the Spanish Civil War

The Spanish Civil War lasted from 1936 to 1939. General
Franco's Nationalists were supported financially and militarily by
Hitler's Nazi Germany, Mussolini's Fascist Italy and the Catholic
Church. Their opponents were the Republicans who were
fighting for democracy in Spain. The elected Republican
Government was only supported by Russia and, to some extent,
by the International Brigades. The latter were made up of
140,000 volunteers, many of them artists, intellectuals or workers,
thousands of whom would die in the war. There was dismay in
the Brigades at the refusal of Britain and France in particular to
support the Republicans. More than a quarter of a million
Spaniards died in the fighting, which ended in a Nationalist
victory. General Franco made himself Chief of State and Head of
Government and there were violent reprisals after the official
ceasefire, with 100,000 Republicans dying in prison or being
executed after the war. Following Spain's neutral stance in World
War II, Franco's 35-year dictatorship, from 1939 to 1975, was
one of the longest lasting non-democratic governments in 20th
Century Europe. It saw Spain isolated by economic blockades,

 The Fame Name Game

*What did Mary Cathleen Collins change her
name to?*

Answer: Bo Derek

excluded from NATO and the UN and mired in economic recession. Franco died in 1975 and the Spanish Parliament made Prince Juan Carlos Head of State. As King of Spain, one of his first political actions was to declare an amnesty for the many political prisoners. This was followed by laws establishing political reform and Spain finally turned back to democracy in November 1976.

The Zodiac

Astronomical observation began in the early civilizations of Asia Minor around 3000 BC, when prominent constellations were recognized and given names. The sky-watchers of Mesopotamia were the first to name the five wandering stars which, together with the sun and moon, form the seven original 'planets' (the word comes from the Greek for 'wanderers'). The Babylonians then came to realize that the sequence in which the sun and the planets appear to move through the heavens could be used as a measure of time. They chose twelve constellations to represent these segments, and gave them the names of animals. The Greeks later inherited this system and named it the zodiac (abbreviated from the Greek for 'animal circle') adding their own links to the gods as an additional layer of meaning. In the 5th Century, the school of Pythagoras proposed an astronomical theory whereby a circular earth revolves on its own axis as well as traveling in an orbit. They believed that this spinning of the earth explained the pattern of night and day. Moving outwards from the earth in the sequence of heavenly bodies, they placed the moon next, followed by the sun, the planets and finally the stars, which they assumed to be fixed on an outer sphere. While this was a significant step forwards, it would take another millennium, until the days of Copernicus, Galileo and Kepler, before Western science finally started to accept that the earth rotated around the sun rather than vice versa.

The Wars of the Roses

The Wars of the Roses were a series of civil wars fought in medieval England from 1455 to 1487. Two branches of the same family, the House of York and the House of Lancaster, claimed rightful descent from Edward III. This set off a struggle for the English throne. In 1455 many barons still resented the Lancaster family's seizure of the throne in 1399, with the coronation of King Henry IV. There was a widely held view that the York family, cousins of the Lancasters, had been cheated out of the monarchy. The ensuing battles became known as the Wars of the Roses because the Lancaster emblem was a red rose while the York emblem was a white rose. (These remain the emblems of the two counties of Lancashire and Yorkshire today, and there is still some friction between the two, even though it is now more about comic one-upmanship than real enmity.) At the battle of Bosworth in 1485, a later Henry Tudor defeated King Richard III, his Yorkist rival. Richard III had been king for two years following the mysterious disappearance of the two younger princes who had been standing between him and the throne. He was the last English monarch to die in battle. After the battle, Henry Tudor was crowned King Henry VII, marking the beginning of the 118 years of the Tudor dynasty on the throne in England. He went on to marry Elizabeth of York thus uniting the two families. In celebration of the end of the struggle, the Tudor rose was created, containing both the White Rose of York and the Red Rose of Lancaster.

A Brief History of the Spanish Armada

In May 1588 a huge invasion fleet sailed from the port of Lisbon. It contained 130 ships fitted with 2,500 guns, along with 30,000 soldiers and sailors. This 'armada' headed for England, which at the time had a relatively small navy, while Spain was the greatest power in the world at the time. There were two main reasons for the attempted invasion. Philip II of Spain was annoyed that Queen Elizabeth had not punished Sir Francis Drake, whose attacks on Spanish ships were little short of piracy. He also hoped to convert England back to the Church of Rome, as it had turned to Protestantism under Elizabeth.

The two fleets met in the English Channel. The English were outnumbered, but they had nimble smaller ships. On 6th August 1588, the Spaniards anchored at Calais. The English sent a large number of small boats with burning material into the midst of the Armada, in order to spread fear and disrupt its formation. The Armada relied on a crescent formation that had been

Thought For the Day

One day, someone showed me a glass of water that was half full. And he said, 'Is it half full or half empty?' So I drank the water. No more problem.

Alexander Jodorowsky

successful previously as it allowed a great number of ships to fire their heavy guns at the same time. The Spanish fled to the open sea, but there they found the bulk of the English fleet awaiting them. Having lost their formation in the open sea, the Spanish ships started to be picked off by the English artillery. In disarray the Armada fled. Attempts to regroup were foiled by terrible weather, in which many ships were lost. To this day, many black haired southern Irish families are descended from Spanish sailors who survived shipwrecks. This victory was the beginning of British naval dominance which would lead to an age of exploration and imperial colonization.

The Elephant in Popular Culture

The first elephants in Europe were military animals. A fighting specimen brought by the Roman army in the time of Claudius terrified the locals, while the exploits of Hannibal riding on elephants have gone down in history. In the 13th Century Louis IX of France gave an elephant to Henry III of England as a present. It lived at the Tower of London and was fed on a sturdy diet of roast beef and red wine, eventually dying as a result of this overindulgence. They were known as majestic, exotic beasts, but most people's knowledge of them came from anatomically inaccurate drawings and dubious legends. It was this idea of elephants as exotic that defined their place in our imaginations. Their unique appearance and size make them objects of awe and, like other African animals including the giraffe, rhinoceros, lion and hippopotamus, they are fascinating if mystifying to the Western mind. This is why 'white elephant' came to mean something expensive, useless and bizarre. Elephants have often appeared in children's stories as well-behaved, wise figures. Famous elephants in fiction include the elephant's child from Kipling, Disney's charming Dumbo, and Dr. Seuss's Horton. Meanwhile, in America, the elephant became a symbol of the Republican Party (United States) following an 1874 cartoon by Thomas Nast.

A Short History of the Beetroot

The beetroot has been cultivated by humans for thousands of years. It was historically used as a medicinal plant for a variety of ailments, both for external application and internal consumption. To this day, the antioxidant properties of the beetroot are under investigation by oncologists to see if it can slow tumour growth, while some medical researchers believe that beetroot juice can lower blood pressure. Beetroots have been used to color food and cloth, make wine, and as an aphrodisiac.

The round beetroot wasn't developed until the 16th Century, although the cultivation of other varieties of beet can be traced back to around 2000 BC. Roman and Jewish literature records its use in the Mediterranean two millennia ago. Archaeologists found beetroot remains in the Third Dynasty Saqqara pyramid at Thebes, Egypt and charred remains were found in the Neolithic site of Aartswoud in the Netherlands. Beet cultivation is recorded in Babylonia from the 8th Century BC, and by AD 850 it had spread to China English and Germanic sources record the beet being widely grown in Medieval Europe and the crop eventually spread across the world. Historically three different types were harvested. Chard is a leaf vegetable similar to spinach. In 1747 Andreas Marggraf discovered that sugar could be extracted from

beets and following on from this development, in the 19th
Century, sugar beet became a major economic crop. During the
Napoleonic Wars the British blockaded cane sugar and as a
response to this Napoleon introduced sugar beet to France.
By 1880 more than 50% of the world's sugar was derived from
sugar beet.

The early medicinal uses of beetroot have some justification. It
is rich in vitamin C, fiber, potassium, magnesium, manganese,
and folic acid while the leafy tops contain high levels of beta-
carotene, iron and calcium. The Romans used it to treat fevers
and constipation, while the Greeks used beet leaves to bind
wounds. Throughout the Middle Ages beetroot (known as the
'blood turnip') was recommended for illnesses relating to
digestion and blood disorders.

In wartime Britain, pickled beetroot was a popular
accompaniment as well as a valuable vitamin source. Pickled beets
are also a traditional food of the American South and in
Australia and New Zealand. Also in the USA, Red Beet Eggs is a
traditional Pennyslvania German dish. These are hard-boiled eggs
that are refrigerated in the cooking liquid of pickled beets and
allowed to marinate until the eggs turn a deep pink-red color. In
Eastern Europe 'borscht' (cold beet soup, often served with sour
cream) is a popular dish whilst in Africa the leaves are often
cooked with meat in a casserole.

Beetroot's tendency to color urine red can alarm the
uninitiated. The deep color of the red or purple beetroot is due
to betanin pigments which are today used industrially as red food
colorants, for instance to intensify the color of tomato paste,
sauces, desserts, jams and jellies, ice cream, sweets and breakfast

cereals. The body is unable to break down these pigments, thus their persistence, and many doctors and nurses have been amused to receive visits from patients who have been unduly worried by this symptom.

Obscure English Language Facts

More Vowel Gymnastics
Suoidea, *seven letters long, is by a long chalk the shortest English word containing all five principal vowels in reverse alphabetical order. Following a long way behind are **duoliteral** and **unoriental** (10 letters) **subcontinental** (14 letters), **neuroepithelial** and **uncomplimentary** (15 letters).*

***Twyndyllyngs** is the longest word in the English language without any of the five principal vowels (at 12 letters), making do with only 'y's. The singular **twyndyllyng** has 11 letters, **symphysy** has 8 letters, while **gypsyfy, gypsyry, nymphly**, and **rhythms** have 7 letters each.*

Amazing Animals

Beaver teeth are so sharp that Native Americans used to use them as knife blades.

Camels have three eyelids to protect themselves from sand that is blown in the desert wind.

Greyhounds were first bred in Egypt in about the third millennium BC. From the 9th Century in England, they were bred by aristocrats to hunt such small game as rabbits and hares.

All pet hamsters are descended from a single female – a wild golden hamster found with a litter of twelve babies in Syria in 1930.

At night dolphins snooze just below the surface of the water. They rise to the surface for air at frequent intervals.

Emus are unable to walk backwards.

There is a species of parrot in New Zealand that often eats the rubber strips that line car windows.

A flamingo can't eat unless its head is upside down.

A group of larks is called an exaltation.

Armadillos are the only animal besides humans that can be infected with leprosy.

The roar of an adult lion is so loud it is audible up to five miles away. As well as warning off intruders they use the roar as a signal for scattered members of the pride to navigate by.

Hard boiling an ostrich egg takes over half an hour.

More Weird Laws

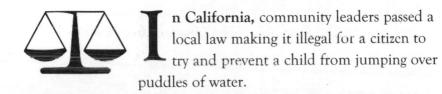 **I**n California, community leaders passed a local law making it illegal for a citizen to try and prevent a child from jumping over puddles of water.

In Wisconsin, it is illegal to kiss or to cut a woman's hair on a train. History does not relate why haircutting for men is not likewise prohibited.

In 1985, one Arizona legislator proposed a law requiring each candidate for the legislature to take an I.Q. test before the election. The scores would have been published on the ballot, if the bill had become law. The fact that the lawmakers voted this bill out makes one wonder what they thought they had to hide.

In California, state office regulations prohibit staff from letting phones ring more than nine times.

A Utah legislator proposed a bill that would have required the TV weather person to provide an ice cream cone to every member of the state House of Representatives any time the forecast was wrong. Sadly for the representatives, the law failed so they never got their free ice creams.

In New York there is a law making it illegal for any person 'to do any thing that is against the law'. Whether or not they remembered to pass another law making it illegal to break this particular law is uncertain.

Federal law no longer prevents garment workers from making mittens at home, so there will be no future prosecutions for domestic mitten makers.

The mayor of Danville, Kentucky is required to annually appoint 'three intelligent housekeepers' to the Board of Tax Supervisors.

In Simsbury, Connecticutt, it's illegal for a politician to campaign at the town dump, though why he or she would want to is another question altogether.

If the city council in Rushville, Illinois doesn't have a quorum, those who do attend can order the police to go out and arrest some of the missing members to force them to come along to the meeting.

In Hartford, Connecticutt, it's against the law to plant a tree in the street.

New York City is known as the city that never sleeps, but it may also be useful to know that it is illegal to have a puppet show in your window there. They really don't like window puppet shows there. Transgression is punishable by a 30-day sentence.

In Boston, cutting firewood in the street is forbidden, as is shooting a bow and arrow in the street.

Washington has proposed a law protecting sports referees from civil suit unless their actions can be shown to be 'willful, wanton, reckless, malicious or grossly negligent.' While in Nashville, North Carolina, punching an official at a youth sports program can incur a three-year suspension from the program. This applies to adult spectators as well as participants.

In Kentucky, it's against the law to use any kind of reptile in any form of religious service. While this seems a bizarre law, it is presumably provoked by the practice of snake handling and the dangers it incurs.

Lawmakers in Robbins, North Carolina proposed the following ordinance: 'In the future, anyone not living within the immediate vicinity of Robbins must have a permit from the Chief of Police and okayed by the Mayor or one of the Commissioners.' However, it was never made clear what the permit was actually for.

The Minnesota tax form is highly detailed. Not only does it ask for your date of birth – it also asks for your date of death.

The Fame Name Game

What did Henry John Deutschendorf change his name to?

Answer: John Denver

North Carolina passed a law saying a political action committee must have a name that accurately describes the group's cause. This is intended to prevent (for instance) pro-smoking lobbyists calling themselves 'Citizens for Good Government.'

In Washington State, any restroom with pay toilets must also have an equal number of free toilets. This law was apparently passed after the speaker of the state House of Representatives was frustrated having hurried to a pay toilet without having the correct change in his pocket.

A minister in Pennsylvania is not permitted to carry out a marriage ceremony if either the groom or the bride is drunk.

If you are ever tempted to do so, it is illegal to loiter in the Detroit city morgue.

A San Francisco regulation makes it illegal to utilize used underwear whilst wiping down cars in a car wash.

Thought For the Day

A man with one watch knows what time it is; a man with two watches is never quite sure.

Lee Segall

Baltimore has some strange regulations. There are laws covering the disposal of hogs' heads, pet droppings and oyster shells. It's also illegal to block the sidewalk with a box. However, this offense only carries a fine of one dollar. Finally it is illegal to throw a bale of hay (or of anything else) from a window on the second story or above.

In New York City it is illegal to carry an open can of spray paint. This may seem bizarre but it was brought in at the height of the graffiti craze, which was a serious problem in the city.

Youngstown, Ohio didn't want any truck with those new-fangled hippies in the 1960s, and a law was passed making it illegal to walk barefoot through town.

Communism is against the law in Haines City, Louisiana. The law was passed in 1950 and remains in force.

New York drivers are notoriously crazy, but pedestrians have also been subject to some confusing legislation in the state. Jaywalking is legal, but not if it is diagonal. So you can cross the street so long as you don't do it diagonally.

A Boston mayor once banned midnight dancing in the city, largely because he didn't like dancing or being kept awake by the music.

Under an 1872 law still on the books, a Chicago alderman can carry a gun.

In San Francisco any 'mechanical device that reproduces obscene language' is illegal. The city also has laws prohibiting kerchoo powders and stink balls.

Town law in Belhaven, North Carolina stipulated that the sewer service charge should be '$2 per month, per stool.' It was later changed to read 'per toilet.'

Members of nine New York Indian tribes are exempt from the city's parking tax.

Albany, Virginia has had a law for many years that prohibits peddlers from using the telephone to either sell things or raise funds. Given the rise of telemarketing you can't help but think this may have been a good idea.

In San Antonio, Texas, you mustn't honk a horn, run a generator, have a revival meeting or do anything else that disturbs the neighborhood. The city also has a four-member noise police squad to enforce this law.

In Boston it's illegal to post advertisements on public urinals. It's also illegal to hang a vending machine on a utility pole.

In North Carolina it's illegal to sell cotton lint at night. However, it is legal to sell cottonseed at night.

Balloons with advertising on them are illegal in Hartford, Connecticutt.

In Minoola, Illinois it's against the law to undress and 'expose the naked person' during daylight or twilight, even if you are simply taking a bath.

In Boston it is illegal to rummage through rubbish containers.

'Dwarf-tossing,' which is the activity of throwing dwarfs wearing padded suits, is outlawed in the bars of Springfield, Illinois. However, while it is regarded as dangerous and exploitative to dwarf-toss in a bar, the practice is allowed elsewhere in town, so long as you have a special permit.

It used to be illegal in Jonesboro, Georgia to say the words, 'Oh boy.'

In Danville, Kentucky, it's illegal to throw soapsuds or slops into the street.

Vermont, as a dairy state, has historically tried to discourage the use of margarine. It is illegal to use colored margarine in

The Fame Name Game

What did Archibald Alexander Leach change his name to?

Answer: Cary Grant

restaurants unless the menu indicates you do. The letters mentioning this must be a minimum of two inches high. Colored margarine can be served only if it comes in triangle-shaped patties.

In Christiansburg, Virginia, it's against the law to imitate a police whistle.

A law in Waterloo, Nebraska once prohibited barbers from eating onions on the job.

In Bloomfield, Connecticutt it is against the law to eat food in your car.

Is a tomato a fruit or a vegetable? Scientists would say fruit, however, in an 1893 tariff case, the US Supreme Court ruled that tomatoes are legally vegetables. This was on the basis that they are normally eaten during a meal and not afterward.

In Salem, Oregon, it's illegal for patrons of nude dancing establishments to be within two feet of the dancers.

Natural Thoughts

A gun gives you the body, not the bird

Henry David Thoreau

In Oakland, California, it is illegal to grow a tree in front of your neighbor's window and block his view. However, if the tree is 'an attractive tree', such as a redwood or box elder, this law may be waived.

Under a 1950s ordinance, stubborn children were classified as 'vagrants' in Jupiter Inlet Colony, Florida.

In Christiansburg, Virginia., it's illegal to 'spit, expectorate or deposit any sputum, saliva or any form of saliva or sputum.'

In Oxford, Mississippi, it's illegal to 'create unnecessary noises.'

In Boston you need to be careful about your manure storage. Don't keep it in your building unless the building is being used as a stable. If it is a stable, you can keep up to two cords of manure. If you have more than two cords, you need a permit to move it, and at all times it is prohibited to leave it in the street.

A Delaware legislator recently proposed a law requiring every minor to inform his or her parents before engaging in sexual intercourse. Reality intervened and the law wasn't passed.

In Provincetown, Massachusetts, it's illegal to sell suntan oil until after noon on Sunday.

In Robbins, North Carolina, anyone who refuses to extinguish or cover lights after hearing the blackout signal is subject to a five dollar fine.

In Miami Shores Village, Florida, all goods made in Communist countries and offered for sale must be clearly marked as such. The ordinance records the problem that such goods are often marked in a 'false, misleading or inadequate manner, to hide their Communist origins.'

Under an 1889 law, the health officer of East Jordan, Michigan could send any non-resident with an infectious disease back to his or her hometown, as long as the person was healthy enough to travel. If not, the officer could rent a house to be used as a pest house.

In Ballwin, Montana, it is against the law to use vulgar, obscene or indecent language except inside your own home.

In Manteno, Illinois you cannot 'throw, drop or place' a used hankie 'upon any public way or public place or upon the floor of any convenience or upon the floor of any theater, hall or assembly or public building or upon the surface or any lot or parcel of ground or on the roof on any building or in any light or air shaft, court or areaway.'

In Tryon, North Carolina it's against the law for anyone to keep 'fowl that shall cackle,' or for anyone to play the piccolo between the hours of 11pm and 7.30am. Presumably the town was once inhabited by an insomniac piccolo player.

You need a permit to run a barbershop in Christiansburg, Virginia. But the wording of the town's law indicates if you're caught operating without a permit, your permit will be revoked.

In Caroline County, Maryland, you can be punished with $100 fine or six months imprisonment for 'forecasting or pretending to foretell the future.'

In Xenia, Ohio, it's against the law to spit in a salad bar.

The World's Oddest Animals

Pygmy Marmoset *Pygmy Marmosets are monkeys native to the rain forest canopies of western Brazil, South-eastern Colombia, eastern Ecuador, and eastern Peru. They are one of the smallest primates in the world, with body length ranging from 14-16cm (excluding the 15-20cm tail). Males weigh around 140g (5oz), and females as little as 120g (4.2oz). It has a tawny coat, and a ringed tail which can be as long as its body. In a trait unique to the species their claws are specially adapted for climbing trees; as their favorite food is tree sap. They also have specialized teeth for gouging holes in bark and can spend up to two-thirds of their waking time up in the trees penetrating the tree bark to reach the sap. They also feed on fruit, leaves, insects, and sometimes even small reptiles. Unfortunately, because of their diminuitive size and speed, it can be very hard to observe them in the wild. In captivity however, the Pygmy Marmoset can live for up to 11 years.*

In Washington it's against the law to pretend you're a rich person's child and entitled to his estate.

Wyoming required that every inmate of the state's training school for girls be issued with crinoline bloomers.

Wisconsin law mandates a fine of $2 to $20 for anyone under the age of 17 who is caught 'jumping onto a railroad car while the train is in motion.'

In Hawaii there used to be a law requiring children to obey all 'lawful and moral' commands of their parents.

In Marblehead, Massachusetts it was once illegal to cross the street on Sunday, unless absolutely necessary.

In Olympia, Washington minors are still prohibited from attending pool halls.

'Coasting on Beaver Street' is illegal in Edgeworth, Pennsylvania. Whether or not this is a euphemism is unrecorded.

Strangers in Simsbury, Connecticutt, were required, under a 1701 ordinance, to leave town within a month if they didn't have at least 20 shillings. This law was only repealed late in the 20th Century.

In Rockwell, North Carolina, if you violate the terms of a proclamation, for instance failing to appropriately celebrate

Hilarious Misprints

One In Three British Men
Ready To Give Birth
Reuters

Mercury Plunges To Bone-
Chilling 68
Dallas Morning News

Spaniard Hits Girlfriend At
Anti-Violence Rally
Reuters

Oil Barge Breaks Off Texas
AP

National Slacker Day May Be
Too Much Effort
Reuters

Quintuplets Born 15 Months
Early
Dateline Moorhead, Minnesota

Rape – The New Way To
Defend Yourself
Ladies Home Journal

Parking Lot Floods When
Man Bursts
Durham Herald-Sun

Priest In Fatal Crash
Improves
Lakeland Ledger

17 Remain Dead In Morgue
Shooting Spree
The News & Observer

Ottawa May Tackle Homeless
Toronto Star

Shooting Suspect Said Hot-
Tempered
AP

Woman Sues Caterpillar For
Sexual Harrassment
UPI

Mike McGrew, deputy US
marshal in Oklahoma City
has carried his son's first baby
as a good luck charm for
thirteen years. He has had it
hanging on the rear-view
mirror of four automobiles
and, during the war, kept it in
the socks of his Army
uniform.
New Jersey newspaper

Peanut Day or Jaycees Week, you can be found guilty of a misdemeanor.

A 1950s anti-obscenity law in Irondale, Alabama, made any showing of anyone nude or 'in a substantially nude state' illegal, unless it were a baby.

In Jonesboro, Tennessee, a slingshot was once classified by law as a deadly weapon.

In the Code of 1650 in the New Haven Colony (now Connecticut), a 16-year-old boy could be sentenced to death if he 'cursed, struck or disobeyed' his parents or was 'stubborn or rebellious.'

In Iowa it is legal to gamble on a riverboat, but there is a maximum bet of five dollars.

In Washington State it's illegal to sell comics to minors if there is a possibility that the comics might incite them to violence or depraved or immoral acts.

In North Carolina, an 1866 law makes it illegal to dig ginseng on other people's property between the months of April and September.

A Wisconsin legislator recently introduced a bill making it illegal to tattoo someone under the age of 18.

A historic Washington law sent participants in a duel to jail for ten years. This was assuming that they survived the duel in the first place.

It's illegal in North Carolina to take and sell labeled milk crates. This is because at one point they were commonly being used as a cheap alternative to furniture.

In the state of Washington it's against the law (as well as unsporting) to catch a fish by throwing a rock at it.

If you own a marl bed in North Carolina, it is mandatory to put a fence around it. (A marl bed is a rock quarry.)

Under Delaware law, any person of good moral character may keep and operate a bowling alley. However, no gambling on the premises is permitted. Meanwhile in Hawaii shooting galleries are legal, but they may not offer liquor as a prize. This is to discourage winners from drinking their prize and then returning for another game.

In Las Vegas you can legally bet on any team, other than the University of Nevada at Las Vegas.

Marathon dancing has been illegal in the state of Washington since the days of the Great Depression. In addition marathon skipping, sliding, gliding, rolling or crawling are also prohibited.

In Kennesaw, Georgia. law makes it mandatory for homeowners to own a gun, unless they are a convicted felon, conscientious objector or disabled.

In Washington State it's illegal to sleep in an outhouse without the permission of the owner.

In San Francisco, it's against the law to beat a rug in front of your house. While in New York City it is forbidden to shake a dust mop out a window.

In Colorado it is legal to remove the furniture tags that say, 'Do Not Remove Under Penalty of Law.'

In Washington State, until quite recently, you could have theoretically have been fined up to $500 for the serious criminal act of removing or defacing the label on a pillow.

In colonial times, there was an ordinance in Hartford, Connecticutt that permitted any resident to rent the town chain for 2 pence. However, the resident had to fix it if he broke it.

In Los Angeles, years ago it was illegal to sleep in your kitchen but not to cook in your bedroom.

The city council of West Palm Beach, Florida, once decreed that the roofs of all outhouses be fireproof.

A law in Columbus, Georgia once made it illegal to sit on your porch 'in an indecent position.'

In Baltimore it's against the law to play professional croquet before 2pm on a Sunday. The law also applies to professional quoits. In Delaware horse racing of any kind is prohibited on Good Friday and Easter Sunday.

Both Massachusetts and New Hampshire had historic laws that penalized gamblers who lost money. In Massachusetts you would face a fine, if you had any money left to pay it with. In New Hampshire it was illegal to pawn the clothes you were wearing to pay off gambling debts.

In recent years, there have been several attempts to legalize camel racing and ostrich racing in New Mexico, but thus far both remain illegal. However, the legislature has recently allowed gambling on bicycle races.

You need a license if you want to sell condoms in Washington State.

In Nevada a man caught beating his wife used to be punished by being tied to a stake for eight hours a day with a sign that read, 'Wife Beater' on his chest. Meanwhile in South Carolina, wife beaters weren't allowed to hold any public office.

In Missouri, male legislators apparently once introduced a resolution urging their female colleagues to strap snub-nosed, 38-caliber revolvers to their ankles.

The Fame Name Game

What did Caryn Johnson change her name to?

Answer: Whoopi Goldberg

An ordinance in Linden, Alabama required all women of
'uncertain chastity' to be off the streets by 9pm. It is unclear
whether the certainly chaste (or certainly unchaste) women of the
town were allowed out on the streets to a later hour.

In Wisconsin you need a cheesemaker's license to make most
kinds of cheese. However, if you want to make Limburger, you
need a master cheesemaker's license.

It's against the law in Florida for an unmarried man and woman
to live together in 'open and gross lewdness.' Connecticut once
had similar legislation, but only the woman was to be penalized.

Taxpayers of Bainbridge, Indiana once had to swear a solemn
oath that the values they placed on their taxable property were
the fair market values. (Some say that modern bankers should
have to take a similar oath when describing their assets.)

A recent proposal that ministers patrol with police officers in Belmont,
North Carolina, noted 'the ministers will carry a Bible instead of a gun.'
While in Mooresville, North Carolina it's against the law to
attach anything to a pool table.

In North Dakota, charitable groups can hold stud poker games to
raise money, but they are restricted to doing so twice a year.
In Indiana it is mandatory for a sports agent to give a college ten
days notice before tempting a star athlete into the ranks of the
professionals.

It's against the law to clam at night in Connecticut.

The Santa Monica City Council recently proposed that men should be allowed to use women's public restrooms when there's a line of three or more at the men's room, and vice versa.

A Maryland law prohibits 'female sitters, also known as shills,' that is to say women who are paid by owners to sit in bars and encourage male patrons to buy drinks.

A Vietnamese lawmaker once proposed the country should ban the practice of women wearing 'falsies.'

A typographical error in the law code of Tempe, Arizona means that a shooting range can be run by the 'Amateur Crapshooting Association.'

In Maine it's against the law to catch lobsters with your bare hands.

If you take your giraffe to Atlanta, Georgia, remember not to tie it to a telephone pole or street lamp. To do so would be illegal.

In Illinois, it is against the law to offer a cigar that has been lit to cats, dogs, or any other domesticated animal that is being kept as a pet.

Leaders Have Their Say

Leaders grasp nettles.
David Ogilvy

Leaders are people who do the right thing; managers are people who do things right.
Warren G. Bennis

When the leaders choose to make themselves bidders at an auction of popularity, their talents, in the construction of the state, will be of no service. They will become flatterers instead of legislators; the instruments, not the guides, of the people.
Edmund Burke

Leaders don't create followers, they create more leaders.
Tom Peters

The more responsibility the Scoutmaster gives his patrol leaders, the more they will respond.
Robert Baden-Powell

Cruel leaders are replaced only to have new leaders turn cruel.
Che Guevara

We are not educated well enough to perform the necessary act of intelligently selecting our leaders.
Walter Cronkite

Elected leaders who forget how they got there won't the next time.
Malcolm Forbes

Blessed are the people whose leaders can look destiny in the eye without flinching but also without attempting to play God.
Henry A. Kissinger

Strong people don't need strong leaders.
Ella Baker

Our leaders are acting like lemmings.
Jack Herer

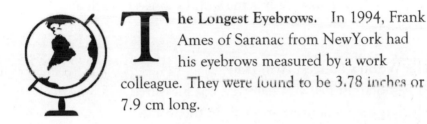

The World's Longest...

The Longest Eyebrows. In 1994, Frank Ames of Saranac from New York had his eyebrows measured by a work colleague. They were found to be 3.78 inches or 7.9 cm long.

The World's Longest Abbreviation
The longest abbreviation in the world contains 56 letters:

NIIOMTPLABOPARMBETZHELBETRABSBOM
ONIMONKONOTDTEKHSTROMONT

This stands for: Laboratory for Shuttering, Reinforcement, Concrete and Ferroconcrete Operations for Composite-monolithic and Monolithic Constructions of the Department of Technology of Building Assembly Operations of the Scientific Research Institute of the Organization for Building Mechanization and Technical Aid of the Academy of Building and Architecture of the USSR.

The Longest Fall That Was Survived
On 26th January 1972, Vesna Vulovic from Serbska Kamenice, Czechoslovakia fell 33,300ft and survived when a Yugoslav DC9 exploded in mid air, as a result of a suspected terrorist bombing.

Her life was saved because she landed on a snowy slope and, although initially paralyzed from the waist down, she later recovered and re-learned to walk.

The World's Longest Beach
Cox's Bazar in Bangladesh is the world's longest beach at 75 miles long.

The World's Longest Arm Hair
Robert Starrett had arm hair that was measured at 5.3 inches which is the the longest arm hair in the world.

The World's Longest Banana Split
The world's longest banana split was created in Selinsgrove, Pennsylvania on 30th April 1938. It took 33,000 bananas, 2500 gallons of ice-cream, 600 pounds of nuts, and a wide variety of other toppings. When complete it measured 7.32km or 4.55 miles.

The Longest Bus
Volvo launched the longest bus in the world October 2004. The B12M is 26.8m or 87.93ft long and is able to carry up to 300 passengers.

The Fame Name Game

What did Charles Hardin Holley change his name to?

Answer: Buddy Holly

The Longest Song Title
Swedish band, Rednex, are the proud owners of the world's
longest song title. At 52 words and 305 characters, (including
spaces) it is:
*The Sad But True Story Of Ray Mingus, The Lumberjack Of Bulk Rock
City, And His Never Slacking Strife In Exploiting The So Far
Undiscovered Areas Of The Intention To Bodily Intercourse From The
Opposite Species Of His Kind, During Intake Of All The Mental
Condition That Could Be Derived From Fermentation*

Longest Tongue
The longest tongue measures 9.8 cm (3.86 in) from the tip to the
middle of his closed top lip and was achieved by Stephen Taylor
(United Kingdom), at Westwood Medical Center, Coventry,
United Kingdom, on 11th February 2009.

The World's Longest Slinky
A 21 meter (71 foot) long Slinky suspended on 418 elastic
threads is free to move in three dimensions.

Longest Ear Hair
Anthony Victor (India) has hair sprouting from the center of his
outer ears (middle of the pinna) measuring 18.1 cm (7.12 in) at
its longest point.

The Longest Book
During the Ming Dynasty at least 3000 scholars spent four years,
beginning in 1403, to work on the Yongle Dadian, an

encyclopedia with 11,095 volumes and 22,877 chapters.
There are an estimated 370 million Chinese characters used.

Longest Time Breath Held Voluntarily
The longest time to hold your breath underwater is 18 min 32 sec
and was achieved by Karoline Mariechen Meyer (Brazil) at
the Racer Academy swimming pool, Florianopolis, Brazil, on
10th July 2009.

The Longest Job Title In The World?
An advert in a London newspaper read:
'Wanted: Temporary part-time libraries North-West inter-library
loan business unit administration assistant'. It was a request
for a librarian.

Longest Word In The English Language
Pneumonoultramicroscopicsilicovolcanoconiosis:
This 45-letter word was coined to serve as the longest English
word and is the longest word ever to appear in an English
language dictionary. It is listed in the current edition of several
dictionaries.

The World's Longest Hiccup Fit
In Iowa in 1922, Charles Osborne got a case of the hiccups whilst
weighing a hog. The fit lasted 68 years until they mysteriously
stopped in 1990; in the meantime he hiccuped an estimated 430
million times. He married twice and had eight children. He died
one year after his hiccups stopped.

The World's Longest After Dinner Speech
Dr. Donald Thomas performed an after-dinner speech at City College in New York from 1st April 1988 until 3rd April 1988 about Vegetarian Athletic Nutrition. Not including a bunch of 5 minute rest breaks, Dr. Donald Thomas' speech lasted an incredible 32 hours and 25 minutes.

Longest Hair
The world's longest documented hair belongs to Xie Qiuping (China) at 5.627 m (18ft 5in) when measured on 8th May 2004. She has been growing her hair since 1973 from the age of 13.

The Longest Balloon Flight
On 19th June 2002 Steve Fossett, aboard the Bud Light Spirit of Freedom, began an epic journey lasting 14 days 19 hours and 51 minutes and covering 20,602 miles or 32,963km, in which he became the first person to circumnavigate the earth, solo, in a balloon. The Bud Light Spirit of Freedom launched from Northam, Australia on and landed at Lake Yamma Yamma, Queensland, Australia on the 4th July. He actually finished the circumnavigation almost a day earlier, but due to the winds was unable to land.

Thought For the Day

Weak eyes are fondest of glittering objects.

Thomas Carlyle

The Longest Beard

When he died in 1927, the beard of Hans Langseth of Norway, was measured at 17.5 feet. Hans Langseth's beard can now be seen at the Smithsonian Institution. Currently the longest beard belonging to a living person is that of Shamsher Singh of India. His beard last measured in at 6 feet.

The Longest Album Title

The longest album title that actually made the charts is by Fiona Apple. It is:

When the Pawn Hits the Conflicts He Thinks Like a King What He Knows Throws the Blows When He Goes to the Fight and He'll Win the Whole Thing 'Fore He Enters the Ring There's No Body to Batter When Your Mind Is Your Might So When You Go Solo, You Hold Your Own Hand and Remember That Depth Is the Greatest of Heights and If You Know Where You Stand, Then You Know Where to Land and If You Fall It Won't Matter, Cuz You'll Know That You're Right

The World's Longest Coin

In 1644, due to the silver shortage, Sweden produced copper plate money. The ten daler coin measured 1 foot x 2 feet and weighed about 20 pounds.

The Longest Feet In The World

The world's longest man has the world's longest feet. Robert Pershing Wadlow's feet measured 18.5 inches and he wore size 37 shoes.

The World's Longest Escalator

The longest escalator in the western hemisphere is located at the Wheaton station of the Washington Metro subway system. It has an overall length of 155 meters or 508 feet and takes over 3 minutes to ride. The world's longest escalator is the four-section Ocean Park outdoor escalator system located at the Ocean Park amusement

The World's Oddest Animals

Star-nosed Mole *The Star-nosed Mole is a small North American mole found in eastern Canada and the north-eastern United States. Living in wet lowland areas it normally eats small invertebrates, aquatic insects, worms and molluscs. It is a strong swimmer and finds food by foraging along the bottoms of streams and ponds. Like other moles, it digs shallow tunnels which lead underwater to aid its foraging. It is not nocturnal, and does not hibernate in winter, when it has been observed tunnelling through the snow and swimming in ice-covered streams. The unique thing about the Star-nosed Mole is its nose. It has a circle of 22 mobile, pink, fleshy tentacles at the end of the snout which are used to identify food by touch. The rest of the animal is covered in a thick blackish brown water-repellent fur and it has large scaled feet and a long thick tail as a fat storage reserve for the spring breeding season. Adults are 15- 20cm in length, weigh about 55g, and have around 44 teeth.*

and entertainment center Hong Kong. The escalator has a vertical rise of 377 feet and stretches out to 225 meters or 745 feet in length.

The World's Longest Dog Tongue
Brandy, a seven-year-old boxer dog, has a tongue that is 17 inches long and it is still growing. At birth, Brandy's tongue was already the size of an adult boxer and as she grew so did her tongue.

The Longest Insect In The World
In 1995, Dr. Francis Seow Choen discovered a stick insect that measured 55 cm, just under 22 inches long.

The World's Longest Paperclip Chain
A team from Eisenhower Jr. High School, Taylorsville, Utah, on 26th March 2004 linked together 1,560,377 paperclips which totaled 22.17 miles in length. Dan Meyer holds the record for the longest paperclip chain made by one individual on the 13th and 14th February 2004, consisting of 54,030 paperclips with a total length of 5340 feet or 1627.6 meters.

The Fame Name Game

What did Eleanora Fagan change her name to?

Answer: Billie Holiday

The World's Longest Great White Shark
The world's largest great white shark officially measured 21 feet but there have been many claims of much longer sharks. Back in 1930 fishermen were emptying out a herring weir in New Brunswick when they found a great white shark. The shark measured a monster 37 feet and weighed 24,000 pounds.

The World's Longest Hole
The record for the world's longest hole or world's deepest hole, now belongs to Maersk Oil.

The hole was completed in May 2008 at Al Shaheen Field, just offshore of Qatar. It is 40,320 feet or 12.3 kilometers in length.

The World's Longest Jigsaw Puzzle
The puzzle was created by Royce B. McClure for EDUCA© and released in March 2007. It is called 'Life: The Great Challenge', measures 168.5 inches in length, 61.8 inches in width and contains 24,000 pieces.

The Longest War In The World
The Hundred Years War between England and France lasted 116 years from 1337–1453.

The World's Longest Nail
The world's largest tire stands in Allen Park, and in 1998, to promote their puncture-resistant Tiger Paw Nailgard tire, Uniroyal stabbed the tire with the world's longest nail. The nail weighed 250 pounds and took the record for world's longest nail at 11 feet. In 2003 the nail was removed and sold on eBay to Ralph Roberts for $3000.

The Longest Leg Hair
Tim Stinton of Australia let his leg hair grow and on 2nd February 2005 he was recognized as having the world's longest leg hair. It measured in at a 12.4cm or 4.88 inches.

The Longest Pizza Delivery
On 17th November 2004 Domino's Pizza set a charity event to benefit the Make-A-Wish Foundation UK so they baked a Vegetarian Supreme pizza in Feltham, London. On 19th November 2004 the pizza was delivered by Domino's franchisee Lucy Clough to 30 Ramsey Street, Melbourne, Australia, a distance of 10,532 miles.

The World's Longest Ladder
The Coast Guard uses a 320 foot ladder, named the 'debarkation ladder', which can be rolled up and unrolled as needed, for just such emergencies.

The Longest Toenails In The World
Louise Hollis of California has the longest toenails with a combined length of her 10 toenails of 2.21 meters or 87 inches.

 # Thought For the Day

We waste a lot of time running after people we could have caught by just standing still.

Mignon McLaughlin, *The Neurotic's Notebook*, 1960

The World's Longest Rabbit Ears
An English Lop rabbit, named Nipper's Geronimo, has been recorded as having the longest ears on a rabbit. The complete span of the ears measured at 79 centimeters, or 31.12 inches, which is longer than the average rabbit's entire body.

The Longest Motorcycle Jump
On New Year's Eve 2007, at the Rio All Suite Hotel & Casino in Las Vegas, Robbie Maddison managed to jump 322 feet or 98.15 meters to earn him the right to claim he made the world's longest motorcycle jump.

The World's Longest Swimming Pool
The world's longest swimming pool is in the San Alfonso del Mar in Algarrobo, Chile. The pool is made with seawater and measures 1013 meters in length. The area of the pool is eight hectares, or 19.77 acres. Construction of the pool was completed in December 2006.

The World's Longest Roller Coaster Ride
Richard Rodriguez, a 43-year-old American, set the record for the world's longest roller coaster ride.

    At Holiday Park in Western Germany, Richard Rodriguez spent 192 hours or exactly eight days riding two different roller coasters. He received only a 15-minute break every 8 hours, but did manage to sleep during the rides. It seems that there was a toilet installed on the coaster for emergencies.

The World's Longest Wedding Dress Train

The world's longest wedding dress train was made by the Green Leaf bridal shop in Paphos, Cyprus by Andreas Evstratiou on 18th February 2007. The train was 1362 meters long.

The Longest Train In The World

The longest train ever was a freight train 7.353km long with 682 cars and eight diesel engines. It belonged to the BHP Iron Ore Company in Australia.

The World's Longest Swim

In 2002 Martin Strel swam down the Mississippi river, a total of 3885km or 2360 miles. He covered the distance in 68 days.

The World's Longest Xylophone

The Kingdom of Busoga in Uganda is home to the 'Kisoga embaire', the world's longest xylophone.

The 'Kisoga embaire' is over 12 feet long and comprised of 20 large keys arranged in a pentatonic scale. It takes six people to play it.

The World's Longest Jellyfish

The Arctic Lion's Mane's tentacles can grow to over 100 feet in length. These jellyfish are found throughout all the world's oceans and even in freshwater.

The Longest Traffic Jam

From Lyon to Paris, France on 16th February 1980 there was a traffic jam that was 109 miles (176km) long.

The Longest Tattoo Session

From 16th to 18th September 2005, at the Outta Limits Tattoo and Body Piercing Studio in Dubbo, New South Wales, Australia Glen Keizer was tattooed for 42 hours and 10 minutes straight.

The World's Longest Scuba Dive

On 3rd September 2004, exactly five days after going under, American Jerry Hall surfaced from Watauga Lake with the new world's longest scuba dive record of 120 hours.

The World's Longest Scarf

A team of 2,000 knitters knitted a scarf to aid Ty Hafan, a children's hospice in Wales. When they were finished the world's longest scarf measured 33.74 miles. The scarf has since been cut up into squares and sold to benefit 'Feed the Children'.

The World's Longest Laughter

In 1962 a group of 12- to 18-year-old schoolgirls in Tanganyika started laughing and couldn't stop. The laughter soon spread to the adults, then to nearby villages affecting thousands of Tanganyikans.

The Fame Name Game

What did Jerome Silberman change his name to?

Answer: Gene Wilder

It wasn't long before the laughing was no laughing matter as symptoms of pain, fainting, respiratory problems, rashes, and crying fits were experienced. Eventually the school had to be shut down so people could be isolated and get over the Tanganyika Laughter Epidemic.

The World's Longest Venomous Snake
The world's longest venomous snake is the King cobra. King cobras average about 15 feet in length. The longest recorded King cobra lived at London Zoo and reached a length of 18 feet 9 inches. (If you get bitten by a King cobra you have about 15 minutes to live.)

The Longest Palindrome In The World
The longest non-English palindrome is saippuakuppinippukauppias with 25 letters. It is a Finnish word meaning 'soap cup dealer.'

The World's Longest Ice Bath
Dutchman Wim Hof spent 1 hour 8 minutes in a tank full of ice, setting the new full body ice contact record in September 2004.

The World's Longest Salami
The world's longest salami was 486.8 meters or 1597 feet long. It was made in Italy in November 2003 by Rino Parenti and Pro-Loco Zibello and on 23rd November 2003 it went on display at Piazza Battisti, Zibello, Italy.

The World's Longest Feathers
In 1972 in Japan an ornamental chicken was bred with tail
feathers that measured 10.59 meters (or 34.75 feet). The longest
feathers for a wild bird belong to the Crested Argus Pheasant
whose tail feather often grows to just under six feet.

The World's Longest Popsicle
The official record for the world's longest popsicle stands at 21
feet and was set in Holland in 1997.

The Longest Earthquake
On 26th December 2004 in Sumatra, an earthquake lasted for 10
minutes and measured 9.3 on the Richter scale. Normally
earthquakes last only a few seconds. The energy released equals
the power of a 100 gigaton bomb. This quake also created the
longest fault ever recorded in the sea floor at about 800 miles
long. The Sumatra earthquake is believed to be the second largest
ever recorded. Nearly 300,000 people lost their lives as a result.

The World's Longest Drowning That Was Survived
In 1986, two-year-old Michelle Funk was playing near her home
in Salt Lake City with her brother by Dry Creek when she slipped
in and sank under the water. Her mother and several neighbors
tried to find her for 66 minutes. When she was found she had no
heartbeat and her core temperature was 70°F. She was taken to
Primary Children's Medical Center where a machine warmed up
her blood. When her temperature reached 91°F her heart started
beating and she opened her eyes.

The World's Longest Animal Name
The animal with the world's longest name is a fly, commonly known as the Stratiomyid Fly or Soldier Fly.
Its full scientific name has 42 letters:
Parastratiosphecomyia stratiosphecomyioides

The Longest Eyeballs In The World
On 13th June 1998, Chicago resident Kim Goodman popped her eyeballs 11 mm. or 0.43 inches out of her sockets. When she was hit on the head one time she noticed one of her eyeballs popped out farther than normal and kept practising for the world's longest eyeball.

The Longest Champagne Cork Flight
Heinrich Medicus opened a bottle of champagne in 1988 and the cork travelled 177 ft 9 in.

The World's Longest Crab
The world's longest crab, a member of the snow crab group, is the giant Japanese spider crab. The body of the giant Japanese spider crab reaches 15 inches in length and the leg span is 12 feet, providing about 50 pounds crab meat. They are found off the Pacific coast of Japan 150 -1000 feet below the surface.

The Longest Egg Drop In The World
On 22nd August 1994 David Donoghue threw an egg out of a helicopter onto a golf course in the UK, from a height of 700 feet. He was trying to get the egg to move forward at the same

speed as it was falling, then have it land on a grassy slope. He now has the record for the longest egg drop without breaking in the world.

The World's Longest Goat Horns
The goat that has the longest goat horns in the world is called 'Uncle Sam'. On 16th April 2004, the horns measured 132 cm, or 52 inches long from tip to tip.

 # Memorable Movie Quotes

This house is so full of people it makes me sick. When I grow up and get married, I'm living alone.
Home Alone

In this life, it's not what you hope for, it's not what you deserve – it's what you take.
Magnolia

Until mankind is peaceful enough not to have violence on the news, there's no point in taking it out of shows that need it for entertainment value.
Clueless

Amazing Animals

Elephant tusks grow throughout an elephant's life and can end up weighing more than 200 pounds. Both sexes of African elephants have tusks, but only the male Asian elephants do.

The bones of a pigeon weigh less than its feathers.

During World War II, the very first bomb dropped on Berlin by the Allies tragically killed the elephant in the Berlin Zoo.

The average canary has over 2000 feathers.

All swans in England are property of the Queen or King.

A bird requires more food in proportion to its size than a baby or a cat.

A group of ravens is called a murder.

The average robin lives to be about 12 years old.

The penguins who live at the tip of South America are called jackass penguins.

There are more bald eagles in the province of British Columbia then in the whole of the United States.

Crows have the largest brains, relative to body size, of any bird.

The clock on Big Ben in London lost five minutes one day when a group of starlings chose the minute hand of the clock as a resting place.

An ostrich's eye is bigger than its brain.

Mockingbirds can imitate any sound from a squeaking door, to a lawnmower to a meowing cat.

Rasputin, 'the Holy Sinner'

Grigory Rasputin's body was taken from the frozen river Neva, in Petrograd, on 1st January 1917. He had been murdered three days before, and was one of the most notorious figures in Russia. Now that he was dead, he would become a legend all over the world – a symbol of evil, cunning, and lust. Most stories about Rasputin are full of lurid details of how Rasputin spent his days in drunken carousing, his nights in sexual debauchery. They tell us how he deceived the Tsar and Tsarina into thinking he was a miracle worker and how he was the evil genius who brought about the Russian Revolution and the downfall of the Romanov dynasty. It is all untrue. Yet it makes such a good story that there is little chance that Rasputin will ever receive justice. The truth about him is that he really was a miracle worker and a man of strange powers. He was certainly no saint – very few magicians are – and tales of his heavy drinking and sexual prowess are undoubtedly based on fact. But he was no diabolical schemer.

Rasputin was born in the village of Pokrovskoe in 1870. His father was a fairly well-to-do peasant. As a young man, Rasputin had a reputation for wildness until he visited a monastery and spent four months there in prayer and meditation. For the remainder of his life, he was obsessed by religion. He married at nineteen and became a prosperous carter. Then the call came again; he left his family and took to the road as a kind of wandering monk. When eventually he returned, he was a changed man, exuding an extraordinarily powerful magnetism. The young people of his village were fascinated by him. He converted one room in his house into a church, and it was always full. The local priest became envious of his following, however, and Rasputin was forced to leave home again.

Rasputin had always possessed the gift of second sight. One day during his childhood, this gift had revealed to him the identity of a peasant who had stolen a horse and hidden it in a barn. Now, on his second round of travels, he also began to develop extraordinary healing powers. He would kneel by the beds of the sick and pray; then he would lay hands on them, and cure many of them. When he came to St Petersburg, probably late in 1903, he already had a reputation as a wonder worker. Soon he was accepted in aristocratic society in spite of his rough peasant manners.

It was in 1907 that he suddenly became the power behind the throne. Three years before, Tsarina Alexandra had given birth to a longed-for heir to the throne, Prince Alexei. But it was soon

 The Fame Name Game

What did Leslie Townes Hope change his name to?

Answer: Bob Hope

apparent that Alexei had inherited haemophilia, a disease that prevents the blood from clotting, and from which a victim may bleed to death even with a small cut. At the age of three the prince fell and bruised himself so severely that an internal hemorrhage developed. He lay in a fever for days, and doctors despaired of his life. Then the Tsarina recalled the man of God she had met two years earlier, and sent for Rasputin. As soon as he came in he said calmly: 'Do not worry the child. He will be all right.' He laid his hand on the boy's forehead, sat down on the edge of the bed, and began to talk to him in a quiet voice. Then he knelt and prayed. In a few minutes the boy was in a deep and peaceful sleep, and the crisis was over.

Henceforward the Tsarina felt a powerful emotional dependence on Rasputin – a dependence nourished by the thinly veiled hostility with which Alexandra, a German, was treated at court. Rasputin's homely strength brought her a feeling of security. The Tsar also began to confide in Rasputin, who became a man of influence at court. Nicholas II was a poor ruler, not so much cruel as weak, and too indecisive to stem the rising tide of social discontent. His opponents began to believe that Rasputin was responsible for some of the Tsar's reactionary policies, and a host of powerful enemies began to gather. On several occasions the Tsar had to give way to the pressure and order Rasputin to leave the city. On one such occasion, the young prince fell and hurt himself again. For several days he tossed in agony, until he seemed too weak to survive. The Tsarina dispatched a telegram to Rasputin, and he telegraphed back: 'The illness is not as dangerous as it seems.' From the moment it was received, the prince began to recover.

World War I brought political revolution and military catastrophe to Russia. Its outbreak was marked by a strange coincidence: Rasputin was stabbed by a madwoman at precisely the same moment as the Archduke Franz Ferdinand was shot at Sarajevo.

Rasputin hated war, and might have been able to dissuade the Tsar from leading Russia into the conflict. But he was in bed recovering from his stab wound when the moment of decision came. Conspirators planned Rasputin's end in the last days of 1916. Prince Felix Yussupov lured him to a cellar, a man he trusted. After feeding him poisoned cakes, Yussupov shot him in the back; then Rasputin was beaten with an iron bar. Such was his immense vitality that he was still alive when the murderers dropped him through the hole in the ice into the Neva.

Among his papers was found a strange testament addressed to the Tsar. It stated that he had a strong feeling he would die by violence before 1st January 1917, and that if peasants killed him, the Tsar would reign for many years to come. However, if he were killed by aristocrats – as he was – then 'none of your children or relations will remain alive for more than two years'. He was right. The Tsar and his family were all murdered in July 1918 – an amazing example, among many, of Rasputin's gift of precognition.

Religious Anecdotes

During the baptism of King Aengus (in the 5th Century), St. Patrick leaned on his sharp-pointed staff and inadvertently stabbed the king in the foot. After the ceremony was over, Patrick suddenly realized what he had done when he saw a growing pool of blood and begged the king's forgiveness. 'Why did you suffer this pain in silence?' he asked. The king allegedly replied: 'I thought it was part of the ritual!'

*Saint Patrick, (c.389–c.469) Christian missionary
and patron saint of Ireland.*

Rumor has it that St. Augustine was once asked, 'What was God doing through all the eternity of time before He created heaven and earth?' 'Creating hell,' he is said to have replied, 'for those who ask questions like you.'

*Saint Augustine, of Hippo, (354–430) Algerian Christian theologian
and philosopher, bishop of Hippo (in Algeria, 396–430)*

Did you know that the Donatists of 4th Century North Africa were so committed to martyrdom that they would stop strangers and demand (under threat of death) to be killed on the spot?

4th Century

Theodoric's trusted Catholic minister, hoping to ingratiate himself with the king, one day declared that he was renouncing his Catholicism to embrace the king's Arian faith. Theodoric was not impressed. 'If this man is not faithful to his God,' he remarked, 'how can he be faithful to me, a mere man?' He had the minister beheaded.

Theodoric ['The Great'], (c.454–526) Ostrogothic king (497–526) [noted for his foundation of the Ostrogoth kingdom in Italy (493), and for his court at Ravenna, the focus of late Roman culture]

When a chapel in which Saint Beuno's bones were supposedly buried was renovated, it became necessary to open the tomb itself. An anthropologist, invited to inspect the saint's skeleton, was surprised to find that its pelvis apparently contained what appeared to be bones from a fetus. 'Well,' the supervisor of the renovation is reoprted to say, 'Saint Beuno was a very remarkable man.'

Saint Beuno, (?–c.440) Welsh abbot of Clynnog (in North Wales)

The great writer St. Augustine once prayed for repentance for his sinful youth. 'Give me chastity and continence,' he pleaded, 'but not yet.'

St. Augustine of Hippo, (354–430) North African Catholic theologian

---

Thought For the Day

You can't reason someone out of a position they didn't reason themselves into.

Author Unknown

Saint Lawrence, as a church deacon during the reign of Emperor Valerian (253-260), was responsible for keeping watch over the church's possessions. He was arrested one day and ordered by a prefect to hand the church treasures over to the government. Lawrence agreed but explained that he would need eight days to assemble them. On the eighth day, Lawrence visited the prefect and presented him with hundreds of impoverished and disabled men, women, and children. 'These,' he said, 'are the riches of the church.' The official was apparently so enraged that he promptly ordered Lawrence to be stripped, bound, and slowly roasted to death above a bed of coals.

Saint Lawrence, (?–258) Roman martyr

Apparently, Catholic Popes have not always lived up to the rigorous standards they expect from their congregations. Several historians have criticized the Roman Catholic Church for its sale of indulgences (basically a license to sin). Though the Church espouses celibacy, Popes Leo VII (936–939), Leo VIII (963–964), and Paul II (Pietro Barbo, 1467–1471) all died while having sex.

Leo VII, (?–939) Italian Pope (936–939)

In 320 BC, an army led by Ptolemy I of Egypt attacked Jerusalem. The city – which had withstood the formidable Sennacherib and Nebuchadnezzar with admirable tenacity – fell easily. Why? The Egyptians had attacked on a holy day and, unlike the Israelis in 1973, the ultra-pious Jews of yore refused to fight on the Sabbath, even in self-defense.

Ptolemy I, (c367–c283) Macedonian king, general under
Alexander the Great, ruler of Egypt (323–285)

Hypatia, the female Neo-Platonist philosopher, mathematician, and astronomer, was the last recorded member of the great museum of Alexandria and the only noted scholar of ancient times. Though several Christian bishops were among her pupils, her adherence to pagan scholasticism literally led to her undoing at the hands of Christian zealots. Hypatia was murdered one day by a mob of fanatic monks. It was a cruel death. They are said to have sliced her body to pieces with oyster shells gathered from the Alexandrian harbor.

Hypatia, Egyptian Neo-Platonist philosopher, mathematician, and astronomer (c.370–415)

According to a 12th-Century chronicle, King Canute, became tired of the excessive flattery of his retainers and ordered that his chair be brought to the seashore, where he commanded the waves not to touch him. Naturally, the incoming tide soon demonstrated the futility of human demands. Canute thereafter hung his crown upon a statue of the crucified Christ to point out that he was not as powerful as his people had supposed him to be.

Canute, [also Cnut or Knut] ['The Great'] (c.994–1035) English monarch, King of England (1016–1035), Denmark (1018–1035), and Norway (1028–1035)

St. Hugh of Lincoln (the Bishop of Lincoln) tried to acquire a sample from a bone said to derive from the arm of Mary Magdalen during a visit to the celebrated monastery of Fecamp. Apparently, a biographer later recalled that the bone had never been taken from its wrappings by the abbot or the monks present at the time. It was said to be sewn very tightly into three cloths, two of silk and one of ordinary linen. No monks dared to accede even to the bishop's prayer to be allowed to see it. St Hugh, however, took a small knife from one of his notaries, and hurriedly cut the thread to undo the wrappings. He examined it and apparently then kissed it. He then tried unsuccessfully to break it with his fingers, then with his teeth. By this means he broke off two fragments, which he handed immediately to the writer...

St. Hugh of Lincoln, (c.1135–1200)
English clergyman, Bishop of Lincoln

The medieval monk Caesarius of Heisterbach was apparently amused to overhear a Cistercian lay brother praying: 'Lord,' the man is said to have declared, 'if Thou free me not from this temptation, I will complain of Thee to Thy mother.'

Caesarius of Heisterbach, (c.1170–1240)
Cistercian monk and chronicler

Saint Francis of Assisi is said to have visited Egypt in 1269, intending to convert the sultan, al-Malik al-Kamil, to Christianity.

The Fame Name Game

What did Reginald Kenneth Dwight change his name to?

Answer: Elton John

The sultan, however, had laid a trap for him: a carpet, decorated with crosses, placed before his divan. 'If he treads on the crosses,' the sultan explained, 'I will accuse him of insulting his God, and if he refuses to tread on the carpet, I will accuse him of insulting me.'

Sure enough, Francis stepped upon the carpet, prompting an outburst from the delighted sultan. Francis, however, was not easily duped: 'Our Lord was crucified between two thieves,' he apparently declared 'We Christians have the True Cross. The crosses of the thieves we have left to you, and I am not ashamed to tread on those.'

Saint Francis of Assisi, (c.1182–1226) Italian friar,
founder of the Franciscan order, patron saint of ecology
[noted for his dissipated youth and for his later conversion (1205)
and devotion to prayer and charity]

The French army, under the guidance of Pope Innocent III, took the town of Beziers near the Mediterranean coast during the Albigensian Crusade in 1209. When the town was seized, the question arose over how its upstanding Christian inhabitants could be distinguished from the damned heretics. It is said that Simon de Montfort had the solution. He ordered them all to be killed, pointing out 'The Lord will know his own.' As a result,

Thought For the Day

We often repent the good we have done as well as the ill.

William Hazlitt, *Characteristics, 1823*

tens of thousands of men, women, and children were
indiscriminately slaughtered.

Simon de Montfort, [Earl of Leicester] (c.1208–1265)
French-born English nobleman

An eminent preacher is said to have once admonished Richard I
to marry off his three daughters, lest he be severely punished by
God. The king protested that he had no daughters. 'Your Majesty
has three,' the priest apparently replied: 'Ambition, avarice, and
luxury. Get rid of them as fast as possible, else assuredly some
great misfortune will be the consequence.'

'If it must be so,' Richard retorted, 'I give my ambition to the
templars, my avarice to the monks, and my luxury to the prelates.'

Richard I ['The Lion-heart'], (1157–1199) English king (1189–1199) [noted
for his leadership of the Third Crusade (1190–1192) and for his capture and
imprisonment in Austria by Holy Roman Emperor Henry VI (1192–94)]

When St. Catherine of Siena was a young novice of the Sisters of
Penance, she supposedly nursed a woman with breast cancer. The
lesions were suppurating and gave off a nauseating smell. Because
she aspired to dominate her physical sensations in the name of
submission to God's higher power, the future Doctor of the
Church drained some of the fluid into a ladle and drank it. That
night, it is rumoured that Jesus came to her in a vision and
invited her to drink the blood spurting from His wounds.

Catherine of Siena, (1347–1380) Italian religious leader
[noted for her mediation of the peace agreement between
the Florentines and Pope Urban VI in 1378]

Italian humanist scholar and writer Bracciolini Poggio – as a secretary in the papal Curia – wore ecclesiastical dress though he was never ordained a priest. It is said that a cardinal once chided him for having children, pointing out that this was unbecoming of a man in clerical garb. He was also disapproved of for having a mistress, which the cardinal noted as unbecoming even of a layman.

'I have children, which is suitable for a layman,' Poggio supposedly retorted. 'And I have a mistress, which is a time-honored custom of the clergy.'

Bracciolini Gian Francesco Poggio, (1380–1459)
Italian humanist scholar and writer

In 1505, after a quarrel with Julius II, Michelangelo was forced into a year-long project creating a giant bronze statue of the man. When the sculptor suggested depicting the Pope with his right hand raised and a book in his left, Julius demurred. 'Put a sword there,' he demanded, 'for I know nothing of letters.'

Fittingly, the statue was later melted down – so the bronze could be used to build cannons.

Julius II, [born Giuliano della Rovere Savona] (1443–1513)
Italian Pope (1503–13)

When he was on his deathbed, the Renaissance painter Pietro Perugino is said to have refused to send for a priest. Supposedly, his last words were 'I am curious to see what happens in the next world to one who dies unshriven.'

Pietro di Cristoforo Vannucci Perugino, (1446–1523)
Italian painter [noted for his graceful frescoes in the Sistine Chapel
and for his mentorship of the painter Raphael]

While working on 'The Last Supper', Leonardo da Vinci is said to have remarked that if he could not find a face to paint that was sufficiently evil for Judas he would happily substitute that of the prior in whose abbey he was working.

Leonardo de Vinci, (1452–1519)

It is said that Erasmus was once reproached for having failed to observe the Lenten fast. His supposed response was 'I have a Catholic soul, but a Lutheran stomach!'

Desiderius Erasmus, (c.1466–1536) Dutch Renaissance
humanist scholar and Roman Catholic theologian

Halley's comet could be seen in the night sky on 29th June 1456 and mankind feared it could bring on a plague, famine, or some other disaster. Pope Calixtus III, who had ruled for one year, issued a papal bull or official decree against the comet. His decree asked Christendom to pray that the comet – or symbol of 'the anger of God,' as he allegedly put it – be diverted from Earth or that, as Bartolomeo Platina wrote in 1479, the comet 'be entirely diverted against the Turks, the foes of the Christian name."

Calixtus III, (1378–1458) Italian Pope

Michelangelo was frequently pestered by Pope Paul III's master of ceremonies whilst painting his famous 'Last Judgment' fresco in the Vatican's Sistine Chapel. The man is said to have wanted a glimpse of the emerging masterpiece. When the work was unveiled at last, the man found himself depicted in the painting among the damned in hell, being tormented by demons. The man was horrified and promptly complained to the Pope, who supposedly refused to intervene. He is said to have declared 'God has given me authority in Heaven and on Earth, but my writ does not extend to Hell'.

Michelangelo [Buonarroti], (1475–1564) Italian Renaissance
sculptor, painter, architect, and poet

Hugh Latimer and Nicholas Ridley (the bishop of London) were condemned to be burned at the stake after their show trial for heresy in 1555. As the fire was lit, Latimer turned to the bishop. 'Be of good comfort, Master Ridley, and play the man,' he advised. 'We shall this day light such a candle, by God's grace, in England as I trust shall never be put out.'

Hugh Latimer, (c.1485–1555) English bishop and Protestant martyr
noted for his part in the Oxford disputations against a group of Catholic
theologians (1554) and for his refusal to recant his Protestant faith

Pope Julius III supposedly asked a shoemaker to fashion special papal slippers. When they were presented to the new Pope for a fitting, they were found to be too small. The shoemaker apologized, 'I am afraid they don't fit you, Holy Father'. Apparently the Pope replied, 'On the contrary, no shoes ever fitted me better than these in my life.'

Julius III, (1487–1555) [born Giammaria Ciocchi del Monte] Italian Pope

 The Fame Name Game

What did William Board change his name to?

Answer: Billy Idol

Michael Servetus was declared a heretic for his denial of the doctrine of the Trinity and narrowly escaped the Inquisition in Calvin's Geneva. However, he was eventually caught, tried for heresy, and condemned to death (to be burned at the stake). 'I will burn, but this is a mere incident,' he declared before his judges. 'We shall continue our discussion in eternity.'

Michael Servetus, [born Miguel Serveto] (1511–1553)
Spanish-born theologian and physician

Saint Teresa was approached by a young nun who confessed to a plenitude of spiritual tribulations and terrible sins. After listening to her for some time, Saint Teresa gave her a word of advice: 'We know, sister, that none of us is perfect,' she said. 'Just take care that your sins don't turn into bad habits.'

Saint Teresa of Avila, (1515–1582) Spanish Carmelite nun and writer
[noted for her foundation of convents at Avila (1562) and (with the aid
of Saint John of the Cross) several other religious communities in which
the reformed Carmelite rule was practiced]

Mary Queen of Scots was famously devoutly religious. It is said that the linen sheets upon which she slept were fashioned from the fibers of stinging nettle plants.

Mary, Queen of Scots (1542–1587) British monarch (from 1542), daughter
of James V of Scotland [noted for her forced abdication (in favor of her one-
year-old son, James VI, later James I of England) and her imprisonment and
execution (by Elizabeth I) for complicity in the Babington plot (1586)]

Even though the theory had been pronounced a heresy, Galileo published his *Dialogue on Two Chief World Systems* in 1632. He had made a number of important astronomical discoveries that convinced him of the validity of Nicholas Copernicus's geocentric theory (that the earth moves around the sun rather than the reverse). The Inquisition promptly summoned him to Rome, where he reluctantly recanted and was sentenced to house arrest for the rest of his life. As he rose from his knees after his solemn renunciation of the Copernican doctrine, however, he is said to have muttered: 'Eppur si muove!' (But still it moves!)

Galileo Galilei (1564–1642) Italian astronomer and physicist [noted for his pioneering use of the telescope to study the stars (1610), his espousal of Copernicus's geocentric theory of the solar system, and for his consequent persecution and imprisonment by the Inquisition (1633)]

Because he felt it was blasphemous to name constellations after characters from Greek mythology, the 16th-Century German astronomer Johann Bayer introduced a new system in which the northern constellations were named after New Testament characters and the southern constellations after Old Testament characters. Needless to say, the scheme did not catch on.

Johann Bayer (1572–1625)

Natural Thoughts

No snowflake ever falls in the wrong place.

Zen saying

According to history, a preacher famed for his fearless social criticism was invited to speak before King James I in the 16th Century. The man stood in the pulpit and began:

'James One, Six. "But let him ask in faith, nothing wavering. For he that wavereth is like a wave of the sea, driven with the wind and tossed."' 'God's faith!' the king is said to have cried. 'He's at me already.'

James I (1566–1625) English monarch, king of England and Ireland (1603–25) and of Scotland (as James VI) (1567–1625), son of Mary Queen of Scots

While working on his chronology of the Bible, *Annales Veteris et Novi Testamenti* one day in the mid-17th Century, Bishop James Ussher is said to have calculated what he believed to be the time of the Creation. His estimate was very precise... Sunday, 23rd October, 4004 BC – at 9:00 am!

James Ussher, (1581–1655) Irish bishop

Regular processions were organized around Hereford Cathedral to mark holy occasions at the end of the 16th Century. Prior to one such procession the Dean of Hereford, Dr. Price, decided that in view of his own importance he would not, as had previously been common, walk on foot with the rest of the lowlier canons. He decided instead to ride on horseback so that he might be more easily seen reading from his prayer book. The proud cleric mounted his mare, opened his book and took to the streets. 'His reading was at an early stage when a stallion broke loose, saw his mare and mounted her. The dean was trapped,

read practically nothing and swore he would never ride in a
procession again.'

Dr. Daniel Price, Dean of Hereford, (17th Century) British cleric

The Austrian general Raimund Montecuccoli, an observant
Roman Catholic, ordered an omelet for dinner one Friday
evening. He was unusually hungry and saw no harm in adding a
few small slices of ham to the meal. As his meal was served, a very
loud clap of thunder issued from the darkened sky, clearly the
start of a violent storm. Silently, the general stood up, marched
across the room, and threw his omelet through the nearest
window. 'What a lot of noise for a ham omelet!' he is said to
have exclaimed, gazing heavenward.

Raimund Montecuccoli, Duke of Melfi (1609–1680) Austrian general

On 17th February 1673, French playwright and actor Moliere,
although desperately ill, insisted on perfoming in a scheduled
play rather than let his company down. After the performance he
was carried home, where he died a short time later. Given that
religious prejudice against the theater was so strong, it was
customary for a dying actor to formally renounce his profession
in order to obtain permission for burial in consecrated ground.
His sudden death, however, prevented this. Appeals to the
archbishop of Paris were rejected, and Moliere's grieving widow
sought the help of the king. King Louis asked the ecclesiastical
authorities how deep into the ground the earth was considered
consecrated. The supposed response was fourteen feet. Louis
declared that Moliere's grave be dug in the churchyard sixteen
feet deep where it could be said that he is buried in consecrated

ground without scandalizing the clergy. His grave however, has never been found.

> *Jean-Baptiste Poquelin Moliere, (1622–1673)*
> *French playwright and actor*

In 1683, John Sobieski's military skills drove the invading Turks back from the walls of Vienna, altering forever the history of central Europe. He soon announced victory to the Pope. 'I came, I saw...' he declared. And? 'God conquered.'
[A play on Julius Caesar's famous remark: 'I came, I saw, I conquered' (Veni, vidi, vici).]

> *John III Sobieski, (1624–1696) King of Poland (1674–1696)*

The author of *The Pilgrim's Progress*, John Bunyan, had little worldly success. He became a lay preacher in the army at 16 and his friend was killed standing next to him. At 17, his mother died. At 21 he was a husband, and at 27 he became a widower, the father of four young children, one of them blind. At 32, he was jailed for preaching without government license and his second wife suddenly went into labor and delivered a child who died soon after. He was offered his freedom if he would stop

The Fame Name Game

What did Arnold Gerry Dorsey change his name to?

Answer: Engelbert Humperdinck

preaching the gospel, but is famously said to have replied, 'If I am freed today, I will preach tomorrow.' Bunyan spent the next twelve years of his life in prison. In spite of his difficult life, he faithfully wrote and preached of God's grace and goodness.

John Bunyan (1628-1688) English preacher and writer

In the 18th Century, during a debate in the House of Lords on the Test Laws, which obligated candidates for public office to profess allegiance to the Anglican faith, the Earl of Sandwich is said to have remarked, 'I have heard frequent use of the words "orthodoxy" and "heterodoxy" but I confess myself at a loss to know precisely what they mean.' Bishop Warburton explained: 'Orthodoxy is my doxy,' he whispered. 'Heterodoxy is another man's doxy.'

William Warburton, (1698–1779) English clergyman and literary scholar, bishop of Gloucester (1759–1779)

Lord Chesterfield's sister (secretly entertaining hopes that he would be converted to Methodism) tried to persuade her ill brother to visit a Methodist seminary in Wales to recuperate. Apparently, as she extolled the virtues of the setting's spectacular mountain views, Chesterfield, suspecting what she was up to, interrupted her: 'I do not love mountains,' he is said to have announced. 'When your ladyship's faith has removed them, I will go thither with all my heart.'

Philip Dormer Stanhope, Fourth Earl of Chesterfield, (1694–1773) English politician, diplomat and writer

As the great Puritan leader John Owen lay on his deathbed, his secretary wrote a letter on his behalf to a friend containing the words 'I am still in the land of the living.' Owen then ordered his secretary to stop. He requested that she change that to 'I am yet in the land of the dying, but I hope soon to be in the land of the living.'

John Owen, (17th Century) American Puritan leader

The 18th-Century English preacher George Whitefield was so popular that the Privy Council one day discussed how to control his vast evangelical rallies. 'Make him a bishop,' Lord Chesterfield is said to have suggested, 'and you will silence him at once.'

Philip Dormer Stanhope Fourth Earl of Chesterfield, (1694–1773) English politician, diplomat and writer

Shortly after Louis XIV named Jacques Bossuet bishop of Meaux, the king solicited some of the town's citizens for their opinions of the new bishop. They liked him fairly well, they replied. 'Fairly well? Why, what's wrong with him?' Louis asked.

'Well, to tell Your Majesty the truth, we should have preferred a bishop who had completed his education,' the villagers explained to him. 'Whenever we call to see him we are told that he is at his studies.'

Jacques Benigne Bossuet, (1627–1704) French Roman Catholic bishop and preacher, bishop of Meaux (1681)

 Thought For the Day

Sometimes the questions are complicated and the answers are simple.

Dr. Seuss

The great physicist Robert Boyle was a surprisingly devout man. (He was best known for his pioneering studies of gases culminating in 1662 with his formulation of Boyle's Law). After being frightened by a thunderstorm in Geneva as a boy, he turned to God and wrote essays on religion, later learned Hebrew and Aramaic, and financed missionary work in the Orient. He also left a bequest for the establishment of the Boyle Lectures for the defense of Christianity against unbelievers.

Nonetheless, in 1680 he was elected president of the eminent Royal Society. He apparently declined to accept because he disapproved of the form of the oath.

Robert Boyle, (1627–1691) Irish-born English physicist and chemist [noted for his pioneering experiments with gases and chemical elements, culminating in his formulation of Boyle's Law (1662)]

Not long after the London debut of Handel's *Messiah* (in 1743), the composer was apparently complimented by Lord Kinnoul on his 'noble entertainment.' But the composer was dissatisfied. 'My Lord, I should be sorry if I only entertained them,' Handel replied. 'I wished to make them better.'

George Frideric Handel, (1685–1759) German composer,

 The Fame Name Game

What did Mary Isobel Catherine O'Brien change her name to?

Answer: Dusty Springfield

It is said that while preaching a sermon one day, John Wesley was dismayed to find that quite a few members of his congregation were asleep. Apparently he cried 'Fire! Fire!' to get the guilty parishioners to wake up. 'Where?' they asked, looking around. 'In hell,' Wesley is said to have replied, 'for those who sleep under the preaching of the Word!'

[In his life, Wesley, the founder of Methodism, preached an incredible 40,000 sermons.]

John Wesley (1703–1791) English evangelist
[noted for his role in the foundation of Methodism]

Dr. Johnson's biographer James Boswell once attended a Quaker meeting one Sunday morning, where he heard a woman preaching for the first time. Apparently he later related the remarkable experience to Dr. Johnson. 'Sir,' Johnson is said to have remarked, 'a woman's preaching is like a dog's walking on his hind legs. It is not done well, but you are surprised to find it done at all.'

Samuel Johnson, (1709–1784) English journalist, critic, poet,
lexicographer, founder of 'The Rambler' ['the Great Cham of Literature']

John Wesley's message of repentance and faith was apparently so appealing that one hoodlum, sent by Anglican leaders to disrupt one of their meetings, found himself unable to follow through. As he raised his hand to strike a blow to Wesley's head, he brought it down with surprising delicacy, simply declaring: 'What soft hair he has!'

John Wesley, (1703–1791) English religious leader

Towards the end of his life, Christoph Gluck was asked whether a bass or a tenor should sing the part of Christ in *The Last Judgment*. 'If you wait a little,' Gluck famously replied, 'I shall be able to tell you from personal experience.'

Christoph Willibald Gluck, (1714–1787) German composer

Lord Sandwich is said to have brought in a large baboon whilst hosting a formal dinner one evening. The baboon was apparently dressed in clerical garb and was supposedly there to say grace. His chaplain, grievously offended, immediately rose to leave the room. 'I did not know,' he declared, turning in the doorway, 'that your lordship had so near a relative in holy orders.'

John Montagu Fourth Earl of Sandwich, (1718–1792) British politician, First Lord of the Admiralty (1748–1751, 1771–1782)

A staunch Roman Catholic once confronted the Protestant John Wilkes and asked him. 'Where was your religion before Luther?' Wilkes is said to have retorted 'Did you wash your face this morning?' When the Catholic admitted that he had, Wilkes told him 'Then, pray where was your face before it was washed?'

John Wilkes, (1725–1797) American politician and journalist, member of Parliament (1757–1764) [noted for his libel arrest (1763), exile in Paris (1764–1768), and political revival (as a Middlesex MP from 1774)]

In 1802 Thomas Paine escaped the guillotine (by chance – he had been elected to the French Convention and subsequently imprisoned by Robespierre) and emigrated to the United States. One day while traveling through Baltimore, he was approached by a Swedenborgian minister who had recognized him as the author of *The Age of Reason* whose deistic thesis the minister was clearly eager to discuss. 'I am minister of the New Jerusalem Church here,' he declared, 'and we explain the true meaning of the Scripture. The key had been lost above four thousand years, but we have found it...' 'It must,' Paine testily replied, 'have been very rusty.'

Thomas Paine, (1737–1809) British political theorist and writer

A stern Calvinist minister delivered a sermon one Sunday attended by Ethan Allen and several of his colleagues. 'Many shall strive to enter, but shall not be able,' the minister cried. Indeed, God's grace was sufficient, he continued, to include one in ten, but not one in twenty would endeavor to avail himself of the offered salvation...

Moreover, not one in fifty was the true object of God's solicitude, and not one in eighty was fit... At this point, Allen is said to have collected his hat and left the pew. 'I'm off, boys,' he announced. 'Any one of you can take my chance!'

Ethan Allen, (1738–1789) American patriot, leader of the 'Green Mountain Boys' during the Revolutionary War

The Fame Name Game

What did Roy Scherer change his name to?

Answer: Rock Hudson

According to folklore a number of people sought shelter in a chapel during a heavy downpour. Rowland Hill happened to be preaching there at the time. 'People who make religion their cloak are rightly censured,' he apparently declared, 'but I consider that those who make it their umbrella are not much better.'

Rowland Hill, (1744–1833) British preacher

Richard Porson and a Trinitarian friend were discussing the nature of the Trinity when a carriage containing three men passed by. 'There,' the friend is said to have exclaimed, 'that's an illustration of the Trinity.' Porson however, disagreed and told his friend 'you must show me one man in three buggies – if you can!'

Richard Porson, (1759–1808) British classical scholar [noted for his editions of the plays of Euripides (and for his love of liquor)]

In 1832, John Dalton, known as the father of atomic theory, received a doctorate from Oxford University and was duly presented to King William IV. Though tradition demanded that he wear a scarlet robe, Dalton happened to be a Quaker. Dalton's solution, when the robe was brought before him, was to declare

Thought For the Day

The observer, when he seems to himself to be observing a stone, is really, if physics is to be believed, observing the effects of the stone upon himself.

Bertrand Russell

that the garment was completely gray and therefore wearable. Apparently, Dalton also happened to be completely colorblind.

John Dalton, (1766–1844) British chemist [noted for his study of colorblindness, for his pioneering work on the properties of gases, and for his consequent formulation of the atomic theory]

Lord Melbourne once had to sit through a long evangelical sermon on the consequences of sin. Not noted for his appreciation of religious experience, Melbourne apparently replied that he had always been a supporter of the church, and always upheld the clergy, but pointed out that it was really too bad to have to listen to a sermon like the one that morning.

He is said to have later complained about the fact that preachers actually insisted upon 'applying religion to a man's personal life.'

William Lamb Melbourne, 2nd Viscount (1779–1848) English statesman, secretary for Ireland (1827–1826), home secretary (1830–1834), prime minister (1834, 1835–1841), husband of Caroline Lamb

During a stay with the Scottish preacher Thomas Chalmers and his family, the Swiss divine Jean d'Aubigne was given a kippered herring for breakfast. He is said to have asked about the meaning of the word 'kippered' and was told that it meant 'kept' or 'preserved'.

Apparently as he later led the household in their morning prayers, he asked the Good Lord to see that they be 'kept, preserved – and kippered.'

Jean Henri Merle d'Aubigne, (1794–1872) Swiss Protestant divine

Lionel Nathan Rothschild, of the prominent family of European bankers, became the first Jewish member of the British House of Commons in 1847.

However, because he found the standard oath of office unacceptable to his Jewish faith Rothschild refused to assume his seat until it was changed. Parliament eventually agreed and Rothschild dutifully took his seat...eleven years later!

Lionel Nathan Rothschild, (1808–1879) British banker and politician

The World's Oddest Animals

The Blob Fish Due to the inaccessibility of its habitat, the Blob Fish is rarely seen by humans. This is because this unusually named fish is found on the ocean floor in the deep waters off the coasts of Australia and Tasmania. Here the pressure is 20-50 times higher than at sea level so to remain buoyant, the flesh of the blob fish is primarily a jelly-like mass which is slightly less dense than water. The Blob Fish has what is called a gas bladder – an internal gas-filled organ that enables it to control its buoyancy; this allows the fish to float above the sea floor without wasting energy swimming. It is not much more than a blob of jellyfish but the relative lack of muscle is not a problem as it mainly swallows edible matter that floats by.

Abraham Lincoln ran for Congress as a Whig in 1846 against an evangelical Methodist named Peter Cartwright. Apparently, one day during the campaign, he attended a religious meeting at which Cartwright, after a stirring welcome, invited everyone who hoped to go to heaven to rise. Several of the congregation did so. 'Now,' Cartwright supposedly said, 'those who do not wish to go to hell will stand!' With these words, everyone else stood up, with a single notable exception, Lincoln himself. Cartwright asked Mr Lincoln, 'Where you are going?' Lincoln stood and replied. 'I came here as a respectful listener. I did not know I was to be singled out by Brother Cartwright. I believe in treating religious matters with due solemnity. I admit that the questions propounded by Brother Cartwright are of great importance. I did not feel called upon to answer as the rest did. Brother Cartwright asks me directly where I am going. I desire to reply with equal directness: I am going to Congress!'

Abraham Lincoln, (1809–1865) ['Honest Abe'] American politician, US Congressman (Illinois, 1847-1860). 16th President of the United States (1861-65). Noted for his antislavery election ticket, which precipitated the secession of the Southern states and his leadership of the Union forces during the ensuing Civil War. He also made the Emancipation Proclamation (1863) freeing Southern slaves and his draft of the Thirteenth Amendment (prohibiting slavery in the United States, 1865).

William Gladstone apparently once said: 'One thing I have against the clergy both of the country and in the towns. I think they are not severe enough on congregations. They do not sufficiently lay upon the souls and consciences of their hearers their moral obligations, and probe their hearts and bring up their whole lives and actions to the bar of conscience.'

William Ewart Gladstone (1809–1898) Four-times Liberal prime minister of Great Britain,

During a visit to Henry Ward Beecher one day, Robert Ingersoll noticed a beautiful globe depicting the various constellations and stars of the heavens. Ingersoll asked Beecher who had made it. 'Who made it?' Beecher replied, seizing the opportunity to attack his guest's well-known agnosticism. 'Why, nobody made it. It just happened.'

Henry Ward Beecher, (1813–1887) American Congregational minister and author, brother of Harriet Beecher Stowe [noted for his fervent campaigns for the abolition of slavery]

Not long after composer Louis Antoine Jullien was born (at Sisteron in the Basses Alpes), his father, a violinist, was invited to play a concerto with the local Philharmonic Society orchestra, who graciously decided to invite one of the musicians to be the child's godfather.

A problem arose, however, when each of the orchestra's thirty-six members vied for the privilege. An agreement was finally reached whereby the infant – held by the society's secretary at the font – was duly baptized with all thirty-six names. Jullien's full name, while cumbersome, proved a useful source of pseudonyms for his musical compositions.

Louis Antoine Jullien, (1812–1910) French composer and conductor [noted for his London promenade concerts]

Henry Ward Beecher rejected harsh Calvinism and so concocted an interesting romantic idea of religion as a warm, indiscriminate bath of love. To be truly religious, he said, you must sin, since Christ can't very well save you if you don't.

Henry Ward Beecher, (1813–1887) American Congregational minister and author, brother of Harriet Beecher Stowe [noted for his fervent campaigns for the abolition of slavery]

A married clergyman is said to have once reproached the famous feminist Elizabeth Cady Stanton as she spoke in public at a women's rights convention in Rochester, New York. 'The apostle Paul enjoined silence upon women,' he apparently told her. 'Why don't you mind him?' 'The apostle Paul also enjoined celibacy upon the clergy,' Stanton replied. 'Why don't you mind him?'

Elizabeth Cady Stanton, (1815–1902) American feminist and social reformer

Natural Thoughts

The fish trap exists because of the fish. Once you've gotten the fish you can forget the trap. The rabbit snare exists because of the rabbit. Once you've gotten the rabbit, you can forget the snare. Words exist because of meaning. Once you've gotten the meaning, you can forget the words. Where can I find a man who has forgotten words so I can talk with him?

Chuang Tzu

The Russian archeologist Daniel Chwolson was apparently once asked whether his decision to join the Orthodox Church had been made out of conviction or expediency. 'I accepted baptism entirely out of conviction,' Chwolson is said to have replied, 'the conviction that it is better to be a professor in the Academy in St. Petersburg than a teacher in a school in Vilna.'

> *Daniel Abramovich Chwolson, (1819–1911) Russian archaeologist,*
> *professor of Oriental languages at the Uniuersity of St. Petersburg*
> *(1855), professor of Hebrew at the St. Petersburg Academy (1858)*

During his time as chaplain of the US Senate, Edward Hale was once asked, 'Dr. Hale, do you pray for the Senate?' 'No,' he allegedly replied. 'I look at the Senators and pray for the people.'

> *Edward Everett Hale, (1822–1909) American clergyman*
> *and writer, nephew of Nathan Hale*

The poet Matthew Arnold was apparently famed for his staunch reserve and critical eye. There was much comment after his death in 1888. Robert Louis Stevenson is reputed to have said 'Poor Matt. He's gone to Heaven, no doubt, but he won't like God.'

> *Matthew Arnold, (1822–1888) English poet and critic,*
> *professor of poetry at Oxford (1857–1867)*

In Oxford in June 1860 there was a historic meeting between the supporters of Charles Darwin's theory of evolution and the Church In opposing corners were Samuel Wilberforce, the bishop of Oxford, and Thomas Huxley, who spoke for the Darwinian camp. Wilberforce unexpectedly delivered a savage speech against Darwin and Huxley: 'If anyone were to be willing to trace his descent through an ape as his grandfather,' he demanded of Huxley, 'would he be willing to trace his descent similarly on the side of his grandmother?' 'A man has no reason to be ashamed of having an ape for his grandfather,' Huxley is famously said to have declared. 'If there were an ancestor whom I should feel shame in recalling, it would rather be a man who, not content with an equivocal success in his own sphere of activity, plunges into scientific questions with which he has no real acquaintance!'

Thomas Huxley (1825–1895) ['Darwin's Bulldog'] British biologist, philosopher, and paleontologist [noted for his eloquent defence of Charles Darwin's evolutionary theories, and for his coinage of the term 'agnostic']

Stonewall Jackson once blamed the date, a Sunday, for a failed attempt to destroy the canal leading to Washington. In order to avoid breaking Sabbath again, Jackson planned to attack on a Monday – using gunpowder obtained on the previous Saturday. The quartermaster however, unable to find powder on such short notice, was obliged to procure it on Sunday. When Jackson learned of this unfortunate fact, he promptly sent for 'Monday powder.' 'I desire,' he told his colonel, 'that you will see that the powder that is used for this expedition is not the powder that was procured on Sunday.'

Thomas Jonathan Jackson, ['Stonewall'] (1824–1863)
American Confederate general

A businessman, renowned for his ruthlessness, is said to have made a vow in the presence of Mark Twain. He apparently declared that before he died he intended to make a pilgrimage to the Holy Land and climb Mount Sinai to read the Ten

Commandments aloud at the top. Twain is said to have replied. 'It would be better if you could stay home in Boston and keep them.'

Mark Twain, (1835–1910) [born Samuel Langhorne Clemens]
American humorist, writer, and lecturer

During his lifetime, Andrew Carnegie endowed 2,811 libraries and many charitable foundations as well as the internationally famous Carnegie Endowment for International Peace. He also bought 7,689 organs for churches. He apparently said they were 'To lessen the pain of the sermons.'

Andrew Carnegie, (1835–1919) Scottish-born American steel
magnate and philanthropist

The Fame Name Game

What did Ehrich Weiss change his name to?

Answer: Harry Houdini

The Mind Bending Quiz

1   According to the proverb, what is the better part of valour?

2   Who composed the Moonlight Sonata?

3   Which cartoon sailor has a tattoo of an anchor on his arm?

4   The Leaning Tower of Pisa was built for what particular purpose?

5   Which famous brothers made a movie called *A Night At The Opera*?

6   What is Ripley's first name in Patricia Highsmith's *The Talented Mr Ripley*?

7   In which year were East and West Germany unified?

8   Which Sondheim musical tells the story of a murdering barber?

9   Which rock superstar's first wife was Cynthia Powell?

10 How many letters are there in the Greek alphabet?

11 How many stomachs does a cow have?

12 Which murder victim was named in the trailers for the enigmatic TV series *Twin Peaks*?

13 In which country were the 1980 Olympics, boycotted by the Americans?

14 Which animal can be described as vulpine?

15 What is the name of the medical oath taken by doctors?

(Answers on Overleaf)

Answers

1 Discretion. 2 Beethoven. 3 Popeye. 4 Bell Tower.
5 The Marx Brothers. 6 Tom. 7 1990. 8 *Sweeney Todd*.
9 John Lennon. 10 24. 11 Four. 12 Laura Palmer.
13 USSR. 14 A fox. 15 Hippocratic Oath.

How did you do?

12-15
To infinity and beyond!

8-11
Yabba Dabba Do!

4-7
What's up doc?

1-3
Doh!

More Fascinating Facts From History

The Aztec Indians in Central America mixed animal blood with cement as a mortar for their buildings, many of which remain standing today.

Vincent Van Gogh painted one picture every day for the last 70 days of his life.

The Tower of London, constructed by William the Conqueror in 1078, once contained an extensive menagerie, including a slightly deranged lion.

While performing her duties as queen, Cleopatra occasionally chose to wear a fake beard.

In 1907 the first taxicab was seen on the streets of New York City.

Catherine the Great supposedly liked to relax by having one of her courtiers tickle her.

In the north of China it was once a common practice to shave off pigs' bristles. When the evenings drew in the Chinese would take a pig to bed with them for warmth. Apparently this was more comfortable if the pig was clean-shaven.

It took 20,000 men 22 years to build the Taj Mahal.

Until 1796, the state of Tennessee was called Franklin.

The 5-day, 40-hour work week was first established in the steel industry. Henry Ford adopted it for his factory in 1926, and it has now become the norm for workers in many professions.

New Zealand was the first place in the world to give women the vote. The state of South Australia followed their example in 1894, and was also the first place to allow women to stand for parliament.

When the US War Department was established in 1789, there were only 840 soldiers in the regular army. Their allotted tasks were to supervise public lands and guard the Native American Indian frontier.

Obscure English Language Facts

Strengthlessnesses
takes the gold medal as the longest word in the English language that uses a single repeated vowel (18 letters). In second place we have ***defenselessnesses*** *(17 letters), pursued by* ***strengthlessness*** *(16 letters),* ***defenselessness*** *(15 letters) and* ***degenerescence*** *(14 letters).*

Whenever Napoleon wore his lucky black silk handkerchief around his neck during a battle, he came out victorious. At Waterloo, he unfortunately wore a white cravat and lost both the battle and his empire.

Chrysler constructed the B-29s that bombed Japan, while Mitsubishi was responsible for the Zeros that tried to shoot them down. Both of these corporations now build cars together in a plant called Diamond Star.

The ancient Etruscans always painted women white and men red in the wall paintings they used to decorate tombs.

When Gaius Caesar was a boy, Roman soldiers gave him the affectionate nickname 'little boots' because of the boy-sized military footwear he liked to wear.

A female pharaoh was unknown in Egypt before Hatshepsut, who ordered that she be portrayed in male costume, with a beard and without breasts. While performing her duties as queen, Hatshepsut also wore the traditional kilt which was called a Shendyt.

The German Kaiser Wilhelm II had a withered arm. He liked to hide this by posing with his hand resting on a sword, or by holding a pair of gloves.

The 16th-Century astronomer Tycho Brahe had his nose cut off in a duel over a mathematical problem with one of his students. For the rest of his life he wore a replacement nose made of silver.

Marco Polo was born on the Croatian island of Korcula.

The game of Monopoly was designed to demonstrate the economic theories of Henry George.

Napoleon has historically been described as short, but he was actually five feet six inches tall (1.676 meters), which was the average height for a Frenchman at the time.

In the 16th Century, Ivan the Terrible ordered the construction of St. Basil's Cathedral in Moscow. He was delighted with the work done by the two architects. Unfortunately for them, his response was to have them blinded so they would never be able to build anything more beautiful again.

Napoleon took 14,000 old French decrees and simplified them into a set of seven basic laws. This was the first time in modern history that a nation's laws were deemed to apply equally to all citizens.

When Sir Walter Raleigh introduced tobacco into England in the early 1600s, King James I wrote a booklet warning against the practice of smoking or chewing it.

More than 5600 men died building the Panama Canal.

During the Civil War, the Union needed hundreds of thousands of uniforms for its troops. The supply that grew up in response was the beginning of the ready-made clothing industry in the US.

The right arm and torch of the Statue of Liberty crossed the Atlantic Ocean three times. It first crossed for display at the 1876 Philadelphia Centennial Exposition and in New York, where money was raised for the completion of the statue. It went back to Paris in 1882 to be reunited with the rest of the statue, which was then shipped back to the US.

The first telephone book ever issued contained only fifty names.

Houses were first numbered in Paris in the 15th Century. In Britain, numbering did not appear until 1708, on a street in the Whitechapel area of London.

In 1878 Wanamaker's of Philadelphia became the first US department store to install an electric lighting system.

In ancient Greece, courtesans wore sandals with patterned nails studded into the sole so that their footprints would leave the message 'Follow me'.

Special playing cards were issued to British pilots in WWII. If you soaked them in water they could be unfolded to reveal a map for escape.

In 1974 there were 90 tornadoes in the US in a single day.

Before finally winning the 1860 election, Abraham Lincoln lost eight elections for a variety of different offices.

In 1937 the emergency 999 telephone service was established in London. More than 13,000 genuine calls were made during the first month.

 # Memorable Movie Quotes

Jim: <waking up in bed> She's gone! Oh my God! She used me. I was used. <grins> I was used! Cool!
American Pie

You're one of the most beautiful women I've ever seen and that's not saying much for you.
Animal Crackers

She wrote me a 'john-deere' letter... something about me not listening enough, I don't know . . . I wasn't really paying attention.
Dumb & Dumber